THE LAST DAYS
OF DAG HAMMARSKJOLD

Dag Hammarskjold after his arrival at Leopoldville, 13th September 1961, with Prime Minister Adoula
(Photo: United Nations)

ARTHUR L. GAVSHON

The Last Days of Dag Hammarskjold

BARRIE AND ROCKLIFF
with
PALL MALL PRESS
LONDON

First published in Great Britain 1963
by Barrie & Rockliff (Barrie Books Ltd)
with Pall Mall Press Ltd.
2 Clement's Inn London WC2
Printed in Great Britain by
Unwin Brothers Ltd Old Woking Surrey

TO THE SIXTEEN
WHO DIED
ON DOLA HILL

*The Congo**

Then I saw the Congo, creeping through the black,
Cutting through the forest with a gold track.
Then along the riverbank
A thousand miles
Tattooed cannibals danced in files;
Then I heard the boom of the blood-lust song
And a thigh-bone beating on a tin-pan gong.
And "BLOOD" screamed the whistles and the fifes of the warriors,
"BLOOD," screamed the skull-faced, lean witch-doctors,
"Whirl ye the deadly voo-doo rattle,
Harry the uplands,
Steal all the cattle,
Rattle-rattle rattle-rattle,
Bing.
Boomlay, boomlay, boomlay, BOOM."
A roaring, epic, rag-time tune
From the mouth of the Congo
To the Mountains of the Moon,
Death is an elephant,
Torch-eyed and horrible,
Foam-flanked and terrible.

BOOM, steal the pygmies,

BOOM, kill the Arabs,

BOOM, kill the white men,

Hoo, Hoo, Hoo.

Listen to the yell of Leopold's ghost

Burning in hell for his hand-maimed host.

Hear how the demons chuckle and yell

Cutting his hands off, down in Hell.

Listen to the creepy proclamation

Blown through the lairs of the forest-nation,

Blown past the white-ants' hill of clay,

Blown past the marsh where the butterflies play: —

"Be careful what you do,

Or Mumbo-Jumbo, God of the Congo,

And all of the other

Gods of the Congo,

Mumbo-Jumbo will hoo-doo you,

Mumbo-Jumbo will hoo-doo you,

*Mumbo-Jumbo will hoo-doo you."**

Contents

Introduction

The currency of modern diplomatic exchange is secrecy, its goodwill is confidence. The officials of many countries have helped me in the writing of this book. They include most of the principals who played a role in the dramatic last days of Dag Hammarskjold. I can acknowledge their cooperation but without naming them, for to do so would be to debase both the currency and the goodwill.

Apart from these original researches I have made liberal use of information contained in:

1. The official reports of the Federal Rhodesian and United Nations Commissions which investigated the crash that killed the Secretary-General.
2. The verbatim and tape-recorded transcripts of evidence heard by the two Commissions.
3. News conference and other public statements made by authorities involved in the tangled events of the time.

A good deal of personal and political material has come to me also from very close friends of Dag Hammarskjold in various cities. And I have been helped by colleagues of my own in key capitals who, like the diplomats, have preferred anonymity.

My thanks go out to them.

They also go out to my wife who shared it all.

The story that follows is offered as an important and tragically final part of the life and times of a great and solitary man caught up in the new, twentieth-century scramble for Africa.

Dag Hammarskjold's last days belonged to Africa but he gave his life to the world.

A.L.G.

London, December, 1962.

Part One | The Flight of the *Albertina*

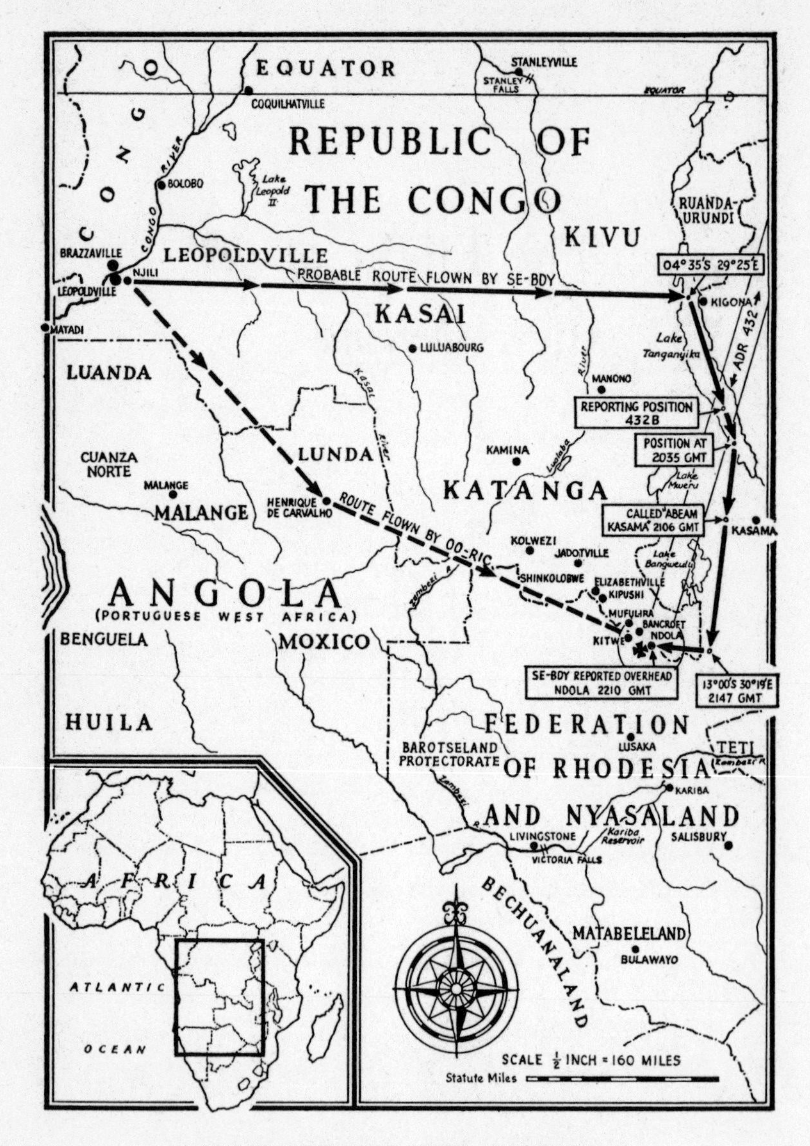

THE FLIGHT OF THE *ALBERTINA*

FIR: FLIGHT INFORMATION REGION

OO-RIC: ROUTE OF LORD LANSDOWNE'S PLANE

SE-BDY: ROUTE OF DAG HAMMARSKJOLD'S PLANE

1 | The Journey

The man in the dark glasses and rumpled gabardine suit took leave of his companions and moved toward the white-painted DC-6B.

Guardsmen in United Nations helmets presented arms in a final salute.

The Congo sun blazed down on the tarmac of Ndjili Airport, outside Leopoldville. In the distance, across the dry bushland, the haze of late afternoon was settling.

Dag Hammarskjold boarded the *Albertina* and, as usual, chose a seat in the rear of the cabin. Beside him, snatching a final few minutes of low conversation, was his good friend and subordinate Sture Linner. Soon Linner rose, shook hands and left.

The six crew members of the Swedish Transair charter plane were at their posts. Three were pilots with captains' ratings on DC-6Bs. Nine of Hammarskjold's own U.N. team—including one woman—already were seated several rows ahead of their chief. It was a motley sixteen aboard the *Albertina,* with names as varied as the lands they came from.

In the nose of the plane Captain Per Hallonquist, with his copilot Flying Officer Lars Litton alongside, gave a signal. Attendants wheeled away the embarkation platform. The door of the aircraft clanged shut, locked by Stationmaster Harald Noork.

The *Albertina* taxied into position on Ndjili's unusually long runway and at 3:51 (all times Greenwich mean time, hereafter G.M.T.), on the steamy afternoon of September 17, 1961, it took off.*

The Secretary-General of the United Nations was off again . . . on a mission of peace that was to become a rendezvous with death. . . .

* Congo time is one hour ahead, and Rhodesian time two hours ahead, of G.M.T.

In the spotless flight control center of Ndola Airport that Sunday evening Moise Tshombe of Katanga was awaiting the arrival of Dag Hammarskjold.

The Central African provincial chieftain had flown into the tidy little copper-belt town in Northern Rhodesia from his capital, Elizabethville, 135 miles away. With him were two lieutenants, Foreign Minister Evariste Kimba and Finance Minister Jean-Baptiste Kibwe, to sustain and guide him in the trials ahead.

Tshombe, moon-faced, big-eyed, had been received with all honors when he crossed into the territory of the Central African Federation. An escort of Royal Rhodesian Air Force Canberra bombers had met his chartered plane. At Ndola he had been welcomed by Federal high-ups and by Britain's High Commissioner, Lord Alport.

For more than a year Tshombe—President of the Katangan Provincial Council of Ministers—had been defying the frail authority of the Central Congolese Government in Leopoldville. He wanted to set up his rich, developed territory as an independent, or semi-independent, state. In his attempts to do so he had run into a head-on political and military clash with the United Nations, the right of which to intervene in the affairs of his land he disputed. Five days earlier fighting had flared between United Nations forces and the Katangans. The battle, then at a peak of bitterness, had plunged the world organization into the most serious political crisis of its existence.

Hammarskjold's meeting with Tshombe had been fixed hurriedly with the aim of negotiating a cease-fire. The Secretary-General hoped it would clear the way for a wider political settlement between the contending Congolese leaders.

The stakes, then, were high for both principals when they headed toward Ndola, whose bright and sunlit streets and flowered gardens belied the gloomy sound of its name.

And the stage was set for a confrontation that looked as if it would contain some of the main elements of the drama of Africa, 1961.

It was to have been a confrontation of two men symbolizing

the wisdom of old Europe and the violence of new Africa . . . the affronted dignity of a peacemaker forced to defend himself and the daring defiance of the lawbreaker conscious of his courage. . . .

To Sture Linner, watching the *Albertina* fade into the eastern sky, the hazards of Hammarskjold's mission were plain enough.

As Chief of the United Nations Operations in the Congo (known, from its French initials, as O.N.U.C.), Linner had been the Secretary-General's constant companion during the past few days of crisis. Fellow countrymen, they had roamed the political landscape endlessly in search of a solution. Now the quest was nearing its climax.

The handsome, lanky Linner was preoccupied mostly with the possibility that Tshombe might at the last moment refuse to meet Hammarskjold. The Secretary-General himself had noted this as a chance he would have to take in flying to Ndola, because the Katangan had put forward his own conditions for a meeting. And he had failed to withdraw them when Hammarskjold had shot back word that the truce talks would have to be held unconditionally or not at all.

That was the first obvious danger in the planned encounter. There were others. Linner knew the outcome could profoundly affect the future of the United Nations and of Hammarskjold's own position. Yet these were now political imponderables, beyond the control of individuals, and Linner had been in his international hot spot long enough to understand that no amount of worry could change the movement of events.

The flash of concern that passed through the forty-four-year-old, aristocratic-looking Swede—and it was not more than a flash—flowed from his awareness of the reckless character of the forces opposing the United Nations. Ordinarily the flight from Leopoldville to Ndola would have warranted about as much attention as a bus ride through the streets of a city. But little was normal in the Congo of 1961. The mood and circumstances of the time injected danger into even the simplest of situations.

Tshombe's power rested on the soldiers of fortune whom he

was paying to fight for him. These foreign mercenaries were sworn foes of the United Nations. It was part of the world body's authorized mission to root them out of the land. Among the highly paid white adventurers deployed by Tshombe were a pair of pilots. One was a bronzed, square-jawed Katangan settler who had learned his flying in South Africa during World War II—Joseph Delin. Another was a Frenchman identified only as M. Magain. They had the run of the Katangan skies with the French-built Fouga Magister jet fighters they were using. These jets had been smuggled out of France earlier in the year in the bellies of big transport planes owned by a private American charter company and flown down to Katanga by way of the Congo Republic (Brazzaville).

Delin's Fouga, nicknamed the Lone Ranger, had in the previous four days played havoc in a series of bombing and strafing raids on U.N. troops, who at that time were without air support of their own. Linner knew that only that morning the Lone Ranger had made two sorties against the U.N. base at Kamina in Katanga; a DC-4 had been set on fire and a pilot and a Swedish soldier wounded. What was more, the *Albertina*, in which Hammarskjold was now flying, had been damaged by gunfire while taking off at dawn from Elizabethville on its way back to Ndjili.

These incidents were ominous. Linner had discussed them with Hammarskjold in arranging the flight to Ndola. Both were pretty sure the *Albertina* would be in peril of attack by the Fouga if the chance arose. As a result they ordered the strictest security precautions, in the hope of attracting as little attention to the flight as possible.

Originally Hammarskjold had wanted to leave for Ndola around 11 a.m., possibly in order to arrive before nightfall, possibly to be sure of being on the spot before any sudden change of mind should cause the unpredictable Tshombe to leave. Quite another flight had been arranged for him, in a different plane. But a combination of factors compelled the plans to be revised. Exchanges with Elizabethville over the terms of the truce meeting went on through the morning. The faster, more comfortable *Albertina* had become available for the journey. It was agreed that the Marquess of Lansdowne, Britain's Under-Secretary of State for Foreign Affairs, should precede Hammarskjold to Ndola to insure that all was ready for the parley on British territory. Lansdowne, at the time, was on a special mission to the Congo and was doing all he could to help end the fighting in Katanga. In the event, Lansdowne took off at 3:04 p.m. in the plane Hammarskjold himself was to have used, and, forty-seven minutes later, the *Albertina* followed.

Linner turned these things over in his mind as he traveled the 10 miles back to Le Royal, O.N.U.C.'s headquarters, in a residential suburb of Leopoldville.

He was a sensitive man dedicated to the U.N. cause, but he was no fusser. He had brought to his job the relaxed confidence of the classical intellectual (he had once translated Homer into Swedish) and of the international businessman (for a while he had headed the Liberian-American-Swedish Minerals Company). He felt that all reasonable precautions allowed by the conditions had been taken.

Yet despite the secrecy, within ten minutes of Hammarskjold's take-off the world was advised that the Secretary-General was flying to Ndola to meet Tshombe. For at 4 p.m. the big international news agencies reported the departure of the *Albertina.*

Hallonquist was an experienced pilot, with 7,841 flying hours to his credit. He was as fit as any of the U.N. pilots operating in the hit-or-miss aviation conditions of the Congo crisis. For twenty-four hours before take-off he had done no flying, and he seemed relaxed and cheerful when he left.

When instructions came through from the Air Transport Office that he was to take the *Albertina* to Ndola, Hallonquist carefully thought out the flight arrangements. Secrecy was the watchword in the plans he made. The state of the aircraft was checked. Transair's chief mechanic and flight engineer, Trygve Jan Tryggvason, reported a bullet had pierced the left engine during the attack earlier in the day. The damage was repaired. The rest of the machine was closely examined. Normally the *Albertina* (registration letters SE-BDY) was used by the U.N. Force Commander, General Sean Mc-Keown. It was a fairly new plane, purchased only two months earlier from the Arabian-American Oil Company. Special care was given to it. About mid-morning it was loaded for the long journey.

Tryggvason and his crew completed their repairs and pronounced the machine flightworthy by 11 a.m. They went to lunch, after locking the doors and removing all ladders. For the next four hours the *Albertina* stood unguarded. U.N. troops were posted at Ndjili's main gates but the airport, as a whole, would have been an easy place to enter if anyone without authority had wanted to do so. And although the cabin of the aircraft was secured, a trained saboteur could have found easy access to the hydraulic compartment, the heating system or the mechanism of the nose wheel.

In charting the route to Ndola—normally a journey of 970 nautical miles, or about four flying hours—Hallonquist and his Transair and U.N. colleagues agreed that the *Albertina* should make as wide a detour as possible around the usual playgrounds of the Lone Ranger. Some danger was recognized as being inevitable. The Fouga was operating from the Kolwezi strip, 230 miles from Ndola. Its combat range was about 150 miles. But there was always the chance that it could use some field nearer Ndola. Already it had sought to prevent U.N. reinforcements from landing in Elizabethville. It might easily attempt the same sort of thing with the *Albertina*.

The thirty-five-year-old Hallonquist did what he could to try to conceal the trail he intended using. Enough gasoline for thirteen hours and twenty-five minutes was taken aboard. He filed a false flight plan in the Ndjili control room for onward transmission, showing his destination as Luluabourg, capital of Kasai Province, northwest of Katanga. As an alternative destination he named Leopoldville. The aircraft would not have been allowed to take off without a flight plan, but he did not want to disclose his true destination for reasons of security.

In a conversation with Major Knut Olov Ljungkvist of

O.N.U.C. Air Operations, Hallonquist and Aahreus discussed their plans shortly before take-off.

Ljungkvist later recalled:

> ...At that time the last beacon to be used on the way down was Luluabourg. After that, he told me, "There is no radio navigation aid for me, so I have to go to Luluabourg, and after that I do not know if I am going to follow the Angolan border or whether I am going to take some other way."
>
> That was all he told me anything about, that he had decided to go to Luluabourg and after that he did not know. He told me, "I am going to prepare the rest of the flight during the flight, depending upon the special conditions."

Hallonquist went even further. He arranged that the *Albertina* would stay out of radio contact with its base during the journey. He planned to fly by dead reckoning, and although this carried the risk of navigational error, he figured it would reduce the chance that an enemy could follow his flight by observing his radio signals.

Nobody in the *Albertina's* crew was listed as navigator, but Hallonquist himself was Transair's chief specialist, and instructor, in navigation. And his co-pilots, Aahreus and Litton, also were qualified to navigate. The three fliers all held licenses as Radio Telephony operators.

The crew was augmented by Sub-Lieutenant Karl Erik Rosen, a member of the Swedish military contingent in the Congo who traveled as radio operator. The reason was that although radio silence was to be observed there was a chance that in an emergency the *Albertina* would need to transmit and receive messsages. A seçond radio operator was installed to monitor Hammarskjold's plane from an O.N.U.C. station at Ndjili. Both were under orders to communicate by Morse code in Swedish so as to render any messages unintelligible to the Katangan forces. In the event, no exchanges took place between them.

After take-off Captain Hallonquist cleared the frequency of the Leopoldville control tower and then maintained radio silence for four hours and eleven minutes. He headed toward Luluabourg and then flew east to a point in North Congo recommended for flights along the Nairobi-Ndola run. At 8:02 p.m. the *Albertina* broke silence and called the Flight Information Center at Salisbury, the Federal capital. The pilot reported his estimated arrival time at Ndola would be in another two hours and thirty-three minutes.

About thirty-three minutes later he called Salisbury again, this time giving his position as over Lake Tanganyika, on the eastern corner of the Congo. Hallonquist then turned south toward a point east of Ndola. Exactly an hour after its last call to Salisbury the *Albertina* checked in with Ndola Control Tower—at Salisbury's request—for the first time.

A. Campbell Martin, Air Traffic Controller at the Rhodesian Airport, reported that the pilot of the DC-6B, who then was not much more than about fifty nautical miles away, gave his estimated arrival time as forty-five minutes, an unusually long advance notice. He gave the *Albertina* routine approach instructions. In reply the pilot told him the aircraft would not be night-stopping in Ndola but might require a little fuel.

Martin, on Salisbury's orders, thereupon asked the *Albertina's* pilot to declare his intentions. If he was not stopping over at Ndola, where was he heading? How many passengers did he have aboard? Was he going on to Salisbury?

But the *Albertina* refused to disclose the information. Martin said he was told simply that he would get his answers when the plane landed.

At 10:10 the pilot of the *Albertina* radioed Ndola again with this message: "Your lights in sight. Overhead Ndola. Descending." Watchers at the airport at that point spotted the plane flying west-northwestward.

Martin gave the pilot an altimeter check and permission to come down from 16,000 to 6,000 feet. Then he was to check in again for further clearance to a lower altitude.

One month later, on October 18, 1961, the Government of the Central African Federation issued an interim statement on the Secretary-General's last journey. In the dry, laconic language of official statements it said: "No such report and no further radio communication was received from the aircraft."

And in a monumental essay in understatement, it added: "The aircraft failed to land as expected."

The occasion of a swiftly arranged peace meeting appeared to overawe self-conscious Rhodesian officialdom that fateful Sunday, and some of the authorities generated confusion and misinformation. Ndola had been advised around 8 a.m. to prepare the office of Airport Manager J. H. Williams for Hammarskjold's truce meeting with Tshombe. Lord Alport, the High Commissioner, had asked the Federal Rhodesian authorities on instructions from London to expect from Leopoldville two U.N. planes carrying Lansdowne and Hammarskjold. Night-landing facilities were to be prepared, although, at that early stage, nobody knew for sure when Hammarskjold would arrive.

Later in the day, when arrangements in Leopoldville began to fall into place, a more precise indication reached Salisbury of what to expect. The British ambassador in the Congolese capital, Derek Riches, sent this signal to Lord Alport at the request of the U.N. authorities: "Lord Lansdowne and Wilford [his private secretary] will arrive Ndola about 1900 hours [7 p.m.] today and will continue to Salisbury, returning to Leopoldville tomorrow afternoon. Secretary-General is due Ndola this evening by separate flight after Lord Lansdowne. *Flight details will be notified direct from the aircraft.*"

The full contents of that message, timed at 1:49 p.m., never reached the Salisbury Flight Information Center or the Ndola Control Tower. Nor was the text, with its crucial last sentence, made known to the Federal Department of Civil Aviation.

Thus, for reasons still unexplained, the essential purpose of the now-famous "Riches telegram" was defeated. That purpose was to alert the aviation authorities of the Federation to expect any relevant flight information from the *Albertina* directly, rather than through the normal aeronautical communication channels, which are in no way secret.

There were a great many cloak-and-dagger security precautions, which the Rhodesians appeared to aim primarily at newsmen. Scores of journalists and cameramen, representing the world's main news media, converged on the town, which was then a center of international attention. But they were barred from approaching the conference area and had to keep off the tarmac, where they would have been able to identify incoming personalities.

Several mix-ups occurred. The meeting originally was expected to begin in mid-afternoon. But Tshombe himself arrived only toward evening. A nervy man at the best of times, he clearly hated having to wait around for hours and made sure everybody knew it. More than once the British and Rhodesians half expected him to walk out. As the hours slipped by he became more agitated and depressed, and finally, as midnight (Rhodesian time) approached, he asked if he could find a place to lie down and sleep. Instead, soon after 9 p.m., he was driven to the residence of the Provincial Commissioner at Kitwe, thirty-one miles away, to rest.

Twice during the warm, starry African night indications were mistakenly given that the Secretary-General had arrived. The second occasion coincided with the landing of a DC-4 bearing U.N. markings, the principal passenger of which was greeted with some ceremony. Newsmen flashed out stories incorrectly reporting Hammarskjold in and the peace talks under way.

The British diplomat, related by marriage to Prime Minister Macmillan, had promised Hammarskjold before leaving that he would in no way interfere with the negotiations, or even talk with Tshombe or remain on the scene.

"It was important that I should limit my activities to the one purpose of helping to make arrangements for the meeting," he recalled. "I was in no way involved in the negotiations."

But he found when he arrived that Lord Alport had told Tshombe he was coming in. The Katangan already was "in a distressed state" because of the long wait, and he might have drawn "strange conclusions" if Lansdowne had refused to see him. And so, Lansdowne explained, a brief meeting lasting no more than ten minutes became unavoidable. Lansdowne said he refused to discuss, as Tshombe wanted him to do, any matter of substance.

Author's note

In the fading weeks of 1962 (and after this book was printed) it became clear that the dossiers on Dag Hammarskjold were not yet closed.

Conor Cruise O'Brien revised his initial assessment of the "September war" and accused the Secretary-General of authorizing a false U.N. account of what had happened in Katanga (Pages 117 to 123). O'Brien insisted that he had been ordered to end Katangan secession but that when the military operations went wrong Hammarskjold, in effect, repudiated him. (*To Katanga and Back*, Hutchinson.) U Thant at once put out an official U.N. denial which described O'Brien's charge as an "irresponsible fabrication." The bitter exchange emphasized the need for an international inquiry into the political circumstances that drew Hammarskjold to his death. O'Brien's reflection on the integrity of the late Secretary-General seems impossible to accept, if only because nobody has yet established just how much of the truth was conveyed to Hammarskjold in the last days of his life in Leopoldville. Yet even if Hammarskjold did fashion the case to serve what he considered to be the vital interests of the United Nations, to this writer his stature would remain undiminished.

At one point the British envoy had a sharp exchange with Tshombe's aide Kimba. The African interjected during the conversation the observation that he felt he could not trust any white man. Lansdowne rapped him for what clearly was intended as an insult.

The impeccably dressed Briton stayed at Ndola for about ninety minutes. As soon as the *Albertina* passed overhead he walked to his DC-4. Clearance for take-off was delayed about thirty minutes by Traffic Controller Martin, who then was expecting the *Albertina* to land. Finally Lansdowne's machine did leave. Almost at once he asked his Belgian pilot, Captain Deppe, to try to make contact with Hammarskjold's plane. Only silence answered him, and this disturbed the veteran flier.

Deppe's concern deepened at the DC-6B's continued failure to answer his signals or to check back with Ndola. He transmitted his worry to Lansdowne and Wilford. Anxiety rode with them all on their three-hour journey to Salisbury.

On landing at the capital, at 1:30 a.m., Lansdowne's first words to the British Deputy High Commissioner, D. A. Scott, who was meeting him, were: "Have you any news of the Secretary-General's aircraft?"

"To my dismay he said that he had none," Lansdowne afterward recounted. "By then I was in a state of very considerable disquiet. I could not think what on earth had happened. I do not think that there was any doubt in Mr. Scott's mind that Captain Deppe, Mr. Wilford and I were all extremely apprehensive."

It was then that the Marquess of Lansdowne feared the worst had befallen Dag Hammarskjold.

If Lansdowne's uneasy forebodings were transmitted to those around him, they made little impact either in Salisbury or in Ndola.

As the minutes, then the hours, slipped by after the *Albertina's* last call to Martin, it became clear that something had happened to change Hammarskjold's plans or to delay his aircraft.

Martin himself tried in vain, he said, to re-establish radio contact. He checked for police crash reports. After eighty-two minutes he sent out an "INCERFA" (uncertain phase) message to Salisbury, Elizabethville and Lusaka, originating the procedure for an overdue aircraft. But no positive word of the vanished plane came back. He consulted with Airport Manager Williams, and Williams talked with Lord Alport. All together, by surmise and speculation, they came to the conclusion that the *Albertina* had veered away for another destination or that it had decided to stand off until daylight.

"Not for one moment did it enter my mind that he had crashed," Martin explained.

At 1:15 a.m., with Salisbury's okay, he closed the tower and airport, left a communicator (a radio operator without authority to initiate action) in charge, and went off duty and home to sleep.

Williams himself formed the impression during the long night that, if the *Albertina* did intend to land, it would not come in until daybreak, when the pilot could see what he was doing. Alternatively he figured that the plane had diverted. He based all this, he said later, on conversations with Alport, Tshombe and other high-ranking authorities present.

"It was reasonable to assume that the pilot had decided either to divert or stand off until daylight," he said.

Williams confessed he was not particularly worried about the plane when it failed to land after its last contact with the tower: "Bearing in mind the nature of the flight and the very circumstances in which this flight started, I was not concerned at this stage."

He went to his hotel between 12:30 and 1:30 a.m. Soon afterward he was disturbed by two police officers who had hurried around to report that a light, or flash, in the sky had been seen near Mufulira, not far from the town, about the time the *Albertina* had passed overhead. The report, they said, was being investigated. Williams told them nothing could be done from his end until dawn. He turned in for sleep.

Lord Alport waited until about 1 a.m. for the DC-6B to come in. While standing, sitting and chatting he formed various theories about the loss of radio contact and conveyed them to his companions, including Williams. At first he theorized that there had been direct contact between one of the American official planes on the Ndola tarmac and the *Albertina* and that these exchanges had led Hammarskjold to hold off.

But then, a little later, when the plane had still not shown up, another idea occurred to him:

> I thought it possible that something had occurred in Elizabethville or that Mr. Hammarskjold had received a message from Leopoldville, or New York, which made him decide to postpone his meeting with Mr. Tshombe and to go elsewhere.
>
> It did not strike me as strange that Mr. Hammarskjold should not notify Ndola of his intentions, partly because of the circumspect attitude of the aircraft in its contact with Ndola Control, and partly because I thought that he would wish, if indeed he had changed his mind, to have a proper opportunity of dealing with the publicity which would ensue. At 2315 hours [11:15 p.m.] Mr. Williams asked me whether I thought that he should put into operation the normal overdue procedures which I understood were due to operate sixty minutes after contact had been lost. I said to him that he should institute whatever procedures were proper in the circumstances and as far as I was aware this was immediately done.
>
> Mr. Williams, at my request, had throughout this period kept me in close touch with the position as far as it was known to Ndola Control and was, of course, aware of my view that something must have caused Mr. Hammarskjold to change his mind and to decide not to land at Ndola as previously intended. It is natural that this, together with the failure of the Leopoldville plane to follow routine procedures, influenced Mr. Williams' subsequent actions.

And so Alport went back to his private aircraft to snatch some sleep.

During their vigil the Rhodesian authorities appeared to pay scant attention to another aircraft that was said to have passed overhead without identifying itself or signaling the control tower. The assumption was that it was a routine overflight. U.N. officers, however, considered it important enough to rate a mention in their official report to the Security Council on the flight of the *Albertina.*

Several Ndola residents later claimed to have seen or heard a second aircraft overhead about the time the *Albertina* was in the region. Timothy Kankasa, African Secretary of the Twapia Town Management Board, asserted he actually saw two planes that night.

One, he said, was big, with lights. The other, without lights, was flying above the first. Both seemed to be moving northwestward.

"Then it seemed as if the smaller plane was beaming lights on the large aircraft," Kankasa said.

Soon they flew apart.

Meantime, in Kitwe, the other principal player, Tshombe, was getting himself a good night's rest too.

They slept well, although all too briefly, most of those authorities in Rhodesia.

But then, about 4 a.m. G.M.T.—shortly before breakfast time, because Rhodesian clocks are two hours ahead of Greenwich time —the skies began to fall.

Senior Air Traffic Controller T. K. Parkes came on duty and at once checked all signal action for news of the vanished *Albertina*. There was none. He swung into action. Within an hour he signaled Salisbury with this "Uncertain Phase" (INCERFA) warning: "Person reported to the police here seen great flash in the sky at airport. 2300 (hours) in direction of Mufulira."

Eight minutes later Salisbury Rescue and Coordination Center proclaimed a "Distress Phase" (DETRESFA) with messages to Ndola, Elizabethville and Johannesburg for Leopoldville: "Request immediate to Ndola signal ZC40 reference SE-BDY overhead Ndola at 2210 [10:10 p.m.] nil arrival Ndola ex Leopoldville stop Send flight plan details—nil departure signal received."

Within an hour Leopoldville came back to say nothing was known there of the *Albertina's* whereabouts. Police throughout the copper belt were alerted for search action.

Then at 8 a.m.—more than eight hours after "overdue action" and more than three hours after "distress procedure" were proclaimed—planes of the Royal Rhodesian Air Force (R.R.A.F.) began an organized search. There were eighteen aircraft on the ground at Ndola. Squadron Leader J. Mussell, Officer Commanding at the station, said he could have had all of them searching at dawn if he had been given an hour's notice. A Canberra that happened to be airborne on a routine patrol soon after first light was ordered to keep a lookout for wreckage. Mussell reported he had not been asked to undertake a search during the night. It would have been pointless anyway, he explained, because a blazing plane could not have been distinguished from a common bush fire.

Police in Mufulira meanwhile checked in to say they knew no more of the flash in the sky seen during the night. But Ndola residents were coming up with clues. David Bermant, a travel agent living on the outskirts, was awakened by the roar of a low-flying aircraft the engines of which were working hard, causing "tremendous vibration." Mrs. Olive Anderson heard three quick explosions. W. J. Chappell, a caretaker, thought the din of a low-flying plane was followed by the noise of a jet—and a little later he heard three loud crashes and shots like a cannon firing.

In Salisbury, Lansdowne was in Sir Roy Welensky's office when—shortly after 7 a.m.—word came through of the Mufulira flash. The Federal Premier assured Lansdowne—prematurely, as events were to prove—that a "big scale" search for the missing plane already had been launched.

The same grim news trickled in to Linner, and consternation raced through the Leopoldville headquarters. The United Nations in New York was warned to stand by for developments.

Soon after 8 a.m. Linner, on the point of tears, telephoned American Ambassador Edmund A. Gullion to plead for help in the hunt. Gullion hurried. He halted all traffic over the State Department's worldwide teletype network. This was done by using a special secret code signal reserved for use in case of war or the assassination of a head of state. The signal gave him absolute priority to consult with Washington without interference.

Within minutes he had full authority for an Air Force search. Three U.S.A.F. planes in the area took to the skies. They were under the command of Colonel Ben Matlick, air attaché at the U.S.

Embassy in Leopoldville, who was named searchmaster of the international operation. Two O.N.U.C. planes joined the hunt. The French pledged three. Linner called also on the British, Portuguese and Congolese to help set up rescue parties with every available aircraft.

Yet by the time the searchers swung into really organized action in the middle of Monday morning (10:20) there were few among them who doubted that the widely suspected disaster was in fact a reality.

And so it proved to be.

For Dag Hammarskjold's aircraft around 10:13 G.M.T.—to judge by some of the watches recovered from the wreckage—had dived to destruction in the darkness of Africa.

The only man who said he actually saw the *Albertina* crash confessed later he had looted the wreckage.

Ledison Daka, who lived in a nearby village, told investigators he had been awakened by an explosion during the night, and said: "It was in the sky and the thing was coming toward the ground. It came breaking branches and trees . . . . about a mile away. . . . I saw a lot of fire."

The noise also awakened, and frightened, Daka's two companions, Posyana Banda and Damson Moyo. As the first pink streaks of daylight slipped across the horizon they picked their way through the forest they knew so well. Flames and smoke drew them to the hill of death. Terror filled their eyes at the carnage. They saw partly burnt bodies. The heat kept them at least 25 paces from the main body of the debris. Banda wanted to run away but felt he could not move.

After a while the Africans calmed themselves. They could see no movement, nobody living. They stared around them, through the trees, in case rescuers were approaching. But none came.

The ragged-trousered Africans walked slowly toward various bits of shattered wreckage. They were charcoal burners and accustomed to ashes and things that smolder. Near a bush something that seemed undamaged in a box caught their attention. To them it looked like a typewriter and therefore valuable. They were not to know that it was a coding machine. They picked it up, looked around and disappeared into the trees.

An Ndola magistrate some weeks later sentenced them to eighteen months of hard labor for theft, after hearing their explanation that the shivers had seized them and that they were much too frightened to call the police.

A Rhodesian Provost spotter plane piloted by Flying Officer Gerald Craxford sighted the wreckage at about 1:10 Monday afternoon. Police and rescuers were directed to the scene, 9½ miles west of Ndola Airport. It took them thirty-five minutes to get there. They found the debris scattered on a 12-foot-high anthill in the middle of a forest of young hardwood trees. The approach of the *Albertina* to its doom was clearly visible—about 300 yards of sliced treetops, with blackened and scorched branches amid the green.

They found a single survivor among the *Albertina*'s sixteen occupants.

Through the lonely night and for most of the long day Sergeant Harold M. Julien had lain amid the hot ruins of the plane, with the smell of the burning flesh of his companions in his nostrils. The thirty-six-year-old former American marine had groaned and mumbled deliriously, twisting and turning on the dry ground.

But only the frightened birds had heard him. They sang no songs.

Julien, acting Chief Security Officer at O.N.U.C., was rushed to Ndola Hospital suffering from burns covering 50 per cent of his body, a fractured, dislocated right ankle, a skull injury and uraemia (a morbid condition of the blood). He had been given sedation by first-aid men.

At the hospital the duty physician was Dr. Mark Lowenthal, Government Medical Officer, and for twenty minutes he talked with the injured man while treating him.

Julien's first words to Lowenthal were: "Will I be all right?"

The doctor asked him why the *Albertina* had not landed.

"Mr. Hammarskjold said to turn back," Julien answered in a lucid, coherent manner.

How had he got out?

"I jumped from the plane—the others were trapped," he said.

The veteran of Korea was followed into hospital by Senior Inspector Alfred V. Allen, Ndola's mustached police chief, who was hoping for clues that might help solve the mystery of the crash. A hospital sister allowed him to approach Julien's bedside the moment he became conscious. The conversation that followed went like this:

Allen bent close and said: "Harry."

Julien: "Where am I?"

Allen: "You are in Northern Rhodesia. I am a British police officer."

Julien's eyes were closed but he seemed to understand.

Allen went on: "The last we heard from you, you were over the Ndola runway."

Julien: "It blew up."

Allen: "Was this over the runway?"

Julien: "Yes."

Allen: "What happened then?"

Julien: "There was great speed . . . then there was a crash . . . there were a lot of little small explosions all around . . . I pulled the emergency tab and ran out. . . ."

Allen: "What about the others?"

Julien: "They were just trapped."

Nursing Sister McGrath of the Ndola Hospital staff, like Lowenthal, also heard Julien mumble that "Mr. Hammarskjold called out 'go back!' " Then, he said, "there was an explosion." One of Sister McGrath's assistants, Nurse Joan Jones, reported that while she was tending Julien she heard him mutter "something about a spark he had seen in the sky."

The injured American had several periods of clarity in the days that followed. He provided the hospital authorities with the name and address of Maria, his Cuban-born wife, and when she reached his bedside after hurrying across the Atlantic he recognized her. His speech was not difficult to follow. He understood some of the questions put to him and answered them.

The brave fight by the doctors and nurses of Ndola Hospital

for the life of Harry Julien nevertheless came to an end after five days. Maria was at his bedside. Next to the bed too was an eavesdropping tape recorder placed there by investigators, who thought that in the depths of delirium or sleep he might provide some useful bit of information. But the Rhodesian authorities announced publicly on October 10 Harry Julien had said "nothing useful concerning the accident" before he died.

There seemed no doubt about one aspect of the Julien affair. Doctors on the spot in Ndola were pretty sure his life would have been saved if help had reached him earlier.

Dr. Donald Matthew McNab, a Government surgeon who attended to him after he was brought into the hospital, said he would have stood a better chance of living if he had been picked up sooner, but that his prospects had faded with each hour of waiting, untended, in the silent forest. And Dr. Hugh Douglas Ross, who headed the medical team that examined the *Albertina*'s dead, declared Julien's chance of survival had been cut after his badly burned body lay exposed for nearly a day in the tropical sun.

Amid the carnage at Dola Hill the body of Dag Hammarskjold was easily identifiable.

He lay clear of the flames—perhaps the grim reward of a man who always had been impatient, or careless, about tightening his seat belt. There were two wounds in his neck, back and front, one seemingly caused by a heavy broken branch nearby; blood had streamed from the one beneath his chin. The upper part of Hammarskjold's spine was fractured, his ribs were injured and the back right side of his head was badly bruised.

Irrelevantly, his left shoe was missing.

Ambulance man Brian Eccles, who helped lift Hammarskjold's body from the scene, reported: "I noticed tucked into his neck muffler a reddish playing card."

Clutched tight in Hammarskjold's left hand were several dead brown leaves and blades of dried grass. His big-dialed watch had stopped at twenty-five minutes after ten. The Secretary-General wore a bow tie, no jacket. Unnecessarily, a silver identity disc was chained around his right wrist. It had been given him one Christmas by William Ranallo, his aide, who was always discreetly lecturing him about his carelessness.

Eccles expressed the view that Hammarskjold had not died immediately when the *Albertina* crashed. Eccles said that when he arrived on the scene—at 2 p.m. Monday—the Secretary-General's body showed no signs of rigor mortis. From the position of the body too he drew the conclusion that Hammarskjold had been able to move from the airplane after impact. The driver conceded he was no expert in pathology, but he claimed a lot of practical experience in dealing with dead bodies.

The Chief Fire Officer of Ndola, A. V. Lowrie, backed up Eccles' theory. "I was struck by the way the body was lying," he said. "I thought he had been thrown from the plane but had got away from the wreckage and lain down."

Dr. Ross, a forensic pathologist who also served as a consultant to the Federal Government, insisted emphatically that Hammarskjold's death must have been instantaneous. "After sustaining [his] injuries it is inconceivable that survival could be more than momentary," he said. "It would be a merciful assumption that he was killed instantaneously."

Ross felt Hammarskjold's nearness to the fire of the burning *Albertina* probably had delayed the onset of rigor mortis.

The detailed report on Hammarskjold's injuries—drawn up by the panel of pathologists, Doctors Ross, P. J. Stevens and J. Hillsdon Smith—was submitted to the Swedish Government for study. The Medical Board of Sweden invited Doctors A. Frykholm and N. Ringertz to comment on the Rhodesian findings. They expressed the opinion that Hammarskjold, in fact, did live a while, although they could not say just how long. Their view was that if he had been rescued at once and given the most modern medical treatment, the survival period might have been lengthened. The Swedish doctors did not dispute the Rhodesian finding that his injuries were fatal, and they were at pains to say the report of the Rhodesians gave an impression of care and reliability. But they set the cause of death as suffocation resulting from internal hemorrhage.

Most of the *Albertina*'s other occupants were horribly charred, some beyond a layman's recognition. Three were identified only by a process of elimination. This was SE-BDY's full complement of U.N. staffers:

Secretary-General Hammarskjold.

Heinrich A. Wieschhoff, American Director and Deputy to the Under-Secretary, Department of Political and Security Council Affairs.

Vladimir Fabry, American Special Counsellor to the Officer-in-Charge of O.N.U.C. (Sture Linner.)

William Ranallo, American personal aide to Hammarskjold.

Miss Alice Lalande, Canadian secretary to the Officer-in-Charge (Linner).

Sergeant Harold M. Julien, American Acting Chief Security Officer.

Sergeant Serge L. Barrau, French Security Officer.

Sergeant Francis Eivers, Irish investigator.

Warrant Officer S. O. Hjelte and Private P. E. Persson, two Swedish infantrymen taken along as guards.

The six Swedish members of the Transair crew were:

Captain Per Hallonquist.

Captain Nils-Eric Aahreus.

Second Pilot Lars Litton.

Flight Engineer Goran Wilhelmsson.

A/P Harald Noork and Sub-Lieutenant Karl Erik Rosen, the Morse radio operator, taken along for the transmission of confidential signals.

In Leopoldville first confirmation of the disaster, with details, came to Linner from Searchmaster Matlick.

Linner at once despatched Colonel Bjorne Egge, Norwegian

chief of U.N. intelligence in the Congo, to the scene from Elizabethville with orders to take charge of the bodies, effects and any documents that might have escaped destruction. He was to act until more formal arrangements were made for the removal and burial of the victims. That sad task later was assigned to Pier Spinelli, European Director of the United Nations, who hurried to the scene next day in the company of Knut Hammarskjold, Dag's nephew.

Egge was given every help by the Rhodesian authorities when he reached the wreckage on Tuesday, September 19. Investigators were already at work. One of the things the U.N. man scoured the area for was Hammarskjold's own battered old briefcase, which, possibly, contained highly confidential personal and official papers. The bag turned up all right, but Egge was not allowed access to it, for the Rhodesians impounded it. They did so on the grounds that U.N. headquarters in New York had formally advised them Spinelli was to be regarded as the authorized representative of the world body.

In fact, the bag was handed to Spinelli only after the intervention of Lord Alport was requested. The bag contained a few books, a clean shirt, a toothbrush and a few personal belongings, a memorandum of no great significance on the Congo, and the first twelve pages of a translation Hammarskjold had started on Martin Buber's *Du und Ich* (Thou and I), an obscure work of philosophy and poetry. If there were any other confidential documents in the bag, their existence was not disclosed.

Watchers at the scene of the wreckage, meanwhile, were filled with a sense of awe and irony.

The Secretary-General and his companions had died while trying to fulfill a basic purpose of the U.N. Charter: ". . . to maintain international peace and security and to that end to take collective measures for the prevention and removal of threats to the peace. . . ."

The stark truth staring from the smouldering debris was that it soon might symbolize the ruins of the United Nations itself.

Equally clear were the ironies. The United Nations, the business of which was peace, had become entangled in an ugly little war. Hammarskjold himself, who hated violence, had met a violent death.

And the truce he was seeking?

It was to come only after he died.

Monday afternoon Moise Tshombe was preparing to fly home to Elizabethville from Kitwe, where he had been waiting for Hammarskjold to show up. Still no official word of the Secretary-General's whereabouts had reached him. But now he felt he must get back to his base.

Aides summoned a news conference. In strong terms Tshombe denounced what he called the "manœuvres and aggression" of U.N. forces. He claimed 1,000 Katangans, civilians as well as soldiers, had been massacred, "even those who surrendered with arms raised high." And he asserted that the damage so far caused in the U.N. attempt to end the secession of Katanga amounted to $50 million.

Tshombe paused.

A British journalist leaned forward.

"Monsieur le Président," he said simply, "Monsieur Hammarskjold est mort."

Tshombe's big eyes widened.

"What a shame!" he lamented. "I am very sad. If Hammarskjold has died it is bad for the Congo. We Africans should be grateful for everything he has done for Africa."

He hurried back to Katanga soon afterward to take stock of the new situation with the help of his cabinet colleagues and some of his white advisers.

In Elizabethville earlier in the day Tshombe's opponent, Conor Cruise O'Brien, the Irishman serving as U.N. political chief in Katanga, was talking informally with reporters in the garden of his headquarters.

Suddenly a jet fighter whined overhead and let loose a load of bombs, one of which exploded on the far side of the headquarters building. The Lone Ranger swooped back and strafed the grounds with machine-gun fire. O'Brien and the newsmen flung themselves to the ground. Bullets sprayed the area.

As he got to his feet O'Brien calmly resumed talking: "Now, I was telling you about Tshombe and the cease-fire. . . ."

In Ndola's control tower Tuesday, September 19, two men started arranging the cease-fire Hammarskjold had set out to negotiate.

It was patently a makeshift truce that Tshombe signed the following evening with Mahmoud Khiari of Tunisia, chief of U.N. civilian operations in the Congo. Formally, it provided for the ending of the eight-day Battle of Katanga. In fact, it tackled none of the deeper issues of that political settlement which the Secretary-General had planned to take up with Tshombe. It left scope for the manœuvrings and violations that in fact followed in Katanga.

The Katangans were exuberant, feeling for the moment more secure, less inclined to compromise and as resolved as ever not to participate in a general Congo settlement, except on their own terms.

The United Nations, reeling from the impact of the Secretary-General's death, felt its authority weakened, its prestige bruised and its future confused and bleak.

And in that charred forest clearing slashed out by the *Albertina* on top of Dola Hill, a bare three flying minutes away, all was still.

2 | The Crisis

The battered body of Dag Hammarskjold rested in state in Saint Andrew's United Church of Ndola.

The fragrance of fresh-cut flowers rose above the mahogany casket, draped with the blue and yellow flag of Sweden. Four sentries, European and African, guarded the bier, their heads bowed, their backs to the coffin.

Dignitaries and diplomats from near and far were there to pay their last respects. Knut Hammarskjold, Dag's nephew, flew in from Geneva to represent the family. Among the visitors was Tshombe. A white handkerchief peeped correctly from the breast pocket of his dark suit as he strode in. The Katangan leader set a wreath of lilies on the coffin, stood silent for a while, bowed and walked out.

"C'est triste. . . ." he murmured to newsmen.

There was sadness too in Leopoldville. The main newspaper, *Le Courrier d'Afrique,* announced the tragedy in a headline above its masthead that said simply "M. 'H.' n'est plus." Alongside the detailed news despatch were several photographs of Hammarskjold, alone and with Congolese leaders. Then, without legend or explanation, a little map of Sweden.

Statesmen attending the sixteenth annual session of the U.N. General Assembly were in their places on schedule in New York, Tuesday, September 19. The outgoing President, Frederick H. Boland of Eire, with Andrew W. Cordier, the Secretary-General's executive assistant, on his left, called the meeting to order.

Suddenly there was a hush in the great hall. The eyes of the delegates were drawn to the empty chair, Hammarskjold's chair, on Boland's right. Its emptiness, for most of them, was as startling as a shout in church.

Boland called upon the diplomats to rise in "the shadow of immense tragedy," and observe a minute of silence in honor of their fallen servant. There were few who did so without a sense of deep personal loss. Even his Communist foes knew him as a friend of humanity. In an age of violence he was the tireless apostle of peace. Remote and shy, he could not conceal his gentleness. Peril was his companion on many of his missions around the world, but he never shirked a challenge. Hammarskjold's ambitions were well known, but they were not for himself so much as for the United Nations he had grown to love as other men love their women.

The empty chair spread forth a feeling of foreboding as well as poignancy among the mourning diplomats. Seldom before had one man's death threatened the destinies of so many millions, or so vividly dramatized the divisions of the great powers.

Over Manhattan's steel and glass skyscraper hung three questions:

1. Who would replace Hammarskjold as Secretary-General?
2. Could the United Nations survive his passing in the face of the East-West feuds over the shape and power of his office?
3. How should the United Nations reassert its authority in Katanga?

These were the main talking points in the lobbies and lounges and delegation offices after Boland adjourned the four-minute opening session. And many weeks were to pass before the answers emerged.

The Assembly began its yearly business next day with the unopposed election of Mongi Slim of Tunisia as the new President. Slim had been at Hammarskjold's side from the first days of the Congo crisis fifteen months before. At that time he spoke for the only African country on the Security Council, and he had played a conciliator's role between Hammarskjold, the African powers and fellow members of the Council. In his tribute to Hammarskjold from the Assembly rostrum Slim found it difficult to hide his feelings:

"The Secretary-General fell, one might say, on the battlefield of peace," he said.

The crash of the *Albertina* did far more than end the reign of a great Secretary-General. It created a crisis of succession, weakened the United Nations and plucked away the one man who seemed able to lead the world body through a dangerous transition to new political frontiers. These tangled issues would have arisen anyway, in time, because Hammarskjold's term was due to run out early in 1963. But the suddenness of the developments found the main power groups split over a solution.

The Soviet bloc wanted the United Nations to carry on, but with its servants chained by a new form of veto. For all their criticisms the Reds appreciated the U.N. role in localizing the Suez affair. But they resented the form of Hammarskjold's intervention in the Congo in 1960, which had frustrated the chance of a Communist take-over—"We do not trust Mr. Hammarskjold and cannot trust him!" cried Premier Nikita Khrushchev in his rumbustious act on the General Assembly stage that year. He called then for a three-man Secretariat-General—made up of a Communist, a neutral and a Westerner, each with a veto—to replace Hammarskjold.

The Western powers were united against Khrushchev's three-headed monster, but they were divided over whether to strengthen the United Nations. The French, British and Portuguese, mindful of their colonies, had been alarmed at Hammarskjold's attempts to arm his office with power to enforce majority decisions. They were less concerned when U.N. intervention was aimed at trouble-spots outside their own preserve, as in Laos, Lebanon or elsewhere. The American view flowed from President Kennedy's dictum that a strong organization was vital to "the independence and security of every nation, large and small."

The neutrals, holding about half the Assembly votes, were not unanimous. Some, like President Kwame Nkrumah of Ghana, were willing to compromise with Khrushchev's scheme for reform.

Others preferred Kennedy's approach. Most had become impatient with what they saw as Hammarskjold's softness and ambiguities in handling the Congo affair.

All these rival pressures surfaced prematurely when Hammarskjold disappeared from the scene. They overshadowed the bewildering program of ninety national and international problems facing the General Assembly, problems ranging from the apartheid (race separatism) policies of South Africa to Russia's renewal of atomic testing.

Soon it became clear that only the rare prospect of an East-West compromise over Hammarskjold's successor stood between the United Nations and the chance that it might wither away and die like its chief.

Yet, after weeks of agonizingly slow give-and-take, a provisional agreement did emerge between East, West and neutrals. The soft-spoken delegate of neutral Burma, former schoolmaster U Thant, whose name means "Mr. Pure," was chosen as Acting Secretary-General with a cabinet of advisers to try to take up where Dag Hammarskjold had left off.

It was a gleam of light, revealing that the powers of the world still considered it to be in their common interest to keep the United Nations in business.

The hard realities of the Congo drama meantime engaged the attention of the assembled statesmen lamenting the loss of their Secretary-General.

As they saw it:

Tshombe's Katanga had now successfully defied U.N. authority militarily as well as politically and seemed likely to get away with it.

Consequently U.N. prestige had sagged throughout the world, even before the *Albertina* had crashed.

The Congo crisis was at the heart of the U.N. problem, and its settlement was therefore a precondition of the world organization's role as an effective peace-preserving instrument.

Mistakes had been made, culminating in the disaster of Hammarskjold's death. Things had gone badly, not because the United Nations in itself was bad, but because it lacked the support of the great powers. If the great powers had unitedly backed U.N. actions there would have been no Congo crisis. The United Nations did not invent the rivalries of its members. Its members brought their feuds into the Congo debates with them.

With most major outside powers pushing their national interests in the Congo, it was inevitable that U.N. actions at various times would thwart or offend this or that country whose ambitions seemed likely to suffer. The Russians came out in fury first when their great red hope, Patrice Lumumba, was checked. President de Gaulle of France feared that the precedent of intervention against Tshombe—whom he favored—might be applied elsewhere, perhaps even in Algeria. The British had nightmare visions of an intrusion in the neighboring Central African Federation or in their dependent territories. Alone of the effective great powers, the United States, under President Kennedy, loyally supported Security Council resolutions—but not before the Eisenhower Administration had tried, without success, to sway U.N. policy through its big financial contribution to the Congo operation.

Those were the facts. The effects contributed to the events that led the United Nations into battle against Tshombe, and Hammarskjold to his death. Khrushchev broke relations with Hammarskjold. France followed the Soviets in refusing to pay a share of the Congo bill. Britain resisted U.N. initiative at crucial stages with quiet skills acquired over centuries of diplomacy. All this added up to a spectacular reminder, or warning, that the great powers could and would prevent the United Nations from trespassing in the forbidden pastures of national interests.

This snarled-up situation had confronted Hammarskjold and his men with an almost impossible task in their attempt to fulfill their mission. There were times when the Secretary-General temporized and when some governments, particularly in Africa and Asia, felt he should have been tough. This gave rise to a good deal of talk among knowledgeable diplomats, and U.N. high-ups too, that an even greater threat to the future of the United Nations might have arisen if Hammarskjold had lived.

Here was how they figured things:

The shock of Hammarskjold's death was so great that it sobered the powers and the politicians into a careful reappraisal of their postures and policies. Coupled with the pressures of world opinion, this forced them into an accommodation with each other.

But if the Secretary-General had flown back from Ndola to New York empty-handed, a totally different situation would have arisen.

The Afro-Asians, pressing for iron-fisted treatment of Tshombe, almost certainly would have accused Hammarskjold of appeasement, if not of surrender. They might even have turned against him in a crushing display of "no confidence."

Such a development—combined with Russia's campaign against him—conceivably might have broken Hammarskjold. The real source of his strength and influence lay in the support he was able to rally among the Afro-Asians and the smaller member-states of the United Nations. If, then, an Afro-Asian turnabout had forced him to resign, the United Nations would have found itself hopelessly and perhaps irrevocably split. In a situation charged with high tension the chances of an agreement on a successor undoubtedly would have been slender.

Sir Roy Welensky gave a strong, although veiled, hint of this possibility in a statement on September 21 urging that Congolese leaders be allowed—without U.N. intervention—to settle their own affairs: "However protracted a business this may be it seems to me to be infinitely preferable to the shedding of blood merely for the sake of *meeting a deadline in the U.N. calendar.*"

And in Paris around the same time, senior French officials expressed a conviction that Hammarskjold's crisis had begun the moment U.N. forces failed to force a military decision against Tshombe in the Katanga fighting. One senior authority commented: "The Secretary-General was 'politically dead' when he found it necessary to ask Tshombe to join him in a cease-fire negotiation."

Dead in the Rhodesian bush, the world found it easy to mourn Dag Hammarskjold.

The statesmen and the politicians chorused their sorrow, the newspapers and radios blared their praises. There was little reason, now that this truly just and neutral man had become a martyr, for conflict or confusion over his motives and methods.

But it was not always so. Some of the historic missions performed by Hammarskjold for the United Nations showed him to be the servant of a world unborn. He was variously portrayed as a Hamlet . . . a Machiavelli . . . a Frankenstein . . . depending on whose interest seemed to be at stake.

Hammarskjold's interpretation of the U.N. charter was as experimental as it was unavoidable. In a more stable, ordered world the United Nations might have been able to afford the luxury of a soapbox structure relying on words rather than on deeds. The postwar world was neither stable nor ordered, and Hammarskjold soon found himself forced into a big role, one perhaps as significant as that of the President of the United States or the Premier of the Soviet Union. As the living symbol of nearly a hundred countries, he found he had to initiate as well as to execute. It was necessary for him to act as the conscience as well as the voice of his organization.

Article 99 of the U.N. Charter says: "The Secretary-General may bring to the attention of the Security Council any matter which in his opinion may threaten the maintenance of international peace and security."

Hammarskjold set about invoking this right of implied powers in the absence of general directives from a divided, veto-paralyzed Security Council. And he used it to augment his interventions on those occasions when the orders he did get were vague or unhelpful.

He made quite a few long-memoried critics. He angered the Belgians over the Congo. Israel charged him with conciliating President Gamal Abdel Nasser of Egypt. A powerful segment of the British people, and notably the Conservative Government, fumed and never quite forgave him when he insisted on total, unequivocal respect for U.N. resolutions during the Suez affair. De Gaulle snubbed him over the 1961 Bizerta dispute with Tunisia and over other issues. And in the wake of the killing of ex-Premier Lumumba, Hammarskjold was, to the Russians, a "man who sullied himself with foul murder." Clearly, when Hammarskjold's initiatives suited the powers, they were pleased. When they felt their national interests threatened by his actions, they were furious.

The Secretary-General had his periods of depression and discouragement, but he tried to keep his feelings to himself. Instead, with a steely resolve, he pressed on with his chosen work. Bit by bit he built up his office and organization as the base for a de facto system of international morality. And he kept above the tumult of the East-West cold war. For that he was sometimes reviled implicitly by voices in the West as well as in the East.

The late John Foster Dulles said one time with scorn that to be neutral was to be "immoral." Khrushchev later insisted, "There is no neutral man." Each really meant, "Those who are not with us are against us."

Hammarskjold, of course, was reared in the tradition of Sweden's international neutrality, but culturally, intellectually and ideologically he was no friend of Communism. This, to him, did not bar a dedicated career as a truly impartial, fair-minded, uncommitted, international civil servant. In his last annual report before his death he set forth his credo, in answer to the Soviet assertion that there could be no neutrals:

> It has become clear that certain members conceive of [the United Nations] as a static conference machinery.
>
> Other members conceive of [it] as a dynamic instrument of international cooperation . . . served by a Secretariat guided solely by the principles of the Charter. . . .
>
> The character of the mandates [from the General Assembly] has been such that the Secretary-General had found himself forced to interpret the decisions in the light of intentions expressed. [The Charter] envisages a Secretariat as a neutral instrument.
>
> [This] principle also indicates an intention to use the Secretariat for such functions as would require that it have an exclusively international character.

> While it may be said that no man is neutral in the sense that he is without opinions it is just as true that . . . a neutral Secretariat is possible. Anyone of integrity can, regardless of his own views, act in an "exclusively international" spirit and can be guided in his actions on behalf of the organization, solely by its interests and principles.

The Katanga crisis that drew Hammarskjold to his death was one that found the U.N. mission under heavy fire from some Western countries. A few American commentators termed the U.N. operation unjustified and a failure. The Belgians raged. Welensky was furious. The British Government protested. In Parliament lawmakers, taking their cue from some newspapers, used such labels as "outrageous," "criminal," "shameful," "aggression" and "murder" to describe it. The French branded it as deplorable.

Thus the general shock and sorrow over Hammarskjold's death seemed to be tempered in places with a certain ambivalence.

"In his watery blue eyes you could see ambition," said a headline in Britain's mass-circulation *Daily Express* on September 19. The newspaper was one of a group that had never liked anything about the United Nations anyway.

The article by George Gale in the "Britain first" newspaper went on to offer an original explanation of the Swede's real political design:

> Hammarskjold was a man of great ambition. It did not show in the rather prissy way he walked or in the meticulous way he spoke, but you could see it in the firm set of his thin pale lips.
>
> No politician is any use unless he is ambitious. Hammarskjold was certainly a politician. He was no international civil servant for there was no one to give him orders except for the permanently divided Security Council and the permanently propagandist sounding-board of the General Assembly.
>
> But Hammarskjold was a politician without an electorate, a would-be statesman without a state. His ambition was to invest the United Nations with some of the attributes of Statehood. And for this the Congo offered 15 months ago an opportunity far too tempting to be missed. . . .

An emphatically favorable view of the man and his motives came from the American political commentator Walter Lippmann, who some might say was better qualified than the *Daily Express* writer to form a balanced judgment:

> I knew Dag Hammarskjold long enough and well enough, I think, to understand why he accepted the risks of opening up new paths in such wild and uncharted country. He was not an innovator because he had an itch to change things. He was a political innovator because there was no decent alternative. He saw no alternative by the United Nations in a crisis where there was a bitter confrontation in the cold war.
>
> No cautious and timid man would have dreamed of staking the prestige and perhaps the future of the United Nations, as well as his personal reputation and his office, on the attempt to pacify the Congo. But great as were the risks of intervention, the risks of letting events run their course were much greater.
>
> If the United Nations now fails in what Hammarskjold inaugurated, the prospects are that the terrible racial struggle between Europeans and Africans will become deeply entangled in the conflict between the western powers and the communist powers of the Soviet Union and China.
>
> It was to avert and to prevent this fatal entanglement that Hammarskjold dared to use the powers of the United Nations. . . .

In the world as it is, it sometimes turns out that dead martyrs achieve more for their causes than live prophets.

Little people all over the world nursed the hope that Hammarskjold's ideas in time would inspire member-countries collectively to create the truly United Nations for which he died.

The nations *were* united for a while in the serene and ancient university town of Uppsala, Sweden, on September 29, 1961. That was the day they buried Dag Hjalmar Agne Carl Hammarskjold, fifty-six, in the grave of his fathers.

It was in this onetime seat of Swedish royalty that Hammarskjold was formed. In the red castle of the provincial Governor on a hill peering over gabled roofs and spired churches, where Vikings once walked. In the school and university, where he shone as a scholar and bent over his essays and economic theories and law books. Along the river and in the lovely countryside and in the nearby mountains, where he skied or walked or cycled with friends, talking, arguing, wondering about life and the world and people. Talking, reading, working, forever working.

Statesmen came to his funeral from all over the world.

The entire diplomatic corps from Stockholm, including the Russians. King Gustav of Sweden and his Queen Louise. Prime Minister Tage Erlander and members of the Swedish Cabinet. Vice President Lyndon B. Johnson of the United States, the Lord Chancellor of Britain, Lord Kilmuir, Trygve Lie from Norway, Madame Lakshmi Pandit, sister of Indian Prime Minister Jawaharlal Nehru.

There were the familiar delegates and officials of the United Nations, looking like their pictures. Mongi Slim, in a place of honor as one of Hammarskjold's closest friends, was there, seemingly overcome. Adlai Stevenson of the United States was there, and so was Frederick Boland. Linner flew in from Leopoldville and Dr. Ralph Bunche, Hammarskjold's American deputy, from New York. There were Israelis, Congolese from Leopoldville, Laotians, Indonesians, Pakistanis.

They all crowded into the austere Cathedral of St. Erik (Sweden's patron saint). The red-brick building is tall and narrow, with saintly murals on its inside walls and the tombs of kings and noblemen and national leaders in its side chapels. Hammarskjold's coffin was set on a bier before the high altar and covered with the Swedish flag. A sea of flowers and wreaths, sent from all corners of the earth, surrounded it. They came from little people and big. From the Irish in Katanga and Queen Elizabeth of England. From newsmen at U.N. headquarters and President Kennedy. From student groups and the King of Laos and the Imam of Yemen.

On one side of the coffin, in high chairs, sat the Swedish King and Queen, on the other side the Swedish family Hammarskjold. At the head of the bier the Archbishop Eidem stood praying, conducting the service, scattering earth on the coffin. Eidem, 81, had long since retired, but he had buried Hjalmar, Hammarskjold's father, in 1955, and so was asked to conduct the service. The elder Hammarskjold once was Governor of Uppland Province and, during World War I, Swedish Prime Minister. This was Dag's home town. The choir sang. Trumpets and violins played.

Elisabeth Söederström sang in English "I Know that my Redeemer Liveth." Students carried the coffin out to the royal funeral car—a blackdraped old gun carriage, drawn by four horses. Silent crowds lined the streets. A cathedral bell kept tolling. The cortege dragged down the cobbled street from the hilltop toward the cemetery, and there seemed to be sadness everywhere.

They buried him in the family grave, marked by an obelisk with the single word "Hammarskjold" engraven on it. At dusk that day, September 29, 1961, the 7,500,000 Swedes throughout the land paused in silence for a minute of national mourning.

The statesmen hurried back to their crises. . . .

3 | The Mystery

The dizzying political merry-go-round that was the Congo once led Dag Hammarskjold to observe wryly to a friend in Leopoldville, "It isn't even anarchy."

Classical realities of power and politics, as taught in London or Paris, Washington or Moscow, had little meaning in the Congolese context during the first year or so of agonizing statehood.

In a world of forest and savannah and weird tribal rivalries, the tidy standards of the white man had to be revamped. The only certain thing was uncertainty, the impossible became possible, the obvious did not always happen. Anything went.

The gaudy term of Patrice Lumumba as the country's first premier, and his later assassination in Katangan captivity, carried its own grim reminder of the Congo game. The kidnaping of Tshombe in Coquilhatville produced the improbable spectacle of Katangans calling for U.N. intervention. Colonel Joseph Mobutu, then a twenty-nine-year-old accountant officer, climbed a barroom table in Leopoldville one night and announced he had given the Soviet ambassador and other Red diplomats forty-eight hours in which to leave the country. In Katanga the incredible story stumbled on, with the build-up of a band of soldiers of fortune—*Les Affreux* as they came to be called, the Frightfuls—leading Tshombe's forces in a stop-at-nothing campaign for independence.

Bloodshed, massacres and hunger stalked the people in their slow awakening. Some of the rich became richer. Most of the poor longed for the material blessings of the white man's world. Conspiracy bloomed like the mauve-flowered jacaranda trees.

But the mines and the plantations worked on. Somehow the grass was cut in the gardens of the towns. Cables were sent, and the telephone kept on ringing. The utilities did not shut down. The slow Congo River went rolling on to the sea.

It was a bizarre interlude for the nicely trained diplomats from abroad. They put away their textbooks, pigeonholed their principles and turned back to nineteenth-century patterns of political intrigue and string-pulling. For them the secret was to be not over-fussy about where diplomacy ended and politics began. The only alignments that mattered were those that preserved the powers of the protagonists, and the diplomats could only hope the protagonists did not switch too often.

In this situation Hammarskjold, the servant of the nations, tried to tread the tightrope leading from disaster to the vision of a new order of world cooperation. He slipped and he stumbled, he wavered and he wobbled his way forward—evading the shots not only of those he knew were his foes but also of some he thought were his friends.

Small wonder that in the aftermath of his sudden death rumor bred suspicion and doubt fed on misunderstanding over why he should have crashed.

There were only three possible explanations:

1. Pure accident through mechanical failure or pilot's error.
2. Sabotage, or attack, inside or outside the *Albertina*.
3. Hammarskjold's own inner despair and shattered hope, which blocked his sense of reality.

Had, then, the Swedish statesman's journey to destruction been the solution of the gods or of men? Or had it been of his own making?

The sight of the *Albertina*'s remains galvanized the Federal Rhodesian authorities into action. Premier Welensky swiftly ordered two investigations.

The first was the normal secret inquiry undertaken to conform with the law of the land and the standard procedures laid down by international civil aviation authorities. State specialists hurried at once to the scene to collect and evaluate every single bit of technical and other information that might bear on the crash. The Swedish Government, the Transair Company, the U.N. authorities, the International Aviation Organization of Montreal, and the International Federation of Airline Pilots Association accepted invitations to participate as observers. They did so, but without committing themselves to accept the findings of Salisbury's probe.

The second was an extraordinary public inquiry held in view of the major international significance of the accident. It was headed by the Federal Chief Justice, Sir John Clayden. Other members of the three-man commission were Sir George Lloyd-Jacob, a Chancery Division judge from England, and Group Captain Jack Newton of the International Civil Aviation Organization.

Welensky's Government kept tight control of all the clues, evidence and investigations—even of the Hammarskjold briefcase. Nobody was allowed near the accident site without special authority. More than 130 witnesses were interviewed inside the Federation and the Congo, and more than 400 pictures relevant to the crash were assembled. Scotland Yard—Britain's famed sleuthing headquarters—sent a specially trained man to Ndola to do some checking. But even he had to obtain the permission of the Rhodesians to inspect the remains of the plane.

The Swedish Government assigned its own police, detective and aviation experts to Ndola under orders from Prime Minister Erlander to take every conceivable factor into account. Stockholm's squad was headed by Otto Danielsson, a senior member of the Swedish Criminal Investigation Department. The significance of the assignment of a criminal investigator, rather than an aviation, legal or political specialist, was not lost on the Rhodesians. They were nettled. Nevertheless, as Erlander told his Parliament on November 22, the Federal authorities provided all help possible in the process of focusing daylight on some of the darker aspects of the tragedy.

After the first shock of Hammarskjold's death had worn off, the attitude of the Swedish Government and people toward the investigation emerged clearly: like many other member-states of the

United Nations, they found it difficult to accept that such a thing, happening to such a man on such an occasion, could have been just an ordinary airplane crash.

It was this sense of uncertainty, or skepticism, or suspicion, that led the General Assembly on October 26 unanimously to decide that an inquiry of its own should be undertaken. One consideration influencing the Assembly was that the Central African Federation was not a fully sovereign state with powers to regulate its own external relations and so to act beyond its frontiers. This circumstance alone seemed likely to circumscribe the scope of the Federal inquiry.

The General Assembly appointed an international commission of five members selected for their legal training. They were Justice Samuel Bankole Jones of Sierra Leone, Raul Quijano of Argentina, who was named rapporteur, Justice Emil Sandstrom of Sweden, Rishikesh Shaha of Nepal, who served as chairman, and Nikola Srzentic of Yugoslavia. Blaine Sloan of the U.N. Secretariat was assigned as Principal Secretary.

The task formally assigned the commission was to check into "all the conditions and circumstances surrounding this tragedy," with special attention directed to four main questions:

1. Why was Hammarskjold's flight undertaken at night without escort?

2. Why was the *Albertina*'s arrival at Ndola delayed?

3. Why was radio contact lost with the aircraft, and what were the reasons for the delay in determining the crash and locating the wreckage?

4. Was the *Albertina*, after the Katangan attack on it in Elizabethville earlier in the day, fit to fly?

The man who led the Federal technical inquiry from that fateful Monday was Colonel Maurice Linton Hilton Barber, forty-nine-year-old veteran flyer and Director of Civil Aviation. The ruddy-faced Rhodesian personally selected three other top aviation experts in the Federation to form his Board of Inquiry.

They were J. Blanchard Sims, Senior Operations Officer in the Civil Aviation Department, M. Madders, Federal Chief Inspector of Aircraft, and Wing Commander E. Evans of the Royal Air Force, who was Air Adviser to the British High Commission in Salisbury.

Barber instructed the specialists from abroad to stay silent during the inquiries in order to avoid prejudging the outcome and to discourage rumor and speculation. He alone had the authority to issue statements in the name of the investigating board.

He and his men got down to work, knowing their findings would have to stand the test of microscopic scrutiny by technicians, politicians, partisans, governments and critics around the world.

Political factors apart, their task was a gigantic one.

There was not much left of the *Albertina*—about one-fifth of the original total of the material that went into it. Its debris lay scattered over a wide area, and much of it was burnt out. Yet the experts took on the laborious job of trying to physically reconstruct the entire plane from its bits and pieces.

There was not much left of some of the bodies. Yet a team of pathologists undertook to examine every available scrap of physical evidence to try to determine identity, cause of death, presence of disease factors, and anything else that might have been relevant.

The scene of the crash was surveyed, the height and thickness of trees in and alongside the path of the descending machine were measured and every inch of the 800-foot wreckage trail was scoured for clues and signs of fire and explosion. Technical studies were undertaken on all instruments, the radio and electrical equipment, elements of the flight system, the autopilot and the altimeters. Inspections were made not only by experts on the spot but also by the manufacturers in America. Flight tests were carried out simulating the actual passage of the *Albertina* in the vicinity of the Ndola field. Altogether 201 live rounds, 342 bullets and 362 cartridge cases were recovered from the crash area and from the dead bodies.*

The search extended fanwise along the plane's visible track through the trees and, beyond it, over an area covering 2 miles by 1½ miles. But the 180 men engaged in the hunt reported they

* Ammunition had been taken aboard the *Albertina*—in the charge of the Swedish guards Hjelte and Persson—as a precaution against attack or sabotage during the mission. There had been several previous attempts to kill, or destroy, U.N. personnel or equipment, since the Congo operations began.

found nothing in the bush that might have thrown new light on the accident.

Thick forest reserves, bush country, lie between Ndola and Mufulira, and it was in one of these reserves that Hammarskjold's plane crashed. The hardwood trees grow to about 35 feet and range in diameter from 8 inches to 2 feet. The grass beneath the trees is also thick, sometimes up to 8 feet high, and since the dry winter season ends about September, bush fires are common.

Soon enough, it became clear that the starting point of the Rhodesian investigators was that the crash was purely accidental rather than the work of saboteurs or attackers. First indications of this were given unofficially to newsmen by Rhodesian experts within hours after examination of the wreckage.

Then Barber himself and the Rhodesian authorities followed through with a succession of four public statements that seemed designed to allay international anxiety over the cause of the disaster:

On September 23, Barber announced his board's explanation of the presence of bullets found in the bodies of the two Swedish guards. "The bullets . . . were definitely not fired from any weapon," he said. "It was known that the aircraft had arms and ammunition on board which was exploding in the intense fire which followed the crash." He observed he was unable "to refute continually reports and allegations which might prejudge the outcome of the inquiry."

On September 26, Barber said it was unlikely that an early decisive statement would be issued on the widely current "sabotage charges."

On September 27, he issued a summary of the preliminary conclusions reached by the pathologists, which said in part: "There is no evidence from our examination of the casualties to support any suggestion that this aircraft was fired upon or suffered in-flight explosion."

On October 18, eight days before the General Assembly debated the circumstances of the tragedy, the Federal Government announced that investigations thus far had failed "to determine any positive cause of the accident." It suggested strongly, however, there could be no question either of sabotage or attack. The relevant section of the statement said:

> Damage to trees at the accident site indicated that the aircraft crashed on a heading of 120 degrees magnetic at a shallow angle. The position of the wreckage was at a point where an aircraft making an instrument approach to runway 10 would be completing a procedure turn. The undercarriage was down and locked and the flaps were partially extended. Examination of the propellers and engines indicated that all engines were operating under some power at the time of impact. The aircraft was destroyed by impact and subsequently the wreckage was largely consumed by fire.

As the Rhodesians pieced together the shattered bits of the macabre jigsaw, a pattern began to emerge that looked to them as if it would fit their initial theory of accident through pilot error.

The nature of the fire showed there was enough fuel. Nothing was found to suggest mechanical or control failure. The radio was passed as working until the time of the crash. Four of the bodies were found with safety belts fastened and two other bodies showed signs of fastened belts, which indicated a normal landing had been intended.

Five altimeters were recovered, three on panels and two spares. The barometric readings on the three working instruments corresponded to the settings that Air Traffic Controller Martin said he had given.

One of the altimeters at the moment of impact indicated the plane was at a height of 4,600 feet. This at once aroused speculation among the investigators, and among experienced Rhodesian flyers, that an erroneous instrument or a misreading by a weary pilot might have contributed to the crash. Dola Hill, rising from the plateau that slopes undulatingly to the airfield, is 4,300 feet above sea level, or 140 feet higher than the runway.

Wing Commander Evans, a member of the Board of Inquiry, explicitly put forward the idea of a misreading through crew fatigue: "At the time of impact one altimeter was indicating 4,600 feet—and this could be the classic case of misreading the altitude as 6,400 feet."

Captain Michael O'Donovan, a pilot with thousands of flying hours behind him, had the same thought. A misreading through weariness, coupled with the strangeness of the terrain, would have been compounded by the fact of the night flight. In daylight most pilots would have been able to make a visual appraisal of the plane's height whether an instrument was misread, in error or not.

The searchers recovered from the wreckage four flight manuals and, after closely studying them, Barber personally formed the view they might provide the vital key to the riddle of the crash.

One was a Jeppesen Manual, published in Denver, Colorado, containing loose-leaf charts showing instrument-approach procedures for various airports. The chart for Ndola had been removed from the Manual. This in itself was not necessarily significant. Pilots usually detach the chart they need and clip it to their map board. The detached page may have been burned in the fire. Each Transair pilot is supposed to carry a Jeppesen. Other Jeppesen Manuals that may have been aboard the *Albertina* could have been destroyed.

The other three were bound copies of the U.S. Air Force Approach Chart Manual, which does not contain a page for Ndola. But it does contain an approach chart for *Ndolo,* an airfield six miles from Ndjili that was abandoned for use by big planes in 1959. Ndolo is 951 feet above sea level, near the Congo River.

One of the American military manuals was found to be folded back at the page for Ndolo. The chart was clearly marked, top and bottom, "Ndolo (Leopoldville, Congo)." It also contained some handwritten notes, in green ink, that included the height of the Ndola runway and the approximate seasonal barometric pressure for Ndola.

Barber felt all these discoveries amounted to more than coincidence and pointed to the possibility that the captain of the *Albertina* "may have got mixed up" between the two airfields. He thought Hallonquist might have been using the map of the wrong field and therefore the wrong let-down procedure.

But Barber's theory won little support from aviation authorities inside and outside Africa. Few could accept the proposition that a flyer of Hallonquist's caliber would have confused two airfields the only similarity between which lay in the spelling of their names. Also, the procedures defined in the Manuals related to instrument approaches, and the Rhodesians were working on the assumption, supported by available evidence, that Hallonquist was making a visual descent. In any case, as Transair pilot Flight Captain Lars Erik Starck pointed out, it was at least as reasonable to assume that fire destroyed Hallonquist's true Ndola chart as it was to suppose that no such chart was aboard the airplane carrying the Secretary-General of the United Nations.

The possibility that outsiders might have caused Hammarskjold's crash arose, in the first place, out of a political assessment.

The suggestion originally was made by the Leopoldville Government, which, of course, was an interested party.

Leopoldville's view was not disputed by authorized spokesmen of the United Nations in the Congo and in New York.

An O.N.U.C. official said he could not rule out that Katanga's Fouga jets were directly or indirectly responsible for the crash. He added that the flight was arranged at night partly in order to avoid those planes. (In fact, Katanga had only one jet active at that tim The man in charge of it, Major Delin, claimed it did not take off o the night Hammarskjold died.)

At New York headquarters, another official said the cause of the crash was "an open question."

Swiftly, around the world, the "foul play" theory snowballed.

In New Delhi, Prime Minister Jawaharlal Nehru commented with visible emotion: "Whether this [death] was due to an accident or some kind of sabotage, I do not know. Conditions in the Congo are such that anything is possible."

Few knowledgeable authorities could dispute Nehru's observations. Nevertheless, they offered something of a blank check to amateur—and semiprofessional—sleuths. A variety of explanations were offered. One of the most novel was given considerable prominence in some Scandinavian journals. Copenhagen's *Ekstra Bladet* and Stockholm's *Se* in January, 1962, carried a copyrighted article by a Danish newsman, P. G. Lindstrom, asserting that the *Albertina* had carried a seventeenth passenger. He was said to be a would-be hijacker, of the Fidel Castro vintage, who had attempted to compel Hallonquist to fly his aircraft into Katanga. Lindstrom also claimed some of Tshombe's men were waiting at Kolwezi airfield to seize Hammarskjold. In the fracas that Lindstrom said followed in the air above Ndola, the DC-6B plunged to disaster.

Lindstrom's version, which he claimed was disclosed to him by one of Tshombe's agents in Europe, was very carefully checked by the U.N. commission, even though it seemed to be no more than a sensational rumor.

Linner and others who saw the plane take off from Ndjili testified that they knew or were introduced to all persons who went aboard. The Rhodesian pathologists who checked the bodies in the wreckage said it was highly unlikely that a seventeenth person was aboard. And the police, who were not told at the outset how many people were in the *Albertina,* examined the scene of the crash for traces that might have been left by anyone wandering off into the bush, but found none.

In London, New York, Salisbury and key capitals of Europe, Asia and Africa, newspapers speculated openly on the possibility of sabotage or attack.

It was early evening September 18, before the ashes of the *Albertina* had turned cold, when Congolese Prime Minister Adoula issued this statement in Leopoldville:

> Immediately after the radio and press announcement of the disappearance of the airplane carrying Mr. Dag Hammarskjold, Secretary-General of the United Nations, a special meeting of the Council of Ministers was called by Mr. Cyrille Adoula, the Prime Minister, for the purpose of considering the domestic and international repercussions of the death of a man who had successfully borne up under great strain and had remained the link between east and west and the guardian of the interests of small states threatened by the western imperialists and neo-colonialists.
>
> Important decisions were taken.

> The Republic of the Congo owes a great debt of gratitude to Mr. Hammarskjold, who, despite a crushing burden of work, recently visited Leopoldville at the invitation of the Central Government of the Congo.
>
> *Therefore, in order to pay a tribute to this great man, now vanished from the scene, and to his colleagues, all of whom have fallen victim to the shameless intrigues of the great financial powers of the west, and in order to demonstrate publicly our indignation at the scandalous interference in our affairs by certain foreign countries, the Government has decided to proclaim Tuesday, 19 September, a day of national mourning.*
>
> Flags will be flown at half-mast throughout the country.

The die—the first official governmental accusation that Hammarskjold's death might have been plotted—had been cast.

The official declarations of Barber's Board did little or nothing to counter the predispositions of people and governments to suspect foul play. Nor were the honest doubts of others who questioned the impartiality of the Rhodesian investigators dispelled.

In part, the explanation was that Sir Roy Welensky had long since taken a political position of strong sympathy and support for Tshombe. The husky Rhodesian leader, who used to be a locomotive driver, also thus gratuitously indulged his need to let off steam against the United Nations. It was as if he resented the right of the United Nations, or anyone else who did not share his views, to concern themselves with the affairs of Africa.

Whether or not Rhodesians were capable of conducting an objective and penetrating inquiry was one thing.

It was quite another when accusations of murder and villainy began to arise as a grim postscript to the Hammarskjold affair.

As if by magic the charges spread through Asia, Africa and Europe.

They implicated not only Tshombe and the soldiers of fortune in his employ but also the British, Belgians and Rhodesians.

What lay behind these allegations? What precisely were they? Why did they persist?

By chance, the day before Hammarskjold died Prime Minister

Nehru charged Britain with obstructing U.N. operations in the Congo. He termed the policy of the British in Katanga "scandalous," yet without listing specific complaints in public.

After the crash, a great storm burst in the Indian press. The British were accused in some newspapers not only of moral but also of actual complicity in the tragedy.

"Never even during Suez have Britain's hands been so bloodstained as they are now," proclaimed the *Indian Express*, the country's biggest daily, in an editorial on September 20. "His death might be a coincidence but could be a calculation."

Bombay's *Free Press Journal* devoted a leader page editorial that same day to an analysis of "Who Killed Hammarskjold?" It asserted that the crash was no accident. "Those who flew into an impotent rage when the U.N. went into action against Tshombe's renegade regime could have had a direct and deliberate objective," it said. It defined this objective as the restoration of Katangan strength.

Africa echoed similar outbursts. Nationalist leaders in the Central African Federation itself claimed the circumstances of the Secretary-General's death were "suspicious." Both Dr. Hastings Banda, the Nyasaland Minister of Natural Resources and president of the Malawi Congress Party, and Joshua Nkomo, president of the African National Democratic Party in Southern Rhodesia, called for an independent international inquiry into the crash.

"The fact that this incident occurred in a British colonial territory in circumstances which look very queer is a serious indictment of the British Government," said Nkomo.

In Accra the *Ghanaian Times*, which usually voices the views of President Kwame Nkrumah but which this time was disowned by him, delivered itself of an editorial salvo under the heading "Britain: The Murderer":

> The history of the decade of the sixties is becoming the history of political and international murders. And one of the principal culprits in this sordid turn in human history is that self-same protagonist of piety—Britain.
>
> Britain was involved, by virtue of her NATO commit-

> ments, in the callous murder of the heroic Congolese Premier, Patrice Lumumba.
>
> But Britain stands alone in facing responsibility for history's No. 1 international murder—the murder of United Nations Secretary-General Dag Hammarskjold.
>
> We declare with the gravest conviction that Hammarskjold was the victim of a deliberate attack, inspired by Britain, and executed by Roy Welensky and that African traitor, Moise Tshombe of Katanga.

The newspaper added that the *Albertina* must have crashed after an attack by what it called "the jet fighters of Katanga-Britain-Rhodesia conspiracy," or through the planting of bombs on the plane by British officials in Leopoldville.

In softer but no less direct terms came this comment from a usually level-headed opposition journal in the pro-Western, Commonwealth state of Nigeria.

"Whatever may have accounted for the sad fate of the U.N. Secretary-General Mr. Hammarskjold," said *The Service* in an editorial, "the British Government cannot easily wash itself of the charge of complicity in the crime committed."

Here was rumor rampant in Asia and Africa.

In parts of Europe feeling ran high too, but suspicions emerged more elegantly.

Anger mingled with sorrow came out of neutral Sweden, Hammarskjold's homeland, and harsh words were heaped on the several hundred mercenaries leading Katangan resistance against the United Nations. They "systematically sought to sabotage the U.N. work for peace in the Congo," said Foreign Minister Osten Unden in Stockholm on September 18.

Unden, some time later—October 26—told the General Assembly in New York: "Considering the political consequences of the catastrophe and the flood of speculation which soon afterward spread among the public and in the press there seem to be well-founded reasons for a complementary investigation [of the crash] under the auspices of the United Nations."

The Swedish Government itself cast no suspicion on the work

of the Rhodesian investigators. But the Swedish press as a whole stressed that it would have been more reassuring if an international commission had taken charge of the inquiry from the start. Hammarskjold's death came for the Swedish people only as a dramatic climax to the concern they already had been feeling over casualties sustained by their troops serving with U.N. forces in Katanga.

National anxiety was deepened further by the views put out in the name of the management of Transair, the Swedish charter company that owned the *Albertina*. From beginning to end they sought to dismiss every possibility of an accident, defending the quality of their planes and pilots and putting forward the theory that the machine probably had been attacked from the ground while approaching the runway.

Compounding these factors, in the Swedish mind, was the mystery of the bullets found in the six bodies. The first vague statement put out by Barber that this was a discovery of "no significance" and that the ammunition clearly had exploded in the flames served only to crystallize the suspicions of the Swedes.

The whispers first, and the public accusations later, of some sort of British-Rhodesian-Katangan conspiracy against Hammarskjold infuriated the Governments of London and Salisbury. They were compelled, first of all, to notice and to answer with scorn charges they regarded as outrageous. They felt bound, next, publicly to redefine their attitudes toward Katanga and the Congo in general. And in a conscious effort to diminish their unpopularity over Katanga, the British and Central African authorities took pains to say the right things on the issues involved whenever the chance arose.

The Foreign Office jumped in on the night of September 18 with a statement affirming London's support for U.N. efforts to "establish a united Congolese state" with Katanga in it. But a settlement must come peacefully. And the British added pointedly that it was Hammarskjold himself who had suggested Ndola—on British soil—as the site of the peace talks.

British High Commissioners in New Delhi and Accra protested the charges of complicity leveled against London by Indian and Ghanaian newspapers. Sir Paul Gore-Booth dealt with specific complaints at a news conference in New Delhi. Sir Arthur Snelling branded as "disgraceful" the accusations of the *Ghanaian Times.*

A cabinet minister in London joined the rare international name-calling match with a denial of what he called "wild accusations." The intervention of Lord Privy Seal Edward Heath was rare because it is unusual for governments—especially in Britain—to reject unofficial charges.

Heath, deputy chief of the Foreign Office, said: "While of course it is unthinkable that our Government could in any way have been responsible for the crash of the Secretary-General's aircraft—and I utterly deny such wild accusations—I do not think I should say any more until the official inquiry is completed."

Welensky in Salisbury felt no such inhibitions.

This onetime professional boxer had for a long time been trading long-distance political punches with Nehru, and in a statement on September 20 he called attention to the "strange outbursts" of the Indian leader in these words: "Mr. Nehru's frequent observations on the Congo situation in the past few days confirm the widespread suspicion that the Indian Government has a special fish to fry in that part of the world."

Welensky denied supporting Tshombe in his conflict with the United Nations—but went on to blame the world body for precipitating the war through actions he called "ill-considered." He noted the Federation has 2,000 miles of open frontier with Katanga and therefore could not remain indifferent to anything that might disturb the stability of the region, which was to the Federation its "most vital interest." And in so many words he asked Nehru to shut up.

It all seemed to be very much a case of point, counter point. . . .

The shooting subsided but the shouting went on.

Only one thing looked sure: Doubt and uncertainty would linger for a long time over the wreck of the *Albertina* in the woods near Ndola. . . .

Hateful suspicion followed the long, lonely trail of the DC-6B all the way from Ndjili to its doom. There were mysteries to be solved in Leopoldville, in the air and in Ndola.

In Leopoldville:

The *Albertina* was a suspect aircraft after the dawn attack by Katangans. Engineers carried out repairs, but could there have been further undetected damage that made it less than safe to fly? Linner advised Hammarskjold to use it, rather than another machine, for reasons of security and greater comfort.

O.N.U.C. showed a proper concern over the perils attending Hammarskjold's flight, but was it not obvious that an overemphasis on security factors could lead to lower safety standards? In any case, was secrecy about the *Albertina*'s route—however much Hammarskjold himself may have favored it—the right answer? Would it not have been better if the Secretary-General had been pressed to make an open, direct, swifter flight, with an escort if necessary, so that all the world could have followed the journey? Is it likely that any would-be assassins would have dared to attack in such circumstances? Why should the Secretary-General, the servant of the world, have had to fly by night, in secret, almost furtively? And, if there was so great a preoccupation with security, why was the *Albertina* left unguarded for four hours after its engineers went to lunch?

Linner claimed an unexplained five-hour delay in Lansdowne's departure caused Hammarskjold to delay his own take-off. What made Hammarskjold consider it so essential that the British diplomat should precede him? It would have been useful to have Lansdowne check the Ndola arrangements—but was it absolutely necessary? And if it was necessary, why could Hammarskjold not have deferred his own departure until next day—especially since Tshombe had not yet withdrawn his conditions for attending the truce talks? The two principals could hardly have transacted any real business at once, anyway, if Hammarskjold had arrived late Sunday night.

Certain of the U.N. security precautions seem almost obsessive, even allowing for the surrealist circumstances of the times.

The Fouga's operations led to the decision not to file a flight plan with Salisbury, but it fails to explain why O.N.U.C. Air Operations was not advised in advance of Hallonquist's route. If anything had befallen the *Albertina* before reaching Rhodesian territory, U.N. authorities simply would not have known where to look for it. It is clear that Hammarskjold himself was aware of some of the precautions. But did any of his advisers try to make him understand that the overelaborate arrangements for concealing his tracks could increase, rather than decrease, the risks? And if any attempt was made to bring these things to his notice, why did he ignore the red flag?

In the air:

Nobody can ever know for sure exactly what went on aboard the *Albertina* from the time it departed. Any attempted reconstruction of its flight therefore has to be based on incomplete, circumstantial and second- or third-hand evidence. Yet some features stand out owing to their strangeness. Hammarskjold's plane flew an estimated 1,500 miles on its roundabout route to Ndola, compared with 973 miles covered by Lansdowne's slower machine. Yet even so, its flying time of six hours and twenty-two minutes seems long for a journey that should have taken about four hours in normal conditions.

One unanswerable question, of course, will always be whether Hammarskjold changed his landing plan at the last moment, as Sergeant Julien's listeners claimed he said. If he changed his mind, what made him do it? If he did not, why did Julien say so (unless he was delirious)? Could there have been sudden recognition of physical danger? Was there a political element that so far has not seen the light of day? Is it conceivable that he learned something from someone aboard, or over his radio, that made him think again?

Another mystery is why Ndola Control, knowing the importance of the occasion, did not use its tape-recording unit to preserve the radio exchanges with the *Albertina*. If this had been done the investigators would not have had to rely on one man's memory, or notes, of what passed between the tower and the pilot.

Then again, having decided on a detour and radio silence for greater security, why did Hallonquist reveal to Salisbury his true destination before he had flown past the Katangan danger area? Having spoken to Salisbury and Ndola, why did Hammarskjold not feel free to radio Lansdowne in the air? The British diplomat tried several times—in vain, he has said—to make contact with the *Albertina before* he landed at Ndola. He also tried reaching the *Albertina after* leaving Ndola, but by then, of course, it seemed to have been too late for Dag Hammarskjold's plane to pick up any signals from anywhere ever again.

In Ndola:

The airport authorities lagged painfully in recognizing that something untoward might have happened to the overdue *Albertina,* and it wasn't till morning that they snapped into action. The broad explanation was that they thought this unusual V.I.P. plane, which had attracted so much attention to itself by breaking so many rules, had veered off to another unknown field. Yet is this a good enough explanation in the circumstances? Would it not have been equally valid to judge that just *because* its behavior and its main passenger were so unusual, greater caution than ever should be displayed? If similar circumstances had attended a flight by Welensky, or Macmillan, would the same assumption have been made, and allowed to stand unchecked so long?

The hunt began in earnest about mid-morning. There were two police reports of flashes or fire in the sky that the police themselves rated important enough to investigate. Yet even with the knowledge that the *Albertina* had failed to check in anywhere, the air authorities somehow did not get around to coordinating the police information on a map until after midday.

Finally, when the police observations were charted and passed on to the pilot of a spotter plane, it took less than half an hour to locate the wreck of the *Albertina.* And within forty minutes rescuers were on the scene. Alas, poor Julien!

One of the most puzzling aspects of the whole affair centered on conflicting reports over the presence of a second aircraft in the Ndola skies about the time the *Albertina* crashed. The implication of accounts suggesting the presence of such a plane was that Hammarskjold's plane might have been attacked and brought down.

The mystery began when Sture Linner in a "special report on the tragic flight of the Secretary-General" told the Security Council on September 19: "At 0800 hours (gmt), UN base operations at Ndjili airport reported that an unidentified aircraft had been reported overflying Ndola airport late the previous night but that no communication contacts had been made between this plane and the control tower." (S/4940/Add. 5, September 19, 1961.)

The Rhodesian authorities, so far as is known, never referred directly to the Linner report. Suspicions about a sky attack on the *Albertina* were consistently and vigorously discounted by Barber and later by the Federal Commission. Suggestions by the African Kankasa that he had actually seen two aircraft, and by others that they had heard more than one, on the night of the crash, were brushed aside as fanciful or unsubstantiated.

The theory of an outside attack, however, was never completely dismissed by Swedish authorities, who also paid a good deal of attention to the riddle of the bullets. Transair's chief engineer, Bo Virving, visited the crash site daily looking for evidence of sabotage. He expressed doubts about the origin of several holes in the aircraft, notably to the right of the co-pilot's seat. In particular he thought that damage to a window frame in the cockpit, and to fiber glass in the radar nose cone, might have been bullet holes. He told the Rhodesian Commission four months after the crash: "I am still suspicious about those two specimens."

Virving's evident preoccupation with the possibility of sabotage, or an attack, did not endear him to the Rhodesians or British. Wing Commander Evans said so bluntly. There was no evidence of sabotage or murder, he insisted. And he said he resented the Swede's suggestions because they gave the impression that the investigators were "not looking for the truth."

Evans continued: "Virving was concentrating on looking for sabotage and enemy action. He has made an allegation of murder against someone. On pure evidence there is nothing to support this statement. No rockets have been found along the path of the aircraft. Exploded rocket heads would leave shell splinters in the fuselage. None has been found."

The wing-piece and window frame of the *Albertina* were examined by spectrographer J. Coles. Afterward he told investigators that metal traces or the holes in them did not appear to be consistent with the entry of bullets.

The mystery of bullets and bullet fragments found in the bodies of the *Albertina's* passengers for a long time absorbed the specialists, who also were divided in their judgments.

A ballistics expert, Superintendent R. H. Els of the Northern Rhodesian police, publicly expressed certainty that bullets found near the wreckage could not have been fired through gun barrels. The only damage he said he saw that might have been caused by a fired projectile was in the radar nose dome, and that this was consistent with damage done by a military bullet at the end of its velocity and tumbling over in the air after traveling more than 2,000 yards. If this, in fact, had been the case the bullet most likely would have been shot from the ground, not from the air. Barber himself had asserted that bullets exploded in a fire could—and in the case of the *Albertina* did—have the power to penetrate a human body.

Some Swedish and Swiss ballistic authorities disputed this claim. Major C. F. Westrell, with a twenty-year background of experience in ammunition factories, was quoted in Swedish newspapers as saying: "I can certainly describe as sheer nonsense the statement that cartridges of machine guns or pistols detonated in a fire can penetrate a human body." He based his assertion on large-scale experiments conducted to determine dangers for members of fire brigades who have to work near ammunition depots.

Other Swedish experts asserted that bullets in a box, placed in an oven and heated until the point of explosion, cannot achieve velocity sufficient to penetrate that container. Some Swiss experts arrived at similar conclusions after carrying out, and filming, tests. But from this general rule they excluded single bullets present in loaded guns.

Rhodesian authorities took steps soon after the crash to try to calm Swedish opinion, which had become agitated on the point. Barber put out a more detailed explanation of the bullets mystery based on evidence at his disposal. The Rhodesian High Commissioner to Britain, A. E. P. Robinson, took time out in Stockholm to meet press and radio men in an attempt to explain Salisbury's views with greater precision.

The findings of the Federal and U.N. investigations meantime were awaited with anxiety by sober men around the world.

Final judgments stood suspended.

Pure accident? Sabotage on board? The bullets of a marauder on the ground or in the sky?

Each of these theories concerning the mysterious death of Dag Hammarskjold is possible. But pending final proof they must remain hypotheses only.

One fact, however, is indisputable. It is that Hammarskjold went out on his mission of peace knowing he was exposing himself to grave dangers.

If, before dying, he had recognized his vulnerability, why did he press forward aware that he might never return?

If he did not recognize the truth, what was blocking his thoughts?

Somewhere along the line there is a missing component. The missing component is the state of mind of the Secretary-General himself.

Dag Hammarskjold was not a simple man. For years he had lived in the blazing lights of world attention. But few people ever got to understand what lay behind the image they saw of a diplomat, polished and politically courageous, calm and quiet. They could not guess at his sensitivity, or at a degree of sentiment, which he had drawn from a gentle mother. They recognized his energy, ambition and idealism. But they were not to know these qualities reflected a burning need to comply with the perfectionism of his autocratic father, Hjalmar, who before his death at ninety-one had been Prime Minister, Judge-President and a Governor of Uppland Province.

Youngest of Hjalmar's four sons, Dag represented European man reared in the finest and most honorable tradition of Old World civilization and service. He was far more than the political diplomat *par excellence.* Aesthete, art and music lover, scholar, mountaineer, poet too, his passion was people and the affairs of men. Always he had wanted to live and shine at living, and he loved the sun and watching birds in flight. Once on a mountaintop he had shouted out the words of *The Waste Land*, by T. S. Eliot.

Dag Hammarskjold never knew failure, or, if he did, could not bring himself to acknowledge it. Why should he? At twenty-nine his highly theoretical studies in economics had earned him a teaching post at the University of Stockholm. Inside two years he was Under-Secretary of Finance, a post he held until 1945. Until 1951 he was top civil servant in the Swedish Foreign Office. In between, from 1941, when he was thirty-six, to 1948, he presided over the Board of Sweden's Riksbank (Central Bank). His various post-war missions included a spell as a non-party member of the Swedish Cabinet in charge of foreign economic relations and several international assignments—including a brief term as Swedish Chief Delegate to the United Nations. He was only forty-seven when he was chosen in 1953, seemingly a dark-horse compromise candidate, to be Secretary-General of the United Nations.

"If I had been as brilliant as Dag and had his ability to deal with people, I might have gone far," his father, the former Prime Minister, commented once.

Here on September 17, 1961, in Leopoldville, then, was Hammarskjold, one of the most important men alive, undertaking to fly 1,500 perilous miles to patch up a peace with the pretender-president of an unrecognized rump territory in Central Africa. And he was not even sure that Tshombe would agree to meet him.

Hammarskjold's real feelings as the *Albertina* soared above the bush and game of Africa, with the sun setting behind it, can never be known. Yet is it possible that his thoughts were on another inexorable sunset? The sunset of his dreams for the sort of United Nations he wanted? Dreams that depended on a U.N. success in the Congo? A success menaced by the pretensions of that lawbreaker Tshombe? There is evidence to show that Hammarskjold regarded the Katangan leader with some distaste—distaste that showed in his face in pictures recording his first meeting with Tshombe in Elizabethville in 1960.

It could be argued that Hammarskjold was politically and morally lost even before he embarked on his last journey. It has been argued that he, Hammarskjold, Secretary-General of the United Nations, was suing for peace with a man he despised in the white-supremacy territory of the Rhodesians. If Katanga was not restored quickly to the Congo fold, his friends, the Afro-Asians, very possibly would have turned on him during the imminent session of the General Assembly. That, presumably, was why some of his staff gambled the authority of the world body on the success of a quick military operation designed to settle Tshombe once and for all. The gamble had not come off, partly through errors of his planners, who had underestimated the temper of Katangan resistance, partly because U.N. chiefs on the spot failed to recognize the scope, the strength and the resolve of the international forces supporting the mercenary bands they were battling.

To some authorities at that time, therefore, Hammarskjold seemed to be entering a negotiation from a position of political and military weakness. Almost everywhere U.N. troops were under siege. Almost everywhere the Secretary-General was under attack, either for what the United Nations had set out to do in the Congo or for what it was failing to do.

The Russians had broken with him a year before, essentially because fulfillment of his aims in the Congo would have ruled out the chance of a Red-tinged government there. The French, British, Portuguese, Belgians, Rhodesians, South Africans and some other Western countries were not supporting him—if indeed they were not actively opposing him—because a U.N. success would have destroyed their hope for a tame, white-influenced government. Hammarskjold was aware of the sense of the warning that the London *Daily Telegraph*—a newspaper close to the sources of

Conservative power in Britain—found it possible to address to him in an editorial published September 16 entitled "U.N. Aggression":

> Great Britain is a member of the United Nations. As such, these criminal follies [in Katanga] are committed in our name and also, in at least two respects, at our direct expense.
>
> The British Government has already demanded an explanation and urged a cease-fire. The Irish also may be pardoned for wondering what their poor soldiers have done to deserve their present misfortunes.
>
> For all its public poker-face, Washington, too, is known to be gravely disturbed.
>
> Mr. Khrushchev's *troika* proposal was designed, *inter alia,* to cut the United Nations down to size.
>
> *If Mr. Hammarskjold does not take care, he may find the West tempted to take another and favorable look at it.*

Did the lonely Hammarskjold have any alternative to a meeting with Tshombe at that time?

The alternative he had was to pursue with greater vigor, greater power, the operation the U.N. forces had started, so that he could force a military and political decision. To appeal to nations like India, Tunisia, Ethiopia and others for more men, more arms, so as to win the Battle of Katanga. To summon up air power regardless of the objections or doubts of the British, French and others. The mere appearance of warplanes with U.N. markings before the scheduled truce talks would in itself, perhaps, have swung the odds against the Katangans.

Hammarskjold could not bring himself to take these decisions. Clearly he felt he could not expose beleaguered U.N. forces any longer to the dangers besetting them. It was obvious that for such a moral aristocrat the thought of prolonging violence and killing a moment longer than necessary was unacceptable. With every muscle and fiber and feeling of his being he revolted against the venture.

Instead, the Swede preferred to arrange his rendezvous, and the decision marked for him the tragic point of no return. As he had done once before in the teeth of Khrushchev's assaults, he saved the Secretary-Generalship. But this time he was destroying himself. Here was moral man annihilating all he stood for by an act of conciliation that he must have realized could produce at best only a new compromise—and at worst his own surrender.

From that moment on the pattern of his behavior seemed to be that of a man not daring to move forward yet unable to retreat. Some saw it as the behavior of a man grown careless of living because some central motif of life itself had been lost. The loss? Could it have been the prospect of success?

Hammarskjold arranged his flight in conditions that looked absurd to cautious men. The *Albertina* was a damaged plane. It had no escort. He flew unnecessarily at night. He was out of radio contact with his base. His pilot before take-off acknowledged that a flight by dead reckoning involved the risk of "a good percentage of error in our navigation." He headed for a zone—indeed he was said to have chosen the meeting place near it—controlled by "Frightfuls," whom he had once described as "scum."

Taken together, these were circumstances that appeared likely to cut Hammarskjold's chances of survival substantially.

The morning of the Sunday that Dag Hammarskjold took off from Leopoldville toward Ndola, a lifelong diplomat-friend of his in Sweden was reading the news of the turmoil in the Congo and the plight of the U.N. forces in Katanga.

He turned to his companions, talked about the implications of it all and then said: "It's beginning to look as if there's only one solution left now for Hammarskjold. It is to die a hero's death."

Next morning he was dead.

In the final year of his life Hammarskjold's thoughts were largely about Africa.

He showed himself deeply aware that the continent had become a powder keg and that any explosion could engulf the world.

Somberly he asked the Security Council for firm directives when the Congo troubles first burst loose.

"There should not be any hesitation," he said on July 22, 1960.

"Our attitude will be of decisive importance not only for the future of the United Nations Organization but also for the future of Africa."

He paused to measure his words and added: "And Africa may well, in present circumstances, mean the world."

In the final week of his life Hammarskjold also thought about his own possible death.

Two days before flying to the Congo from New York he considered and followed up an old idea of his private secretary, Miss Hannah Platz.

Hammarskjold that day dictated a letter, which Miss Platz typed, to his old friend Per Lind, who then was Assistant Chief of the Political Department of the Swedish Foreign Office.

In the letter he asked Lind to take charge of all his personal documents in case he should die.

Premonition? Or resignation? Or chance?

4 | The Congo

Dag Hammarskjold traveled far and wide during his eight and a half years as Secretary-General, but no journey affected him so profoundly as the six-week swing he made through nearly thirty lands of Black Africa in early 1960.

He encountered and responded to the stirrings and the strivings of African people for a better life that were evident wherever he went. And history may yet judge that one of his biggest achievements was to insure an active role for the United Nations in helping along an orderly transition from dependence to statehood for the fledgling nations of Africa and Asia.

When Hammarskjold took office in 1953 he found that a major original function of the United Nations was already transformed. The Charter as drawn up at San Francisco had been designed to enable the great victor powers of World War II to keep the peace by conciliation and discussion. But in fact those powers reserved that task to themselves, outside the arena of the United Nations. The world body, with its top organ, the Security Council, partly paralyzed by the veto, was relegated to the role of a talking shop.

But soon enough Hammarskjold recognized that quite another mission—an historic, delicate mission unforeseen by the San Francisco founders—faced the organization. It stemmed from the emergence of new states, first in Asia, then in Africa, born of the great, old, dying, colonial empires, the European rulers of which could no longer keep their grip on the vast tracts they had dominated so long. Hammarskjold accordingly seized the chance for the United Nations to play the part of wet nurse to the babble of infant states groping their way into a world family torn by the jealousies of its biggest members.

The break-up of the British, French, Dutch and Belgian empires in time gave rise to a new concept in Hammarskjold's view of the U.N.'s role in the world. As he saw it two distinct sets of international problems faced the United Nations:

1. The security relations of the East-West power blocs were expressed in disputes over Berlin and Germany, the future of Indochina and Korea, the status of Red China, disarmament and so on. Taken together, all these issues formed the political snakepit of the cold war. The Secretary-General seldom aspired to intervene in them as mediator or arbiter, because he knew the United Nations, and he himself, would be destroyed by them. And when, occasionally, he was invited to lend a hand, or when he ventured near the well-watched precincts, he knocked at all doors to make quite sure everyone knew he was around.
2. The struggle of the emerging nations for higher living standards was a painful process and, unless controlled, could have sucked them into the vortex of the cold war. Most of these countries were poor. Some had big mineral resources, others boundless potentials in hydroelectric power or agriculture. All needed to be developed, especially the African ones. They did not have the funds themselves. Two major sources were open to them—Western governments and private investors or the Communist countries. Clearly the possibilities of trouble would be endless if East and West were to jostle and compete for favors or influence in the new lands.

Thus it was that the Swede led the United Nations into the field to provide a middle-way alternative, as a channel or source of help and advice.

There were times, nevertheless, when the magnitude of the job of leading the peoples of Africa into the modern world left Hammarskjold and his band of devoted advisers aghast.

The problems of Africa seemed as big as the continent itself, covering one-quarter of the world. Nearly all Europe could fit into the Sahara alone. Africa south of the Sahara is three times the size of the United States. About 200 million black and brown people live there, and until the mid-1950s they were ruled by about 5 million whites.

But through the centuries, even before the white man came, Africans had other masters. They were geography and climate and the conditions these produced.

The eastern and western seaboards of Africa are lined by great mountain ranges cutting off the interior from the sea and the world outside. Generally the coastal regions are well watered, the interior parched. And therein lies the clue of the African's fight for survival against jungle, swamp and the diseases they produce on the one hand, and against desert, famine and poverty on the other.

Africa's rainfall varies from an average of an inch a day through the year in the Cameroons to nothing a year in the Sahara. Scientists say the deserts are gradually creeping outward and that forests and bushlands are retreating. On the whole the arid soil is poor, and agriculture pitifully backward.

Only in mineral resources is Africa rich. Metals prized by the world lie beneath the ground in a giant curve from the Congo to the Cape. In seventy years nearly $18 billion worth of gold, diamonds, uranium, platinum and a string of other minerals has been yielded.

Within the two main racial groups—Caucasoid and Negroid—are hidden a dizzying variety of languages, cultures and tribes. The groups range from tribes practicing eerie ritual murders to those that have mastered complex twentieth-century industrial techniques. Yet with all their diversity the people in the restless shantytowns of Johannesburg, the bustling bazaars of Kano, and the jungle villages today share one thing: a groping and a yearning for knowledge, for recognition, and for the benefits of civilization.

The social unit of Africans through the ages has been the tribe. It was a unit as compact as a hive of bees, although not always so industrious. Tribes were bound together by custom, and custom, resting on taboos, shaped all life. These social units were as remote from each other as the old-time nation-states of Europe. Livingstone reported he found tribes who did not know their neighbors

25 miles away. Yet their neighbors were organized in just the same way. The group ruled the habits of its members—the habits of eating, wearing, working, marriage, religion. All the emphasis, for self-protection and survival, was on conformity.

On the whole, the white man has been too busy scrambling for wealth and territory over the past century to care very much about uplifting the African. In the 1880s the expanding powers of Europe drew arbitrary lines on inaccurate maps to create artificial states that still exist today. The Bakongo tribe, for example, starts off north of the Congo River in the Congo Republic (Brazzaville), passes through the Congo Republic (Leopoldville) and winds up in Portuguese Angola.

Europe's uncontrolled lunge for the riches of Africa left some territories with great ports and railroads, while in their neighbors' territories forest tribes had yet to see a plow.

This was the sort of glimpse Hammarskjold got of a continent swept by the winds of change.

And when the political gale hit the Congo in the middle of 1960—Africa Year—Hammarskjold and his staff swung into emergency action like crusaders.

However, he quickly found that the big powers were suspicious of crusaders: the Communists felt he was trying to rescue the West where the West needed help, and some Western powers believed his strict, middle-of-the-road role threatened their interests.

Hammarskjold therefore drew his main strength and support from the neutral and nonaligned nations of Asia and Africa.

The Secretary-General once confided to Ian Scott, then British ambasssador in Leopoldville, soon after reaching the country in 1960: "This is the most difficult mission I have ever had to face."

It was difficult because the Congo had its own built-in contrasts and contradictions, besides the heritage of hatred that the Belgians had left behind on their sudden exit.

It was dangerous because he knew big powers and little ones were ready to pounce the moment the country broke into a score, even a hundred, tribe-states, as at times seemed likely.

It was controversial because his instructions from the Security Council were vague and even the broadest attempts to interpret them aroused the cheers of this set of partisans, the jeers of that. He asked no blessings. He expected the curses. But he did not always appreciate that today's friends among the powers could become tomorrow's foes.

Finally his mission was challenging because the role of the United Nations in the Congo was conceived as perhaps the boldest, most altruistic attempt at international rescue and reconstruction the modern world had witnessed, and it pointed the way to even better things.

To understand the present and to build for the future, Hammarskjold had to survey the past. He studied intensively, read all the books and talked with anyone he felt could contribute to his understanding.

One particular irony struck the Secretary-General, as it has others. The mid-1960 departure of the Belgians from their huge colony was being attended by political terror—just as epic violence had followed their formal arrival seventy-five years earlier, when the Congo was dragged by Brussels into the white man's world as a "Free State."

It seemed to the Swede as if all the turbulence, torture and tension bottled up in the Congolese in the years between had suddenly exploded like a time bomb set off by pain-crazed revenge-seekers.

African leaders thought there was much to seek revenge for, and said so.

The cry went up soon after that fateful June 30, 1960:

"We are the masters now!"

The Congo of today is essentially the political creation of two men. Henry Morton Stanley, born in 1841 in Wales as John Rowlands, ran away from his workhouse home and sailed in a windjammer to the New World, where he jumped ship at New Orleans and adopted the name of a merchant-benefactor. His storied trail into history winds through episodes as a sailor, a soldier who fought on both sides during the American Civil War, a journalist and an explorer. He became an American citizen for a time, then switched back and ended his days as a member of the British House of Commons. The other man was German by descent, with a somewhat different background. Leopold II of Belgium was passionately ambitious, vain, acquisitive, life-loving. Like Stanley, he craved recognition. He was born only four years after Belgium became a state in 1831, but for him the borders of his land were too cramping, too confining. He was a textbook extrovert in search of an empire.

Stanley was assigned by James Gordon Bennett of the old New York *Herald* to find the Scottish missionary Dr. David Livingstone, who had vanished on a trek through Central Africa. It turned out to be one of the greatest newspaper scoops of history. For Stanley, romantically, did meet Livingstone on Lake Tanganyika, on the eastern corner of the Congo. From then on—though not before writing the obvious book under the obvious title, *How I Found Livingstone*—Africa became Stanley's obsession. He devoted himself to its exploration, now with the backing of the London *Daily Telegraph* as well as of the New York *Herald*. And perhaps his most spectacular odyssey, even to the time it took, turned out to be a 999-day journey across Africa from the Indian to the Atlantic Ocean, in the course of which he discovered and followed the trail of the 2,900-mile-long Congo River. About 235 members of his 350-man expedition perished during the journey. But he had achieved his goal, and he returned to Europe dreaming great dreams for the development of the fabulous lands he had seen.

It was politically the right moment for his return. The uneasily balanced powers of Europe were then bracing for their scramble for Africa. Bits of that closed continent were already being snatched and concessions being grabbed.

The Britain of those days ruled not only the waves but also much of Africa. She was at the height of her imperial glory under Queen Victoria. But the British had too much on their plate for new enterprises, especially in Africa. Apathy laced with skepticism greeted Stanley's grandiose schemes for planting the Union Jack around the basin of the Congo.

But Leopold was neither apathetic nor skeptical. Impatiently he waited for Stanley. He had displayed for some years clear-cut intentions of widening his horizons. He had followed the wanderings and journeyings of the discoverers with fascination. He received Stanley in Brussels with pomp and circumstance—and offered support and cooperation that the explorer gladly accepted. Soon returning to Africa as Leopold's personal agent, Stanley opened a chain of trading stations along the Congo and negotiated with local chiefs more than 400 treaties giving Leopold a European version of claim, title and ownership of the prized lands.

Leopold, meanwhile, set out to win a semblance of international recognition and legality for his ever-increasing stake in the Congo. His designs were shrouded in high-flown phrases about bringing civilization, Christianity and uplift to unfortunate "savages." He disavowed territorial or conquering ambitions. He enlisted the patronage of some of the once-great dynasties of Europe. And, under the sponsorship of Chancellor von Bismarck of Germany, twelve other nations, including the United States, agreed to attend a conference in Berlin to check the developing conflict of interests in Africa. The meeting, held in 1884 and 1885, defined the internal frontiers of the continent in a carve-up that evokes little pride among the participants today. Most of the boundaries drawn at Berlin—including those of the Congo Basin—survive to this day.

The Belgian monarch had not only got what he had set out to achieve but also found himself internationally recognized as the personal possessor of a piece of real estate called the Congo Free State. Belgium's Parliament would have no part of the arrangement; however, if the king wanted a private empire he could have one.

Nevertheless, within twenty-three years world opinion forced the Belgian State to take over the money-producing playground of their greedy king.

Those twenty-three years have been acknowledged by world authorities as among the darkest in Africa's dark modern history. The measure of the riches extracted by Leopold and his agents from the Congo never has, and probably never can be, disclosed.

Leopold himself became one of the wealthiest men in the world.

But the evidence of diplomats, writers, politicians, reformers, historians and missionaries (Belgians among them) suggests that in the process between three and five *million* Congolese died. To this day the archives of the British Foreign Office include documents and pictures purporting to show the scale and the kind of atrocities committed on the natives by authorized agents and companies of the king.

Africans were hunted down in the forests, forced to work on the big estates, organized into chain gangs, flogged and manhandled. Workers who failed to fulfill required quotas of production, or otherwise to satisfy their white masters, had a hand, or foot, or sometimes both, amputated. The system of forced labor—usually in lieu of taxes—was the rule, and it persisted until World War II. There were periodic massacres of rebellious tribes. All this had come on top of that peculiar misery which the Congolese had been suffering anyway before Leopold's brand of civilization reached them. They had been decimated by Arab slavers. Disease had taken its unending toll. Starvation was widespread. In its wake followed rampant cannibalism.

As word leaked out about the ravages a shocked world protested. An improbable alliance emerged among men like Winston Churchill, Theodore Roosevelt, Mark Twain, Sir Arthur Conan Doyle (creator of Sherlock Holmes), E. D. Morel, Roger Casement (an Irishman serving as British consul in the Congo who, during World War I, was to be executed on charges of treason), Emile van der Velde (the Belgian Socialist) and British Foreign Secretary Sir Edward Grey. They raised their voices in chorus to condemn the brutalities carried out virtually in the name of Leopold, who himself had never even visited Africa.

The Governments and parliaments of Belgium, the United States, Britain and other countries debated the issues.

The United States joined in with a declaration that Africans in large parts of the Congo seemed to have been reduced to "a condition closely approximating actual slavery."

In Belgium itself lawmakers and newspapers energetically joined in the campaign.

Grey's predecessor as British Foreign Secretary, Lord Lansdowne, branded the Belgian practices as "bondage under the most barbarous and inhuman conditions . . . maintained for mercenary motives of the most selfish character. . . ."

The comments of both Lansdowne and Grey were reinforced by a British Government White Paper listing some of the savageries and fixing the blame on the Belgian king and his servants.

In 1908 an international commission investigated the charges and came out with an exposure of the abuses that had taken place.

The hue and cry produced some outstanding reformist literature, including writings by Mark Twain and a 60,000-word tract by Conan Doyle entitled *The Crime of the Congo.*

One of the most telling pieces came from the pen of Vachel Lindsay: a poem, "The Congo," that helped bring home the personal responsibility of Leopold.*

The bearded Leopold yielded to the national and international pressure. First some reforms were introduced. Then, a year before he died in 1909 at seventy-four, the Belgian Government took over control of the Congo Free State as a colony. The concessionary companies that had been extracting vast profits were bought out handsomely by the Belgian State (which had, incidentally, itself been sharing in the companies' vast profits). Leopold, even in the course of the transaction with his own Government, showed himself a game loser. He tried to exact a heavy price for "his" Congo—but failed. He tried even to salt away several million dollars worth of Congo holdings—but these too were seized after his death by the State.

Steadily but altogether too slowly for the liking of many critics, the Belgians began to clean up the mess Leopold had left. The old concessions were handed out to new companies and combines. They did not exactly plunge into Africa for the health of its inhabitants; no brave new Congolese world emerged after the ousting of Leopold. But bit by bit things did get better, perhaps even slightly

* Vachel Lindsay's poem is reproduced at the beginning of the book.

faster than in some other African territories. This may have been due to the presence of great mineral wealth in the Congo. It may also have been due to the materialistic approach of the Belgians, who took the view that healthy and efficient African workers were a better economic proposition than unhealthy and inefficient ones.

In his classic *African Survey* Lord Hailey expressed the view that the general aim of Belgian policy had been based in part on the resolve that "rule of the colony should be such as to present the strongest possible contrast to the history of the Free State under Leopold II."

Practically, this policy was expressed in measures to spur the economic advancement of the Congolese—but without giving them any sort of role or voice in the political management of their country. Officially there was no color bar of the kind that stares out of South Africa's system of apartheid (racial separation). The starting point was that full bellies, clothing and reasonable housing were the major wants of the Africans, and that if these needs could be generally satisfied they would display no interest in political rights.

For years the Belgian premise seemed to hold. Living standards among the Africans rose faster and higher than in other African territories. An industrial revolution was pushing the Congo into new economic activities. Natives not long out of the jungle began to learn the skills of the outside world on the mines, in the factories, as copper-smelters, furnacemen, locomotive drivers.

Compared with wages paid to Africans in other parts of the continent, the earnings of some Congolese workers were high. More and more Africans escaped from their lifelong rural poverty, and gradually the walls of their tribal prisons began to be pulled down. The Congolese were mixing more with each other through a sharing of techniques in the magnetic, brash, well-lit towns and cities of the industrial areas. And they were starting to prove themselves—not only to themselves but also to their white masters—to be able to perform the basic tasks of a modern society.

But danger signals were evident to outsiders, if not to the Belgians. The Congolese were not prepared to live by bread alone.

Way back in 1955 Chester Bowles—Assistant Secretary of State after President Kennedy's election, but then an ex-ambassador on a private visit—took a close look at the Congolese situation and wrote:

> The weakness of the [Belgian] program appears to be their reluctance to allow the African to secure an advanced education—even a technical education—for fear that he will then demand a growing share of responsibility in the shaping of his own future. Any visitor who has seen the strength of the independence movement throughout the world will wonder if the Belgians, like King Canute, are not trying to curb a force that eventually will become irresistible.
>
> But it would be a serious mistake to underestimate the intelligence of the Belgians and to assume that they will attempt to stand like a rock in the face of strong future demands from the people. The danger lies not so much in the possibility that the Belgians will not compromise eventually with the force of nationalism, but that when they do they will find the Africans almost totally inexperienced in handling the responsibilities which they are certain to demand and eventually to get.

At the time, that remarkable prophecy by Bowles made little impression on the complacent Belgians. They were convinced they could trade jobs for votes. They believed they could buy political stability with economic opportunity, in a continent that was beginning to shake off the sleep of centuries.

The Congo, like the rest of Black Africa, *had* been asleep for centuries. Many of its forest tribes had still to use the wheel. Many would run away at the approach of a white man.

The country covers 904,992 square miles—as big as Western Europe, or the United States east of the Mississippi. Its 12 million people range from the 7-foot-tall Watusi, who can jump their own regal height, to pagan pygmies standing little more than 4 feet high. In between there are the Nilotic Mangbeto, the highly artistic Baluba in the south, and an assortment of perhaps 200 other tribes as well. They speak 40 different languages, more than 400 dialects. But they also share one more or less common tongue, Lingala.

It is a land of almost countless bird species, insects, lions, rhinos, monkeys, elephants, giraffe, leopards, bucks, alligators and lush flowers and vegetation.

It is also a land of surprises, some less mild than others. In November, 1961, an alligator ate the ambassador of West Germany, who was ill-advised enough to go wading along the bank of the Congo at Leopoldville. The same year American ambassador Gullion went to his garage, not unreasonably, to pick up his car. It was there all right, but alongside it was—an alligator. Another time workmen entered a generating plant in Stanleyville during the season when the flooded Congo sometimes bursts its banks, and inside it they found—two alligators.

But not all the surprises of the Congo have to do with alligators. In the northern rain forests trees grow to great heights within three years. A "quinine forest" of cinchona trees was developed by the Belgians for the treatment of malaria, which has long been one of the country's greatest killers. Before independence some of the 70,000 or so Belgian administrators and settlers in the big cities used to have iced oysters and orchids flown to them almost daily from Brussels.

In the pre-independence period nearly 7,000 missionaries—mainly Roman Catholics—were trying to lead the Congolese away from paganism. The Catholics once were given a twenty-year "monopoly" in the field of education. About one-fourth of the Congolese are Christian, another million or so are coming along that way while the rest bow mostly to tribal gods, from the moon to a wide assortment of devils.

The weird religions of the Congolese—indeed, of Africans generally—reflect their realism rather than their backwardness, as some people imagine. European or Asian man, whose environment is so much less hostile than the African's, could think logically in terms of a good, kind, fine deity. But the African's surroundings were essentially cruel, stark, evil, with disease, hunger and pain the everyday realities. Over the centuries life taught him its lesson of being conquered rather than conquering. Nature's sermon was to expect no mercy. The African accepted this, and if there are elements of cruelty in his diverse forms of ju-juism, devil deities and so-called black magic, they show only that Nature's preaching has had its effect. Accordingly, in their own religions Africans rarely *worship* their gods—their impulse rather is to appease or conciliate them with sacrifices in the outside hope of warding off evil retribution.

Some of the Congolese people are as different from each other as, say, American Indians are from the British Royal Family. The Basalampasu in Kasai periodically practice cannibalism, whereas to the southeast in Katanga the Lundu and Baluba have displayed their ability to cope with up-to-date commercial, economic and military techniques. Both the Watusi and Baluba have dynastic traditions reaching back to the sixteenth and seventeenth centuries. Others have finely developed accomplishments in arts, crafts, dancing and singing.

It is a country of contrasts. In certain respects the Congo is about the richest region in Africa—mineralogically Katanga is perhaps the richest in the world—but poverty and ignorance haunt most of its people. The intense assortment of its natural colors deepens the mystery of the ancient rites still performed by some of the folk who dwell in its dark forests. The main natural export products are palm oil and cotton, but agricultural development generally is primitive, with some natives relying on termites for food. In the cities and towns the women wear bright and colorful robes, but in equatorial regions people roam naked. For years a Belgian helicopter used nightly to spray Leopoldville, the capital, with insecticide to combat mosquitoes. In outlying parts the tsetse fly still scourges and decimates tribes and cattle with sleeping sickness. Modern airliners run by the Belgians before independence linked all six provincial capitals, but the road system between Leopoldville, Stanleyville and Elizabethville remains wild, adventurous and disjointed. The Congo, sixth longest river in the world, is the main artery of the country and if harnessed could supply up tc 190 million horsepower of electricity, or more than all the rivers in the United States put together. But only the cities, towns and key mining districts have electricity.

The Congo is mainly an agricultural country, but the Belgians invested almost all their funds, energy, planning and science in the development of its highly abundant and profitable mineral wealth.

In turn the mines lured an expanding network of secondary industries, including building materials, river ships, beer, lemonade and cigarettes, chemicals, margarine, sugar, textiles, cement and lime, rubber, sisal, rope, sacking and canvas, tiles and bricks, paints and varnishes, and so on.

During the final years of its stewardship the Belgian Government bravely set out to right the imbalance in the Congo economy. The idea was to move from over-reliance on the ready rewards of mining toward a more diverse and broader base of activity in all areas. In the mid-1950s a ten-year program was launched to develop labor, soil, communications, transportation and hydroelectric power resources, and to rationalize agriculture literally from the grass-roots.

Total investment planned was around $1.4 billion—or more than double all the Belgian and foreign capital sunk into the Congo between 1870 and 1936. Profits in cash and in kind over that sixty-six-year period cannot be accurately measured but it is certain they returned, many times over, the capital outlay.

John Gunther estimated in his book *Inside Africa* that "in 1950 more than 75 percent of its [the Congo's] total income (32.5 billion Belgian francs or 650 million dollars) went to three percent of the population."*

There is a very special fascination in trying to identify the essential interests that make up that three percent.

Their identity provides clues to the dramatic political events that followed the Congo's emergence as a state—and to Tshombe's attempt at an independent Katanga.

---

*John Gunther, *Inside Africa* (New York: Harper & Brothers, 1955), p. 677.

The real money power in the Congo had long been vested in five main supertrusts, together controlling as much as three-quarters of all business. The Belgian Government owned substantial holdings in each. In some of the hundred or so individual enterprises under the giant umbrellas of the Big Five, the Belgian Government exercised absolute control of the stock.

It would take a very smart Philadelphia lawyer—helped by a band of knowledgeable colleagues from Brussels—to unravel the financial structures of each trust, and their relations with each other. And even then he would be able to guess only very roughly at the value of the total Belgian stake in the Congo and at the average annual profits.

Estimates of Congolese dividends paid range between $50 million and $200 million a year. But even a correct estimate would tell only part of the story. The reason is that the Belgian State's "take" consisted not only of a share of profits but also of taxes. The paychecks of the John and Jane Does of Belgium for the past half-century, therefore, have depended on the energies of the Congolese.

The Congo's Big Five are:

1. Cominiére (Société Commerciale et Minière du Congo), which owns vast agricultural properties throughout the country.
2. Banque Empain, which built up a huge transportation system consisting of river, road and other forms of traffic.
3. Huilever (the Belgian offshoot of the great Unilever empire), which concentrates mainly on the production of palm oil, the Congo's main agricultural export.
4. Brufina (Société de Bruxelles pour la Finance et l'Industrie), which has banking, insurance and manufacturing interests.
5. Société Générale de Belgique, which controls, among a breath-taking range of other interests from Sabena airlines to pharmaceuticals, the extraordinary Union Minière du Haut-Katanga.

To some it may seem as if the Union Minière is as subsidiary to the Société Générale as a dog is to a flea on its back. To others it may look as if the Union Minière is Katanga.

One writer, during a visit to Elizabethville in the pre-independence period, was told by a Belgian employee of the company: "This street you are walking on? It practically belongs to Union Minière. The hotel you live in? It's the property of the company. Those policemen down the road are servants of the Administration. But Union Minière has its own police too. And often they have to take care of the uniformed ones."

The story of the Union Minière is a success story of twentieth-century free enterprise if ever there was one.

To begin with, Katanga never formed part of the Congo Free State recognized by the Berlin powers in 1885. It seemed at that time to be too remote and worthless. But then Cecil Rhodes, the colorful British empire-builder, began dickering with some of the local African chiefs. He already had staked vast tracts to the south, in what became the Rhodesias, named after him. Rhodes had guessed at or been tipped off about, Katanga's riches. But if the Britisher was shrewd, King Leopold was no less so. At once he sent expeditions to the region, staked out his claims and, in 1894, won international recognition for his new annexation.

A few years later a British mining engineer named George Grey, employed by Tanganyika Concessions, or Tanks, wandered into Katangan territory from Northern Rhodesia. Within a mile he came across old native open-cast diggings that, as he found, led to rich copper veins. These are being exploited to this day as the Prince Leopold mine at Kipushi. Tanks won permission from the Belgians to prospect the area and to share the proceeds. And in 1906 Tanks merged with the local Belgian interests to form the Union Minière. It received a concession to mine a 7,700-square-mile area—bigger than Belgium—until 1990.

Neither the Union Minière nor Tanks ever looked back.

The Union Minière in the pre-independence period produced most of the Congo's nearly $500 million worth of minerals—or about half the value of the Congo's annual exports. It provided in direct taxes nearly half the Congo's revenue. It contributed a great deal more indirectly. Millions of tons of mineral output, for instance, were freighted year by year across the Congo by railroad and river to the Atlantic port of Matadi—instead of using shorter routes outside Congolese territory. It developed Katangan production of copper (to 8 per cent of world output), cobalt (to 60 per cent), zinc, silver, platinum, wolfram, tungsten and, lately, germanium, used in making transistor radio sets.

Just before World War II the fabulous earth of Katanga gave the world another long-kept secret—one that helped to change the course of history. All the uranium that went into the atomic bombs dropped on Hiroshima and Nagasaki to hasten the end of the war against Japan came from the mine of Shinkolobwe, near Jadotville, less than 100 miles northwest of Elizabethville.

The story is this: Uranium, the fissionable element that gives atomic bombs their force, was known to exist in great quantities at Shinkolobwe, which was originally worked as a source for radium. As World War II approached, physicists of the great powers, including Nazi Germany, began their researches into the splitting of the atom for military purposes. In circumstances of great secrecy Edgar Sengier, then the head of the Union Minière, was approached by a British scientist to insure that none of Shinkolobwe's known deposits of pitchblende, or uranium ore, would be sold to Germany. Sengier agreed. He went even further. He arranged for the secret transfer of Shinkolobwe's entire stock of uranium ore to the United States. The day he exercised that initiative was the day that split the world in two, for it heralded the dawn of the nuclear age.

In the first year of Katangan separatism under Tshombe, the Union Minière seems to have worked well enough. Copper output rose to a record 300,000 tons. The company provided Tshombe with four-fifths of his $100 million revenue. But political uncertainties depressed the market value of its shares from a peak of 7,000 Belgian francs ($140) in 1956 to 3,000 Belgian francs ($60) in early 1960, and lower still to about 1,200 Belgian francs ($24) in the fall of 1961 after Hammarskjold's death.

The fate of the biggest single shareholding in the company fell into dispute too as a result of Tshombe's break-away movement. An 18.4 per cent block, once held by Leopold and then taken over by the Belgian State, nominally was held in trust in Brussels pending the outcome of the quarrel over the rival Elizabethville and Leopoldville claims to sovereignty. Tshombe in the meantime was paid the considerable yield from that stockholding, and it kept his regime in business.

Tanks appeared just as healthy as the Union Minière. The two companies shared a certain precariousness because of political factors. Tanks' stock was leavened out with the introduction of American and South African capital. It holds a one-seventh share in the Union Minière. Its interests included several of the new gold mines in the Orange Free State province of South Africa, and copper mines in Northern Rhodesia. One plum was a 90 per cent holding in the Benguela railroad, which, since Congolese independence, has carried about half of Katanga's mineral output across Portuguese Angola to the Atlantic. Angola and South Africa, like Katanga, have become gripped by political change and turmoil, but Tanks still stands as virtually the strongest single financial holding company among the mining groups exploiting the wealth of Africa south of the Sahara.

Tanks is interlinked financially, and through common directors, with the three other major groups that run the mining business of Northern Rhodesia. They are the Anglo-American Corporation, headed then by Harry Oppenheimer, Rhodesian Selection Trust, headed then by Sir Ronald Prain, and the British South Africa Company, headed then by Lord Robins. The chairman of Tanks was Captain Charles Waterhouse. He won prominence as one of the bitter-enders in Britain's House of Commons, clamoring for all-out action, including the use of force, to regain control of the Suez Canal after President Gamal Abdel Nasser nationalized it in 1956.

With Britons, Belgians and Americans on the boards directing the affairs and the policies of the giant combines of Katanga and Northern Rhodesia, it was inevitable that the future of the rich region would become a vital economic interest of these nations.

It also was inevitable that the political fate of any one part of Central Africa's troubled heartland would affect all the others.

Shock waves of the Katangan explosion, therefore, spread far and wide beyond the tidy rows of company houses outside Elizabethville where African miners of the Union Minière dwell.

They rumbled through the hushed board rooms of the great mining groups in London and Johannesburg. They were recorded in the chancelleries of member-states of the United Nations. They flashed through the seething slum towns and sprawling cities of Africa. And the beat of tom-toms took the word to isolated bush and forest tribes across the continent.

5 | The Breakdown

The story of the Congo since statehood has been a story of the world game at its worst, yet with flashes of fineness to relieve the dismal picture.

To Dag Hammarskjold, watching, it was the whole human tragicomedy in action at its basest and its best. He saw the greed and goodness of men, their violence and revenge, power politics and the pursuit of peace. The very special fantasies of Congolese affairs tangled with the realities of big business and diplomacy. Ugly crises cut across the comfortable frontiers of the cold war, dividing old friends and creating new foes.

Belgium tossed the Congolese into the deep waters of independence before teaching the infant nation how to swim. Perhaps some Belgians figured they would be called back as lifesavers.

The struggle of the Congolese for life began very soon after the formal proclamation of statehood on June 30, 1960. Like a flash flood the trials and tears of the people were released and spread over the land, soaking, although not always submerging, many of the symbols of a hated past.

White women, mainly Belgians, were ravaged. Old tribal rivalries among the Congolese blazed into violence. High point of all the turbulence came with the mutiny of the Force Publique, the enlisted personnel of which rose against their Belgian officers. Here was irony: The Belgians had created the Force Publique sixty-nine years before partly to help preserve their power, and now this same force was on the rampage trying to break the last vestige of Belgian authority. In the storms that followed the Belgian Government of former Premier Max Eysskens ordered paratroopers back into the Congo to protect the lives and property of its citizens. The rickety coalition headed by the Congo's first Prime Minister, Patrice Lumumba, began to fall apart. Tshombe, then an obscure provincial leader, hoisted the flag of Katangan independence. He welcomed the return of Belgian troops.

This was the background on July 14, 1960, when the Security Council authorized Dag Hammarskjold to rush military aid to the beleaguered land in response to a joint appeal by President Joseph Kasavubu and Lumumba.

Nobody could foresee then that the historic mission launched under Hammarskjold's personal direction would shake the authority and very foundation of the world organization itself.

From the very outset Hammarskjold and his team moved fast, planned big and worked endlessly to assemble a force from the ends of the earth to carry out their assigned task.

Essentially that task was to fill a very perilous vacuum.

For unless the United Nations intervened it was clear that several interested nations were ready to plunge into the giant territory. In the first place, African territorial powers like Britain, France and Belgium were bracing to move in. Secondly, some nearby African states like Ghana were thinking of doing the same. And finally and most important, the United States and the Soviet Union were squaring off to join the scramble. The Congo to begin with, and all Africa later, thus stood in danger of becoming a new battlefield of the old East-West cold war.

Hammarskjold was quick to recognize another danger in the situation. It was that the subsurface conflict between white and non-white might merge with the cold war—the Communists seeming to take the side of the non-whites and the West as a whole lined up with the whites.

Walter Lippmann offered this view of Hammarskjold's undertaking: "The U.N. force in the Congo is the most advanced and the most sophisticated experiment in international cooperation ever attempted.... Among all that is so sad and so mean and so sour in world politics it is heartening to think that something so good and so pure in its purpose is possible."

But not everyone, by any means, shared Lippmann's judgment. An empire-minded British parliamentarian, Lord Hinchingbrooke, saw the U.N. force as "a charging Congo rhinoceros, tearing up the earth in great craters, shattering mines, works and hospitals and sending thousands of simple Africans scurrying back to the barbarism of their forefathers or, perhaps to be infinitely craved for, to death itself."

Perhaps the truth about the mission launched by Hammarskjold on the orders of the Security Council lay somewhere in between the hot praise and the cold hate expressed by Lippmann and Hinchingbrooke.

U.N. intervention in the Congo undoubtedly did help to limit the human tragedy of a people unprepared for power. But that intervention was not authorized primarily in the cause of humanity. It came about because it suited the prevailing interests of the world's three main political groupings. The West feared a red lunge into the African heartland. The Afro-Asians wanted to keep the cold war out of the seething continent. And the Russians were playing to the Afro-Asian gallery and, therefore, resisted any temptation to bulldoze their way into the troubled Congo immediately.

If the outcome was an essay in supranationalism, Hammarskjold soon discovered some powerful states were not yet ready for an experiment so daring. Those countries that opposed the U.N. operations at various crucial stages did so not necessarily in the Congo's interests but in defense of what they thought were their own; those that backed U.N. actions may also have done so in their own interests. (It was a sad commentary on the times that the opponents of U.N. intervention felt able to criticize, question and suspect the motives of nations that showed loyalty to the world body.)

There appeared to be an inability, or resistance, among leaders of several sophisticated powers of the West to face what might have happened in the Congo if there had been no U.N. intervention.

John Foster Dulles once observed in discussing the capability of the world organization:

> I recognize that this [U.N.] Charter does not do what

> many people would like—to guarantee at a single step perpetual peace.
>
> But the world does not move at a single step from a condition of virtual anarchy to a condition of well-rounded political order.
>
> I say that here is . . . a step forward on to new, firm and higher ground.

The huge, although hazily defined, mission of the United Nations was to:

1. restore law and order, prevent civil war and promote a reunion of the Congo's splintering parts.
2. keep foreign powers and personnel out.
3. hold the fort while the Congolese themselves sorted out their difficulties and arranged to take over the running of the state.
4. help cope with the immense human problems thrown up by the political breakdown of the Central Government's authority.

Orders of the Security Council at the best of times are patchwork compromises made up of the raw sensitivities of the eleven member-states.

One of the few things clearly spelled out in the key resolutions passed before September, 1961, was that the United Nations was to steer clear of the Congo's political quarrels. While working for Congolese unity O.N.U.C. was to do nothing that might "influence the outcome of any internal conflict."

That, on the face of things, seemed clear enough.

But Hammarskjold swiftly discovered that there was a hairline distinction—if any existed at all—between, for example, expelling unauthorized foreigners and interfering in political affairs. In Katanga the foreign mercenaries were propping up Tshombe's regime, and their expulsion would have meant his collapse. Katanga's separatism was the issue that throughout 1961 lay at the heart of the entire Congo crisis.

Another big difficulty was that the U.N. peacemaking process depended broadly on a general return to the terms of the Loi Fondamentale, the Congo's stopgap constitution. But the Loi Fondamentale was what Tshombe, sitting on his mineral riches, was quarreling about with Leopoldville, which wanted to share in the jackpot.

Complicating all this was the determination of great international combines, already in the field, to preserve their privileged position in Katanga. Their resolve was reflected in the all-out backing they gave Tshombe's struggle for statehood initially and for semi-independence later.

There was nothing unique about the struggle of a rich provincial regime wanting to keep the fingers of jealous neighbours out of lush-looking pies. The dispute had a familiar ring to Europeans, Asians and North Americans who knew their own history.

But the big snarl came when the squabbles of the Congolese contenders tangled violently with the secret manoeuvrings of outsiders pushing their own special interests.

The scarcely credible pattern of events leading to Hammarskjold's death unfolded as if through one of those wobbly, old-time kaleidoscopes.

Lumumba and Tshombe held the stage most of the time. Others waited in the wings. None seemed so important for a time as the brooding Antoine Gizenga, an acknowledged leftist who claimed to be heir to Lumumba's power. For a while he worked under Cyrille Adoula in a laboriously rebuilt Central Government.

The phantom flittings of Lumumba in and out of power, captivity and even life itself turned him into something of a legend in the brief chronicles of Congolese nationhood. He tilted prematurely at the windmills of tribalism in his dream of molding a single Congolese nationalism that could sustain a strong, modern state. In the process he made enemies of those local and regional leaders who saw their own powers threatened by centralized authority.

Lumumba set out as a reformer, not a radical. He turned to the Communist powers for help only after he felt himself spurned by the West.

"We are now ready to work with the powers which have been in Africa to create a powerful new bloc," he said before becoming Premier in mid-1960. "But if this effort fails it will be through faults of the western powers."

Like so many other Congolese politicians, his political background was less than three years old. He was only thirty-six when he died. He never learned how to compromise. Passion fed his pride. In a land of talkers he could not curb his tongue. Pitchforked, unprepared, into leadership of a revolution, he found no time to learn from mistakes and no tolerance for those mistakes. Within ten weeks President Kasavubu sacked him, in an action of widely doubted legality.

The period that followed deeply involved Hammarskjold. He had rallied 20,000 troops and technicians from eighteen countries to help the Congo off its knees. Those who by then were supporting Lumumba—mainly the Soviet bloc and the Afro-Asians—demanded U.N. action to restore the deposed Premier.

Hammarskjold said his mandate barred that sort of intervention. He was abused and reviled by Khrushchev, who demanded his dismissal. The Russian claimed Hammarskjold was no longer neutral and proposed that a three-man Secretariat-General should run the United Nations. The "troika," named after the three-horse teams that pull Russian sleighs, had come to town.

The disjointed drama stumbled on. Army Commander Mobutu seized power in September, 1960, and by the end of that year had arrested Lumumba. The slender, thirty-six-year-old Lumumba was handed over by Mobutu and Kasavubu on January 17, 1961, to Tshombe in Katanga. On arrival Tshombe's troops beat him up. Twenty-five days later Lumumba's "escape" from captivity was announced by Tshombe. A day or two afterward he was reported slain in flight.

Shock rolled around the world. Few doubted that Lumumba had been murdered. Khruschev assailed Hammarskjold as "an accomplice to murder" because he had not intervened to free Lumumba.

A four-nation U.N. team later, in mid-November, reported its conviction that Lumumba indeed had been murdered, with Tshombe and two Belgian officers actively participating in the crime. Tshombe denied this. He complained the commission had not even visited Katanga to hear evidence.

The U.N. group, consisting of Burmese, Ethiopian, Mexican and Togolese delegates, dismissed Tshombe's version of the killing as "staged" and urged action to bring the accused men to justice. Lumumba was executed "according to a pre-arranged plan," the report said. Godefroid Munongo was singled out for special blame because of "the extensive role" he played in the affair. Kasavubu also was named as partly responsible for handing Lumumba over to Tshombe, "knowing full well in doing so that they were throwing him into the hands of his bitterest political enemies."

The working officials of the United Nations on the spot did not, on the whole, think much of the commission's report. They felt it amounted to a superficial job of investigation. Through their own channels of intelligence they knew pretty certainly who had killed Lumumba and who had inspired or organized the slaying. But their lips were sealed at the time of the probe, and they are sealed to this day.

Lumumba's death deepened the crisis for the Congo, for Hammarskjold personally and for the United Nations.

Gizenga, Lumumba's right-hand man, set up his Stanleyville regime as a government entitled to rule the whole country. It maintained the claim nearly six months and won the temporary recognition of several foreign powers, notably the Communists. The thirty-six-year-old Stanleyville leader was never a Tshombe-type secessionist, although he seemed sometimes to act like one. As a disciple of Lumumba, the one-time teacher, he stood for a unitary Congo, and his manoeuvrings were motivated, not by a wish for the independence of Orientale Province, but by a desire to control the central government of "One Congo."

On February 21, 1961, Hammarskjold was given wide new powers by the Security Council, which ordered him:

1. To reorganize and to discipline Congolese armed units.
2. Immediately to root out all Belgian and other foreign military and political advisers not under U.N. command and to expel the mercenaries.

3. To take "all appropriate measures," including as a last resort the use of force, to prevent civil war.

The sweeping implications of this directive did not emerge for six months. In the intervening period Hammarskjold and his men on the spot exerted all their efforts to promote by patient and quiet diplomacy a political reconciliation of the main contenders and to persuade Tshombe to get rid of the mercenaries. The Katangan strong man was brought face to face with the Leopoldville leaders three times. At their third parley in Coquilhatville he so exasperated Kasavubu and Mobutu that he was arrested by the same troops who had seized Lumumba.

Developments that followed were an ironist's delight. Katangan ministers implicated in Lumumba's assassination pleaded with the United Nations to save the life of the man who had been defying the world body. Tshombe was in the end released after two months, ostensibly for agreeing to join a central government. Safely home, however, he denounced that accord.

The U.N. men then turned their attention to bringing Cyrille Adoula and Antoine Gizenga together. Surprisingly, they succeeded. Gizenga, whatever his reasons—and few credited him with altruism—merged his regime within the national authority. Mobutu withdrew. In August, 1961, Adoula became Premier, on a pledge to end Katangan separatism. Linner was the man who had discovered Adoula and nurtured him toward leadership. "It was natural as a Swede for me to seek out the trade union leader," he once recalled. "And I went into the African quarter and found Adoula. He was astonished. No one had ever sought him out before —at least no European—and no one had ventured into his quarter of Leopoldville before. From that time on we became the closest of friends."

At the time Adoula was forty, a product of Catholic schools, a onetime labor union leader and a Socialist who professed anti-Communism. He once made it clear his "anti-capitalism" did not extend so far as to favor nationalizing the Congo's big money-making industries.

The person mainly instrumental in restoring the Central Government was Mahmoud Khiari, the Tunisian who signed the makeshift truce with Tshombe after Hammarskjold's death. He was a consummate politician who rarely hit the headlines because he performed his main negotiating services in softness and silence behind the scenes. Khiari successfully carried out a long series of mysterious missions. But none was so mysterious as the one that led in September to the first Battle of Katanga and to the flight and crash of the *Albertina.*

At that time of dying northern summer Hammarskjold and O.N.U.C. looked upon some of their achievements with quiet satisfaction.

The Katangan affair aside, several major tasks had been mastered. Somehow Congolese statehood had survived as an international reality. Foreign powers had been barred from establishing themselves in the country.

The mass of the people, again excepting Katangans, gradually were coming around to accept national unity. Ordinary men and women had kept their jobs and drawn their pay, and consequently hunger and revolutionary discontent had been staved off. After an alarming fall, output in many fields was rising again. Exports too were beginning to climb—partly, perhaps, because mining and other companies were getting out all they could while they could. True, the national budget had a monthly deficit of about $16 million, but at least accounts were being kept.

On the workaday level of people's lives there were plenty of accomplishments of the kind that rarely make news. Water had been filtered. Epidemics had been halted or prevented. The sick and wounded were being cared for and utilities kept running. Refugees were being accommodated, fed and clothed.

Nevertheless the oncoming autumn brought Hammarskjold face to face with a grim paradox in the Congo scene.

This was the paradox he saw from New York:

Khrushchev's plan for a three-man secretariat to replace Hammarskjold was born of the Congo crisis. The theory of troika (Communist-neutralist-Western) control had been rejected by everyone outside the Soviet orbit as unworkable for the United Nations.

Yet it seemed to Hammarskjold as if the form and spirit of the troika offered the only hope of giving substance to the shadow of Congolese unity.

Northward in Stanleyville lay Gizenga's leftist influence. Even after joining Adoula he had carefully kept his 9,000-man army with its East European arms out of Leopoldville's reach.

In the center, Leopoldville, were the moderate middle-of-the-roaders, led by Adoula and Kasavubu. They campaigned with equal enthusiasm against what they termed imperialist and Communist intrigues, and did so just as warmly as other neutrals, like Nehru, Nkrumah and Nasser.

To the south, in Elizabethville, the pro-Western Tshombe still was resisting all efforts to return to the Congolese fold.

Hammarskjold may have detected the double sting in that tale of three cities during the last weeks of his life.

For more than a year he had been trying to coax, pull and push Tshombe into winding up his venture in statehood.

If Tshombe had agreed, Hammarskjold would have witnessed the completion of the Congolese troika. That would have carried its own sting.

In fact, Tshombe did not agree in Hammarskjold's lifetime.

And so Hammarskjold died knowing that Tshombe, an obscure forty-three-year-old Lunda tribesman, had defied him, the servant of the world. That was the second, unkinder sting.

Who was this Tshombe? Where did his strength and power rest?

Deep in the Commune Albert, in Elizabethville's African quarter, an old, boarded-up store bears the name Joseph Tshombe across its facade.

Here Katanga's leader was formed.

His father was the son of a tribal blacksmith in a northwest Katanga village. Old Joseph could scarcely read or write, but he was a shrewd merchant. He built up a chain of businesses. He ran a hotel. After World War II he journeyed to Belgium, paying his own boat fare, the first Congolese to do so. He was wealthy enough to see that Moise got the education he never knew himself.

The young Tshombe went through a mission school run by American Methodists. He became a Lutheran. His higher education was spotty and inconclusive. It included several years' study of commerce and law, by correspondence. Moise did not inherit his father's flair for business; at least one of his enterprises ended in bankruptcy.

Tshombe soon proved he had other talents. He showed he had an eye for the main chance. He married the Roman Catholic daughter of the Paramount Chief of the Lunda, so insuring for himself the good life. His talk was fluent, his smile ready. In 1959, when it was safe to do so under the Belgians, he entered active politics and quickly became leader of the CONAKAT (Confederation of the Association of Tribes of Katanga.)

Rarely in that period did he stray far from the side of the governing angels, at least in public. He seemed to conform with the positions taken by other Congolese leaders when the struggle for national independence was on. And during the Brussels negotiations on the transfer of power, Tshombe made no formal demands for Congolese Federation or for a special Katangan status. The furthest he went was, with some others, to argue the advantages of federalism. At that time the Belgians were absolutely insistent that an independent Congo would have to be a united Congo under a strong central government.

The tall Katangan leader oozed sophistry rather than sophistication. He gave visitors the impression he was his own publicity agent. Just the right length of starched, white cuff showed from his jacket sleeves. His pictures, which adorned Elizabethville, bore brave slogans like: "He suffers for us. Be worthy of him." At his frequent public meetings or news conferences he developed the gesture of raising both arms, fists clenched, in a sort of salute.

As the months of Katanga's venture dragged on, his grip on the machine of government tightened. He reveled in the process of building up the trappings of statehood. His orders were obeyed through those parts of the province outside Baluba control. The red and green Katangan flag fluttered bravely whenever and wherever it could decently be raised. He had a special Katangan currency printed—with his own picture on the bills. Automobiles took on new plates bearing the Katangan coat of arms, and they were recognized at least by sympathetic Rhodesians to the south. Official letters bore the heading "Etat du Katanga."

Moise Tshombe was not the living symbol of a truly popular movement among the Africans of Katanga for the sort of freedom yearned for and earned by other peoples in the postwar mainstream of nationalism. There is no such thing as a "Katangan nation," and indeed the ferocity of tribal feuds within the province has matched anything that has happened in other parts of the country.

Essentially the Katangan leader was the political creation of a trinity consisting of the 25,000 local Belgian settlers, the one-time Belgian rulers and the Union Minière du Haut-Katanga. This did not relegate him altogether to the status of a helpless or hapless stooge. He was too shrewd a politician for that. He showed himself resolute enough to use those who were in his debt on occasions, just as he allowed himself to be used. Within the African context he had his own ambition, and that was to promote Lunda nationalism or imperialism as far as he could.

The picture that emerged from measuring Tshombe's Katanga against conventional political standards looked something like this:

1. In the 1960 pre-independence elections, when separatism was not an issue, CONAKAT won 91,116 votes (33.4 per cent), while Congolese Vice-Premier Jason Sendwe's intertribal BALUBAKAT Alliance won 134,916 votes (49.4 per cent). The support of the remaining groups (about 47,000 votes, or 17 per cent) was more or less equally shared by the two main parties. Tshombe, however, managed to form the provincial government with twenty-five CONAKAT members, three allies from the smaller groups and all nine of the appointed members in a legislative body of sixty

elected members. During 1961 more and more ordinary Africans turned against his minority regime. Their opposition was stifled by the use of many classical police state methods, including lashings, political killings, strong-arm techniques that brushed aside the rule of law.

2. Territorially, his regime controlled about half the province, and his writ steadily shrank. To the north the Baluba—hated foes of Tshombe's Lunda and Munongo's Bayake—were in command and kept pressing southward.

3. Financially, about 80 per cent of Katanga's revenue came from taxes, dividends, franchise charges and duties subscribed by Union Minière. Spokesman Arthur Pared estimated in Brussels on December 11, 1961, that the combine's payment to Katanga for that year would run to about $52 million. The payments represented the yield on the 18.4 per cent stockholding in Union Miniére bequeathed by the Belgian State to its successor government. In international, Belgian and Congolese law there was no question that the Central Government of Leopoldville was the successor administration. Katanga had tried in vain—once even by an offer of payment—to win the recognition of foreign powers, and indeed it did not formally aspire to nationhood after the fervor of the first few months. Union Minière's annual report for 1961 explained the money *had* to be paid to Tshombe, because it "had to concede the de facto legal supremacy of the Katanga administration." The company, according to its officials, never had any say in the destination or division of its funds. But, outside of the Union Minière and Tshombe's supporters, most authorities found it hard to see the payments as anything but support of an insurrection.

4. Militarily, the 7,000-man Katangan Army (which, by the end of 1961, had swelled to nearly 10,000) was equipped, officered and trained initially by Belgian officers. They turned over to the Katangans some of the modern arms, ammunition and stores piled up in Belgium's huge Kamina base. U.N. troops later captured a dump that included Belgian submachine guns, bazookas, triple-barrel rocket projectors and other weapons used by the N.A.T.O. armies in Europe.

5. The administrative machine of the Katangan authorities was a small-time operation (outside the police and armed services) that functioned under the watch of foreign specialists, including French, Swiss, Belgian and other European technicians. The cooperation between Katangans and whites was rated as one of Tshombe's major achievements.

6. Internationally, Tshombe's cause was plugged in Western capitals by powerful groups of sympathetic politicians and by investment groups anxious to swing the official policies of their national governments behind him. In places like London, Paris, Brussels, Lisbon, and to a lesser extent Washington, these interested parties came to be known as the "Katanga Lobby." Their activities, information and propaganda were carefully coordinated until they assumed the scale of an outright campaign against the United Nations itself.

It is extremely doubtful, therefore, whether Tshombe would have ventured on so blind and perilous a course without prior promises of support from the unofficial alliance of Katangan white settlers, mining interests and one-time Belgian colonial rulers.

Equally, it was difficult to believe that he could have survived with a resilience apparently so astonishing without the active help of outsiders, including some foreign powers, once he had set up Katanga in business as a pretender state.

Hammarskjold himself never doubted that Tshombe's separatism was financed largely by Union Minière and unofficially encouraged, if not directed, by the personnel of that huge institution. A U.N. Conciliation Commission for the Congo reported in early 1961 that "the Union Minière du Haut-Katanga finances the Katanga authorities to an appreciable extent" (A/4711). In the fighting that flared in September, 1961, U.N. officials knew the company's widespread telecommunications system, its buildings, its workshops, its employees and its world-wide political and propaganda facilities were harnessed to the Katangan cause. The accusations, vehemently denied then by Union Minière chiefs, were not pressed to the point of any legal test.

All these factors, seen together, produced a very definite image of Katanga in other parts of the continent. Reginald H. Green, assistant professor of economics at Yale, wrote a study on the nature of the Katangan regime on January 23, 1962, in a letter to the *New York Times*. He said in part:

> African attitudes to Katanga and its apologists stem from this record. To them the Lunda imperialist, minority nature of Tshombe's regime is clear, as is its dependence on Union Minière payments permitted by Belgium in violation of her agreements with the Congo.
>
> The continued existence of the Lunda state benefits only the Lunda and Union Minière; certainly it injures the Congo as a whole and the anti-Conakat majority in Katanga.
>
> Support for Katangan self-determination is therefore seen as either deliberate or deluded support for tribalist imperialism and monopolist neocolonialism. This position is neither irrational nor extremist, but based on the nature of Katanga's regime and its financial supporters.

The Katangan leadership pressed on, nevertheless, undeterred. Tshombe showed himself to be an adept, energetic politician. He was fond of borrowing the rousing themes, if not the exact words, of Sir Winston Churchill's wartime speeches in order to rally his followers at times of crisis.

But the Katangan became a frightened man as the stakes of his gamble grew higher. He slept badly. He was anxious about his health. He was jittery about his security. He disliked being kept waiting. His temper was short.

Only Tshombe himself could say if Lumumba's staring eyes kept him awake at nights. But there were plenty of other ghosts to haunt him, and they left their telltale traces on the life and times of Katanga.

The tidy streets of downtown Elizabethville gave an impression of peace and order before September, 1961. But tribal clashes left their periodic scars.

The police were polite. But there were an awful lot of them.

The Union Minière was stepping up output. But it could have

been because of declining confidence in the future, a decision to build up great stockpiles in case operations were halted.

And then there was the constant nagging specter of the United Nations, with its mandate to promote the unity of the country, hanging over the land.

It was no wonder that Tshombe's followers, white and black alike, took time out to scrawl slogans on public places and to chant them during staged demonstrations for appropriate visitors. Slogans that said: "Go to Moscow, O.N.U.C.!" and "Down with the United Nations!"

It was no wonder that Tshombe himself came to lean ever more heavily on the ruthless band of mercenaries who led his army.

Where did they come from, these soldiers of fortune? Why were they there? Who were they?

They were a mixed bunch of career soldiers, bush pilots and professional hunters from many lands but mainly from Belgium, France, Rhodesia, South Africa and Britain.

Some went to Katanga to forget or be forgotten.

Others insisted they had a genuine mission to guard that little bit of Africa against Communism.

Early in 1961 there were about 700 of them, but their numbers dwindled as O.N.U.C. rounded them up. At one stage, of 442 foreigners listed by the United Nations as wanted men, 180 were regular Belgian Army officers seconded to Katangan forces. Another 175 were Belgian volunteers from the local settlers who said they were defending their homes. There were 21 Frenchmen under Colonel René Faulques, who masterminded many of his companions' most daring exploits. Faulques tried at one time to persuade Tshombe to employ only French mercenaries but was turned down. Several of the French adventurers had been barred from returning to their homeland for the parts they had played in the vain Algerian revolt against President de Gaulle earlier in the year.

They wore green and brown camouflage blouses, green tropical slacks, Stetsons or berets, green neckerchiefs, heavy jungle boots. Altogether they added a touch of flamboyance to the Elizabethville scene, crowding the saloons and night clubs, drinking fast and heavily.

Swashbucklers, some bearded, some mustached, they looked like fugitives from a Western film set. Their arms included Belgian Sten guns, heavy and light machine guns, rifles and automatic pistols worn loosely, cowboy-style, in holsters around their waists. Always liberally supplied with transportation, they rode around in jeeps and other military trucks.

The "Frightfuls"included among their motley ranks men who had been trained in World War II and in the unofficial wars that followed in distant lands like Indochina, Korea, Algeria and Malaya. At one time there was a complete English-speaking company —including mainly Britons, Rhodesians and South Africans—led by the spectacular brother of a British member of Parliament.

Captain Dick Browne was a huge bull of a man with a bushy beard. Once he led an attack by a white battalion on Congolese troops holding Manono in North Katanga in May, 1961.

Katangese troops had tried for months to recapture the town. Browne drove down the main street on the bonnet of a jeep, firing from the hip. The town was clear of Congolese in forty-five minutes.

Browne would always give the same answer when asked why he fought for Tshombe: "I am fighting Communism. It is the same war I fought for the British in Malaya."

Browne eventually was expelled by O.N.U.C.—only to return some time later on the payroll of Union Minière.

Tshombe's personal helicopter pilot was also a Briton, Peter Wicksteed, a twenty-eight-year-old product of an exclusive school and the British Fleet Air Arm. Friends explained that an unhappy marriage had sent Wicksteed in search of adventure. Before joining Tshombe he flew for Fidel Castro in Cuba.

The first commander of Tshombe's air force was a Belgian-Irish viscount who flew with the Royal Air Force in World War II. The operational command later fell to Delin, the spare South African-trained settler who piloted the Lone Ranger in the deadly raids against United Nations forces during the September fighting. From his headquarters at Kolwezi, a mining town 200 miles northwest of Elizabethville, Delin controlled a force of twenty planes, most of them light transports converted to makeshift bombers.

Tshombe never made any apology for employing white mercenaries in his forces. In his view their presence was perfectly justified. After the 1960 mutiny, with its trail of turmoil, Tshombe and the Belgians disarmed the Force Publique in Katanga. In its place they built a new army from tribes whose loyalty was assured. It had always been a cardinal point of Belgian colonial policy that any Congo province should be policed by men from another province, to reduce the chance of the Force Publique and the local population getting together in an uprising against their colonial rulers. Here was the "divide-and-rule" principle in practice.

Tshombe's new army had a backbone of noncommissioned officers who had served with the Force Publique. But the great majority of his troops and police had no military experience. He needed whites to train his men. Belgium provided them. He needed whites too to form a strike force against the Northern Baluba while his own men were being trained. These were the mercenary irregulars—South Africans, British, French, Rhodesians and others with a taste for adventure and cash. The supreme justification for the employment of whites, in the eyes of Tshombe's protagonists, was the fact that law and order of a homemade kind was maintained through half of Katanga while the rest of the Congo simmered and stewed.

His air force grew out of the sort of government air service essential in any country with primitive communications. At first it consisted of a handful of light planes owned by the Public Works Department. To these were added helicopters, a few de Havilland Dove transports and three Fouga jets. By September, 1961, only one Fouga still remained active. One had crashed and the other was held by the United Nations.

Even when the Dove transports were converted to bombers, and the air force reinforced with brand new Dornier 28s bought from West Germany, Tshombe's pilots still technically were employed by the Public Works Department. Other mercenaries melted away into civilian sinecures. They went onto the payroll of various government departments as engineers, technicians, even teachers.

One of the first acts of the Adoula regime was to decree in August that all foreign political or military men and mercenaries hired by Tshombe must leave the country. They called for U.N. help to see that the order was fulfilled. This made it the duty as well as the right of O.N.U.C. to move against Tshombe's band of adventurers.

Hammarskjold, then in New York, was closely consulted on the operational plan drawn up by Conor Cruise O'Brien and his staff in Elizabethville, and he approved its details.

Accordingly, early on August 28 an Indian contingent of the U.N. force encircled Camp Massart, the main camp of the gendarmerie in Elizabethville. Other units marched in to seize the downtown post office and Radio Katanga as precautionary steps to stall any call to arms by Tshombe. At the same time scores of mercenaries in various parts of the town were arrested. But at least a hundred or so faded into the bush.

The operation against the post office and radio station in some ways duplicated preventive action U.N. forces had taken exactly a year before in Leopoldville, when the airport and post office in the capital had been seized for the declared purpose of preserving peace. At the time, the operation was endorsed by the main Western powers, including Britain, but was furiously denounced by neutral and Communist countries. They felt it prejudiced the position of Lumumba, who was still being acknowledged by important powers as the Congo's lawful premier.

The surprised Tshombe agreed at once to cooperate with the U.N. Command. He broadcast a decree formally ending the contracts of foreign military advisers. For a while it looked as if all was over. In fact, the real crisis was only shaping up. The diplomats began to get busy. There were several swift developments.

A meeting of the consular corps took place first of all, and a course of action was mapped. U.N. representatives were invited —and agreed—to meet the consuls. They got together, and Henri

Crener, the Belgian Consul-General, who presided, pointed out that there were some two hundred Belgian army officers in Katanga and that their arrest would humiliate the Belgian Government and people. He offered with the support of his colleagues to take over responsibility for repatriating these officers, along with all other mercenaries regardless of their nationality. The U.N. authorities accepted the arrangement on condition there would be no filibustering and no arguments over who should be repatriated. These terms were accepted and the U.N. men called off—fatally called off—their rounding-up operations.

Within a day or two Crener came back to the U.N. Command. He said he was extremely sorry, but his superiors in Brussels had overruled his offer to take over the responsibility for the evacuation of all foreign military advisers other than Belgian Army personnel. That was not all.

O'Brien gave his version of what happened next in an article published by the Tuaurim *Bulletin* on February 6, 1962, and reprinted in *The Irish Times* next day:

> ... Neither the British Government, nor any of its supporters, as far as I know, has denied the fact of the flagrant encouragement given to Mr. Tshombe by the call of Mr. Dunnett, the British Consul in Elizabethville, with his Rhodesian deputy, Mr. David Smith, on Mr. Tshombe following the successful mass expulsion of mercenaries on August 28th.
>
> Mr. Smith, in the presumably approving presence of Mr. Dunnett, read out a message of encouragement from Sir Roy Welensky, which, as well as denouncing the United Nations' action, promised Mr. Tshombe "all support legally possible." Fortified by this encouragement and the promise of support, which he prominently featured in his press and on his radio, Mr. Tshombe launched that campaign of anti-U.N. manifestations and inter-tribal hate propaganda which led ... to the outbreak of fighting ... on the morning of September 13th, 1961.

The effect of all this was to loosen the U.N. grip on the situation. Follow-through action had been suspended despite the fact that scores of do-or-die adventurers still were at large. In the pause that followed, several outside powers, including Britain, roundly criticized the action on grounds that O.N.U.C. had overstepped its authority.

Britain's permanent delegate at U.N. headquarters in New York, Sir Patrick Dean, called on the Secretary-General under orders to:

1. Ask the exact scope and purpose of the U.N. move of August 28.
2. Inquire if force had been used before other methods were tried.
3. Say that Britain felt the United Nations had no right to remove essential foreign civilians whose services were needed by the Katangans.

Hammarskjold insisted there had been no breach of the U.N. mandate. He defended the actions of his officials in the Congo to the hilt. And he advised Dean that O.N.U.C. intended, unflinchingly, to fulfill its assigned task of ridding the Congo of all unauthorized foreigners.

Hammarskjold also sent his personal congratulations to O'Brien and his men for their very smooth performance.

On the night of September 11, a few hours before he flew off to the Congo, Dag Hammarskjold invited two couples to dinner at his New York home.

They were Mr. and Mrs. Carl Nordenfalk, fellow Swedes, and Mr. and Mrs. Ben Shahn. Carl Nordenfalk, Director of the National Gallery in Stockholm, had commissioned Ben Shahn, the famed American painter, to do a portrait of Hammarskjold.

For two years and more Nordenfalk had been trying to get Hammarskjold to stay still long enough to have the picture painted. The Swedish Government wanted it hung in the state gallery, where national leaders of bygone centuries look down from the walls. The dinner that night was arranged partly to settle the matter and to fix sittings.

Nordenfalk told the story of the dinner party in the course of a published tribute to Hammarskjold some months later:

> Dag invited us both for dinner together with our wives in his home. It was an extremely stimulating evening. Dag welcomed us, sunburnt and in best vigor after two weeks of vacation.
>
> He and Shahn competed in telling stories about their travel adventures. Dag showed us a set of beautiful photographs from Mount Everest—taken by him. It is a matter of general knowledge that he was far more than an amateur as regards photographing.
>
> The conversation also touched upon the Congo. He talked about the situation there with great confidence. The worst was now over.
>
> One did not speak much about art, but it was decided anyhow that Ben Shahn in the near future should start making some drawings of Dag in his working milieu. We felt at least near the goal. All seemed to be arranged for the best.
>
> This happened on the 11th of September. The following morning his plane left for the Congo.*

The worst was now over in the Congo, Dag Hammarskjold had said less than forty-eight hours before his arrival in the torn land . . . the worst was now over.

* *En Minnesbok* (Stockholm: Bonniers).

Part Two

The Last Days of Dag Hammarskjold

6 | The Wednesday

Dag Hammarskjold arrived in the Congo on Wednesday, September 13, not knowing the fight for the life of the United Nations had started against a foe he despised and with methods he detested.

The noise of battle in Katanga began at dawn while he was flying the Atlantic from New York. At Ndjili Airport, where he landed that scorching afternoon, the atmosphere was electric among the Congolese Government leaders, local U.N. chiefs, members of the diplomatic corps, and foreign correspondents who had gathered for his arrival. They searched his manner and his movements for signs of anxiety. Everyone wondered exactly how much he knew about the confused and quickly changing situation. Nobody was sure if the ominous echoes of the shooting had reached him in mid-air.

But, as usual, Hammarskjold's bronzed face was impassive. His dark-blue suit seemed to shine when he moved in the equatorial glare. He wore no hat and his combed-back hair seemed almost golden. His eyes screwed up when the sun caught them, for he had no sunglasses. Adoula strode forward and greeted the Secretary-General. For a while the two men stood on top of a carpeted pedestal, with Hammarskjold beginning to display his usual impatience at the inevitable news photographers taking their inevitable pictures. Yet as he stood there in the full gaze of the assembled onlookers the tension somehow seemed to subside. This, after all, was Hammarskjold, the representative of the United Nations and the arbiter of their quarrels. His presence offered the sort of relief a family doctor gives at a time of crisis. Magically, the familiar "let-

Dag-do-it" mood began to lift the depressed spirits of his friends and to lower the tempers of his critics.

The top echelons of the Leopoldville regime had come along with Adoula to welcome Hammarskjold. Gizenga, Mobutu, Foreign Minister Justin Bomboko attended, as if to demonstrate the scarcely credible fact of their unity to an honored guest who also was the symbol of world order. Briskly, with Adoula alongside, Hammarskjold inspected an honor guard comprising a Congolese Army battalion and contingents of the Nigerian and Swedish forces serving with O.N.U.C. After the ceremonial, the Secretary-General left the airport in Adoula's car for a brief chat at the Premier's residence. Over glasses of iced orange juice they talked about the work program that lay ahead during Hammarskjold's two-day official visit.

On to Linner's villa next. It was the first chance the two old friends had had to talk alone. Swiftly Linner outlined the Katangan situation. Tshombe's forces had engaged U.N. troops in battle. Initial reports indicated ministers of the provincial government had fled. For a while it looked as if the runaway province's dash for independence was ending.

But, Linner added grimly, later messages were quite cheerless. Fighting still was going on. It was too early to attempt a judgment of the outcome, but—as Hammarskjold well knew—the U.N. troops were not equipped for a long campaign. In that sense the outlook was ominous.

Clearly the U.N. men in Elizabethville had intended the operation as a swift, painless show of force to underpin their security while the roundup of mercenaries was resumed.

Equally clearly, though, something had gone wrong. The shooting was more violent than anyone expected. It looked as if it was spreading. The mercenaries were on the move again, leading Katangan resistance. Their guns had started the battle.

The two Swedes talked in low voices in one of the air-cooled rooms of Linner's modern, two-story home on a hill in Kalina, the residential district of the city. The building sprawled in its own big garden, lush with lawn and trees and flowers.

Outside, the flag of the United Nations drooped listlessly.

The news from Katanga startled Hammarskjold as much as it worried Linner.

Both men knew well enough that during the past fortnight Tshombe and his backers had stepped up their campaign of cold hatred against U.N. forces. Hammarskjold and Linner were also aware that intertribal tensions had been raised almost to breaking point under the lash of Katangan incitement. O'Brien had warned Tshombe to stop this kind of provocation or risk the sort of forceful U.N. intervention that the Security Council had authorized on February 21. Only four days earlier Michel Tombelaine, O'Brien's French deputy, had been detained by Katangan police on the orders of a white man. The mercenaries were emerging from their lairs in violation of Tshombe's latest promise to dismiss them once and for all.

The worsening situation had, about September 9, led O'Brien to recommend to Linner the urgent need for U.N. firmness in the face of Tshombe's defiance. He pressed for action to take over Radio Katanga, to arrest Interior Minister Munongo and others he considered responsible for the provocations, and to round up the mercenaries. And he added, in grim mood, that if it became necessary to use force there should be no letup until Katanga's separatism was ended.

All this, Hammarskjold indicated to Linner, was understandable without being justifiable in terms of the Security Council mandate. But he failed to grasp why the day's action had gone ahead without his explicit authority. Why could the operations not have been held up at least until he arrived in the Congo? Was it not clear to the U.N. hierarchy on the spot that the diplomatic aspects of the situation were dynamite? Even the perfectly legitimate August 28 action, when not a shot was fired, had brought stiff protests from the British and like-minded states. Now, less than a week before the session of the General Assembly, U.N. troops were in a shooting match that could only heighten the crisis for all concerned.

Hammarskjold's manner was cold as he asked these pointed questions. He appeared to freeze still more when he heard Linner's account. It was an account that seemed to deepen the mystery. Linner himself had conveyed to O'Brien a general authority to complete the roundup of mercenaries which had been started on August 28. But the Irishman's specific recommendations for tough measures to end Katangan secession had been set aside—pending advice from New York or Hammarskjold's own word on arrival. Nevertheless, it seemed to some in Leopoldville as if O'Brien was stretching his luck dangerously. He and his staff were creating the impression by their public statements that the U.N. aim in the current operation was no less than the liquidation of the Tshombe regime.

Yet even if that were so, a riddle still remained unanswered. Why did O'Brien submit a series of recommendations to Leopoldville for drastic action—recommendations that called for precise approval or disapproval—if he felt himself free to act anyway?

Puzzlement, distress, anxiety, shadowed the talk of the two Swedes. Neither man could know then that O'Brien had not, as they suspected, overstepped himself by engaging in a gamble that patently imperiled the authority of the United Nations.

The former chief of the U.N. mission in Katanga some time later—on December 17, 1961—gave his own version of how the plan of action he had urged came to be approved.

O'Brien wrote in an article published by the London paper *The Observer*:

> On September 10, Mr. Mahmoud Khiari and Mr. Vladimir Fabry arrived in Elisabethville with instructions for Brigadier-General Rajah, Commander of the U.N. forces in Katanga, and for myself. Mr. Khiari, a Tunisian, was nominally head of U.N. Civilian Operations in the Congo, but Dr. Linner had entrusted, or relinquished, to him great authority in the political field in which he had shown enormous ability. . . .
>
> He is a negotiator of extraordinary skill, and his skill had rendered great service to the U.N. He had merited the high esteem, and he had also won the confidence, of Mr. Hammarskjold. We had received our instructions from Mr. Khiari in connection with the operation of August 28 and it seemed entirely natural to accept verbal instructions from him in so important and secret a matter.
>
> I cannot here attempt a portrait of Mahmoud Khiari, but it is necessary to say a few things about him. He is, in the fullest sense of the word, a fabulous man; towering, mysteri-

ous, exotic, of vast capacities and not entirely worthy of belief. His only purpose was to bring the U.N. operation in the Congo to a successful conclusion. I liked him and admired him; I still like him and admire him but knowing what I now know, my admiration is tinged with caution and regret.

Mr. Khiari gave us our instructions in the drawing-room of Les Roches, my residence in Elisabethville. Those present at the main meeting at which the instructions were given included, as well as Brigadier-General Rajah and myself, and Mr. Khiari and Mr. Fabry, Colonel Jonas Waern, the Swedish Officer commanding South Katanga; Colonel Bjorn Egge, the Norwegian Intelligence Officer; and my deputy, Michel Tombelaine.

The instructions were as follows; to take over the post office, the radio studio and the transmitter; to raid the Sureté and Ministry of Information offices; to arrest any European officials found there and seize their files; and to arrest Godefroid Munongo, the Minister of the Interior; Jean-Baptiste Kibwe, Vice-President and Minister of Finance, and Evariste Kimba, so-called Foreign Minister. Tshombe also was to be arrested if absolutely necessary. Mr. Fabry, who was then Legal Adviser to the ONUC at Leopoldville, and who was to die in the crash at Ndola, produced from his brief-case *Mandats d'amener*—roughly equivalent to warrants for arrest —for Tshombe, Munongo and the others. These warrants bore the seal of the Central Government.

Strictly from the point of view of the situation in Elisabethville they were sound enough instructions, and the necessity for them arose from Tshombe's resistance, encouraged from the outside, to the implementation of the Security Council resolution.

The trouble was that nobody outside Elisabethville, except Mr. Khiari and Mr. Fabry, seems to have known about the instructions.

When I went to Leopoldville, several weeks after the close of hostilities, I found to my bewilderment that neither General [Sean] McKeown nor Dr. Linner knew the instructions I had received. In New York I found that neither Dr. Ralph Bunche [the Assistant Secretary-General] nor General Rikhye [the Military Adviser] knew about them either. Dr. Bunche believes that Mr. Hammarskjold did not know about them at all.

Mr. Khiari claims that he had been in personal, direct

> communication, by a channel unknown to anyone else, with Mr. Hammarskjold by secret unnumbered telegrams.
>
> It may be so; it is probable enough that Mr. Hammarskjold had begun to see the necessity for some strong action. But it seems unlikely to me now that Mr Hammarskjold did know the details—and they were pretty large details, like arresting a President—of the instructions given to us. . . .

The Secretary-General, after trying but failing to discover the precise origins of O'Brien's initiative, asked Linner about attempts for a cease-fire. Here, too, the prospects seemed bleak.

Perhaps the worst feature of the day's shattering developments, Linner reported, was a breakdown in truce exchanges. Very soon after the first shots, Tshombe at 4:45 a.m. in a telephone conversation with O'Brien asked for an unconditional cease-fire. The U.N. man agreed at once. Both issued orders for an end of the shooting, and their orders were acted upon. But then O'Brien and Tshombe lost touch with each other.

A curious episode followed at about 6 a.m.

Tshombe turned up, unannounced, red-eyed and unshaven, at the British Consulate. He knocked at one of the windows of Dunnett's residence and Dunnett invited him in. Cups of steaming coffee appeared. They talked for about an hour—but "did not discuss politics," Dunnett told O'Brien next day in reply to a direct question. The Foreign Office in London insisted that "nothing of substance" came up.

At about 7 a.m. Tshombe left the Consulate. He next appeared on the Rhodesian frontier. But almost as soon as he took leave of Dunnett the Katangans resumed their shooting, according to U.N. accounts. U.N. troops returned the fire. A clandestine radio began broadcasting hot, rousing appeals in Tshombe's name for "total war" against the international force. The short-lived truce had broken down.

To many it seemed as if the Katangan leader's visit to Dunnett offered a golden chance for action to confirm the tentative cease-fire, action perhaps in the form of an invitation to O'Brien to hurry around to meet Tshombe at the Consulate. In later explanations the British emphasized that the idea never came up. "Mr. Dunnett at that stage was not authorized by London, nor invited by the contenders, to work for a cease-fire," a Foreign Office spokesman said.

O'Brien had his own theory about this incident, which he felt fitted into a wider pattern proving "British encouragement to Tshombe to defy and resist the United Nations." *Before* visiting Dunnett, O'Brien maintained that Tshombe was ready to come to terms, and if he had done so the first Battle of Katanga might never have taken place. *After* visiting Dunnett, O'Brien learned the hard way that something had happened to stiffen Tshombe's resistance. The Irishman spelled out his belief—in a highly secret despatch filed to O.N.U.C. headquarters—that the British had encouraged Tshombe to fight on. In public, however, he never explicitly made this allegation, although he implied it in terms that could not fail to be understood.

Attempts to arrange a truce continued even after the fiasco at daybreak. A noon meeting was set up at the U.S. Consulate between O'Brien and Tshombe, but by then Tshombe was at, or near, the Rhodesian border.

Weighing all these shock developments with Linner, Hammarskjold quickly made two tactical decisions. Firstly, O'Brien must be instructed to pursue his cease-fire attempts with the utmost vigor. Secondly, Hammarskjold himself must carry on with the defined purpose of his own mission, for the time being. The visit had been set up primarily with the needs of the General Assembly session in mind. O.N.U.C.'s new budget was to be debated, and an aid program for the Congo was in preparation; its scope and scale obviously would depend on the progress toward a political settlement.

Linner had arranged an important dinner for that night so that Hammarskjold could discuss these and other issues with key Congolese leaders. Adoula, Gizenga, Vice-Premier Sendwe from Katanga, and Interior Minister Christopher Gbenye were coming along. U.N. guests included General McKeown, Khiari and the Chief Administrator, Habib Mahmoud.

At sundown, before the informal party, Hammarskjold retired

briefly to his upstairs room to freshen up. The big, high-ceilinged room was along a short corridor. Linner and his wife slept at the other end. In between the Linners' two sons, fifteen-year-old Allan and thirteen-year-old Lennart, shared a room. Ivory ornaments, wood engravings and other African handiwork collected by the lads on safari decorated the comfortable family home. The boys, at the time, were back at their school in Sweden, the well-known Sigtuna Humanistische.

Alone, while the pink and red sunset glowed through western trees, Hammarskjold unpacked a few things from his bags.

He placed the only book he had brought with him on the bedside table.

A statesman crusading for a better world could hardly have made a more interesting choice.

The book was a French-language edition of the *Imitation of Christ* by Thomas à Kempis.

It is always difficult to know exactly what happened when riots, battles or little wars break out suddenly.

In the case of Katanga the confusion over who shot first was confounded by the hatred for the United Nations expressed by articulate residents. Outside of the Katangan leadership these articulate people were mainly whites. Few ordinary Africans offered their point of view, because they did not dare to.

Tshombe's regime itself issued no communiqués, no coherent, documented account of the dawn drama tracing in detail the sequence of events. The point of view of the Katangans was put forward by sympathetic politicians and news correspondents. Several described the U.N. action, without supporting evidence, as plain, straightforward aggression. In general, the Katangans took the line that they were entitled to act in their own defense the moment U.N. troops began moving forward to take over public and strategic installations. It was as if they had come to believe their own propaganda—that Katanga was a sovereign state and that U.N. troops were invaders.

The U.N. Command took the best part of a day to give the

official documented version of what happened. By that time the world had been fed with some incomplete, confusing, exaggerated and partisan news despatches hurried to cable-heads in Rhodesian border towns. On the basis of such unofficial reports several governments formed rush, and sometimes rash, judgments of the events. They found it difficult later to retreat from their public positions of anger and indignation over what had been portrayed as an attempted U.N. eviction of Tshombe.

The essential elements of the U.N. account of the day's action seemed then, as now, difficult to dispute. The poor preparations for the U.N. operations offered their own evidence to show that no military campaign, no act of "aggression," had been planned. Furthermore, the action taken by Hammarskjold's men was at no stage shown by any power or international authority to have been illegal.

Unwise, mistimed and ill-planned, perhaps.

But not illegal.

What precisely happened in Katanga that fateful Wednesday? How did the situation arise? Where did the fighting start?

The basic document of reference explaining these questions was Sture Linner's official report to the Secretary-General.

It assumed historic importance because of the justification it offered for the U.N. operation. Every government in the world interested in the Congo situation examined it almost clinically. Every word in it had to be chosen with care. No understanding of the events was possible without it.

It is essential to reproduce it here because the story it told was the story Hammarskjold himself had clearly in his mind as he set about the task of retrieving the bruised and battered cause of the United Nations.

Report of the Officer-in-Charge of the United Nations Operation in the Congo to the Secretary-General relating to the implementation of Paragraph A-2 of the Security Council Resolution of 21 February, 1961.

1. Paragraph A-2 of the resolution adopted by the Security Council on 21 February 1961

> "*Urges* that measures be taken for the immediate withdrawal and evacuation from the Congo of all Belgian and other foreign military and para-military personnel and political advisers not under the United Nations Command, and mercenaries; . . ."

By far the largest concentration of such personnel, about 500, was to be found in the Katangese armed forces. Efforts to implement the above provision, which had to be pursued by way of negotiations in view of the lack at this stage of legal authority for the U.N. to take other steps for implementation of the resolution within the Congo, remained for several months without appreciable results.

2. On 24 August 1961, the President of the Republic of the Congo, upon the advice of the Government, enacted Ordonnance No. 70, providing for the expulsion of all non-Congolese officers and mercenaries serving in the Katangese forces, not under a contract with the Central Government. The Prime Minister of the Republic of the Congo requested U.N. assistance in the execution of this Ordonnance and in ensuring the evacuation of the personnel falling under the expulsion decree. These actions gave the UN legal rights within the Congo corresponding to the terms of the aforementioned resolution.

3. On 26 August, Mr. Munongo, Minister of the Interior of the Katanga provincial government, announced that the United Nations was planning to disarm the Katangese armed forces and that 1,500 ANC [Central Government] soldiers in United Nations planes were on their way to Elisabethville to occupy Katanga. This announcement and similar false rumors created an atmosphere of tension notwithstanding the fact that they were immediately denied by the United Nations. The UN was therefore compelled to take security precautions when, on the morning of 28 August, it proceeded to take measures for evacuating foreign military personnel and mercenaries. It placed a surveillance on Radio Katanga, on Gendarmerie headquarters and on other key points and installations in the city of Elisabethville. During the few hours that this surveillance lasted, the radio continued to broadcast normally, with the sole exception that no statements of an inflammatory nature, likely to lead to an incitement to civil or tribal disturbances in violation of paragraph A-1 of the Security Council resolution of 21 February, were permitted. Moreover

an appeal was made to the Katangese gendarmerie to co-operate and to the Katangese population to maintain calm and proceed with their normal occupations. No resistance was encountered from the Katangese armed forces or police in the execution of the evacuation measures, and life continued normally throughout Katanga.

4. Mr. Tshombe was informed by the UN representative of the objectives of the United Nations action. At noon on 28 August Mr. Tshombe stated in a broadcast that his government had approved of the evacuation of foreign military personnel and had terminated the services of all foreigners in the Katangese armed forces effective that day.

5. In the morning and again in the afternoon of 28 August, UN representatives met with the Elisabethville Consular Corps at their request to discuss repatriation procedures. The Belgian Consul, who presided over these meetings, stated that by arrangement with his colleagues he would undertake the responsibility for ensuring the surrender and repatriation and travel of all personnel required to be evacuated, irrespective of their nationality. He introduced two senior officers who had served in the Katanga Gendarmerie and who were to assist the United Nations in arranging an orderly withdrawal of all foreign personnel who served in the Katangese armed forces. The United Nations agreed to this evacuation procedure on condition that the evacuation would not thereby be delayed and that the United Nations retained the exclusive authority to decide who should be evacuated and when. On this understanding the United Nations refrained from continuing to search for and apprehend foreign military personnel, and permitted about 70 Belgian officers to stay in the Belgian Consulate building in Elisabethville until transport for them became available.

6. Unfortunately, these arrangements were not scrupulously observed. Only the officers already stationed in the Belgian Consulate building and officers of the Belgian Army placed at the disposal of Katanga by the Belgian Government were dealt with under this procedure, and even in the case of these officers delays or administrative exemptions were proposed. The foreign officers and mercenaries, profiting from this relaxation of evacuation measures, re-infiltrated into the Gendarmerie, and there were indications that they began distributing arms to certain political or ethnic groupings. The

foreign elements also began exercising pressure on some Katangese ministers to dissuade them from moving towards political reconciliation to the authority of the Central Government. Finally, the foreign military personnel, together with the so-called "ultras" among the non-African residents, exercised an adverse influence on the Katangese government, inciting them to terroristic actions and violations of fundamental liberties.

7. Thus, the actions of the political police (Sureté) which must be regarded as falling under paragraph A-2 of the resolution and which is an instrument of Mr. Munongo largely directed by foreign officers, combined with the inflammatory propaganda broadcast on Radio Katanga and spreading of rumors, caused panic among the Baluba population, who began to throng into UN camps, asking for protection. The influx of Baluba refugees, who constitute the economically and educationally most advanced part of the African population of Elisabethville, began on 24 August following the arrest of their spokesman, Mr. Bintu, and a few other leaders. By 9 September the number of refugees had reached 35,000 and created not only a very serious problem for the United Nations which had to protect, feed, shelter and care for them, but also a situation likely to lead to tribal and civil war.

8. Information obtained by the United Nations from various sources established that Mr. Munongo and his Sureté officials had conspired, or were attempting, to carry out attacks on United Nations personnel, military as well as civilian.

These reports were to some extent confirmed by the occurrence of inspired demonstrations against the United Nations in the first week of September, which resulted in considerable material loss to the UN and in injury to a number of United Nations personnel.

9. Of a much more dangerous character, however, was the menace to the security of the United Nations personnel and property constituted by the terroristic conspiracies and activities of some of the foreign officers in the Katangese armed forces who had thus escaped evacuation measures. Most prominent among them were a group of officers of French nationality, some of whom were unable to return to their own country because of their implication in the recent revolt by French military elements in Algeria. Another group consisted of soldiers of fortune, while a third group were the so-called "volunteers" recruited from amongst foreign settlers in the Congo.

Information received to the effect that one such group planned to introduce plastic bombs into the building in which the UN offices in Elisabethville were located compelled the United Nations on 6 September to move its headquarters to one of the military camps. There was also evidence that these officers were organising a guerrilla group among the *gendarmerie* personnel, that they were maintaining their hold over certain units of the *gendarmerie* preventing them from co-operating with the UN, and that they organized the attack on the UN garage and the burning of UN vehicles.

10. The day of 9 September was set as the time-limit as of which all foreign military personnel had to report to a United Nations unit for evacuation. By that date, however, only 273 foreign officers and mercenaries had been repatriated and 65 were awaiting repatriation. At least 104 foreign personnel were known to have failed to report or to give any account of themselves. The United Nations representative thereupon called once more on the consuls asking them to ensure the immediate departure of their nationals, failing which the United Nations would have to resume action for implementing the 21 February resolution by all means at its disposal.

11. In the morning of 11 September the deputy United Nations representative in Elisabethville was arrested on orders given by a non-Congolese officer of the political police (Sureté). This was the culmination of a long series of wrongful acts by these officers, including the organization of attacks on the United Nations, repeated threats, and incitement to violence. Moreover, it was impossible to persuade the Baluba refugees to return from the UN camp to their homes as long as they were exposed to threats and arbitrary arrests by, or at the direction of, Sureté officials. The United Nations therefore requested that all the non-Congolese officers of the Sureté be evacuated within 48 hours.

12. At the instigation of the remaining foreign officers, as well as of the local extremists, heavily armed patrols and guard posts began to be maintained by the *gendarmerie* at all public buildings and other installations in Elisabethville. The police was reinforced by 300 members of Mr. Munongo's Bayake tribe. Arms were also being distributed to individuals and groups who were not properly trained and disciplined to handle them.

13. On 12 September the "Foreign Minister of the Ka-

tanga Government," Mr. Kimba, announced that negotiations had been opened for reinforcing Katangese units with personnel and equipment from Rhodesia.

14. Also on 12 September, UN representatives met with Mr. Tshombe and members of his government in an attempt to obtain a lessening of the tension, a withdrawal or at least reduction of the military elements from the streets in Elisabethville, an end to the inflammatory propaganda, redress of refugee grievances which would permit their return to their homes, and assurance that the evacuation of all personnel falling under paragraph A-2 of the 21 February Security Council resolution would proceed promptly. UN representatives also attempted to persuade the Katanga government to reconcile their political differences with the Central Government by constitutional means and gave assurances concerning Mr. Tshombe's safety if he wished to travel to Leopoldville for discussions. On all these points the answer of the Katangese government was a negative one; they refused emphatically to permit the evacuation of the foreign officers serving in the Katangese Sureté.

15. In the early hours of 13 September, the UN forces therefore took security precautions similar to those applied on 28 August, and deemed necessary to prevent inflammatory broadcasts or other threats to the maintenance of law and order while the UN resumed carrying out its task of apprehending and evacuating foreign military and para-military personnel. At this point an alert was set since arson was discovered at the UN garage. As the UN troops were proceeding towards the garage premises, fire was opened on them from the building where a number of foreign officers are known to be staying. UN troops were subsequently also resisted and fired at as they were deploying towards key points or while they were guarding installations in the city. UN troops returned fire.

16. While it is yet too early to reconstruct from the incomplete reports the whole story of the events of the day, a report transmitted at noon on 13 September by the Commander of UN forces in Katanga, Brigadier S. K. Rajah, states that the radio station and post office guarded by UN troops were attacked several times and that extensive sniping fire was directed against UN troops and the residence of the UN representative from houses occupied by non-African residents of the city. Non-Congolese officers and mercenaries were ob-

served leading the attacks, directing fire and handling the weapons. On the other hand there is no evidence of any spontaneous or large-scale actions having been taken against the UN by the Congolese personnel of the Gendarmerie.

17. Sporadic sniping and occasional bursts from heavier weapons were reported throughout the day and up to the time of writing this report, the Katanga Radio Station was reported substantially damaged by mortar fire directed at it when the UN sought to use it to appeal for calm and cessation of fire. Casualties so far ascertained include one Indian soldier and one Swedish officer killed, 6 Indian, 3 Swedish, 4 Irish and one Norwegian personnel wounded.

18. The UN representative contacted Mr. Tshombe and attempted to obtain a cessation of the hostilities as soon as possible. A cease-fire was in fact issued by Mr. Tshombe, but was disregarded by the mercenaries involved in the fighting. Throughout the incident, the adjutant of the President, Major Mwamba, assisted the UN headquarters in their efforts to contact responsible authorities who could have used their influence to restore calm.

19. To this end, a meeting was arranged between the UN representative, the United States Consul, Mr. Tshombe and other political and military leaders to take place at noon. Mr. Tshombe and the Congolese leaders did not come to that meeting, however, and contact between them and the UN representative was not re-established up to the time when this report was being drafted. Mr. Kibwe is reported to be in a UN camp.

20. In the afternoon of 13 September, the Central Government of the Republic of the Congo dispatched to Elisabethville a delegation headed by the Commissaire d'Etat for Katanga, Mr. E. D. Bocheley, to assist the provincial authorities in the restoration of law and order. The UN dispatched a team of technical experts to help in the restoration of essential utilities and public services.

The crackle of machine guns and the crunch of mortars in Katanga sent their echoes around the world.

Reactions ranged from bitter resentment to unqualified approval.

In some key capitals of Western Europe and of white-ruled

African states, the sound and fury of criticism of Hammarskjold were intense.

On the whole Afro-Asian comment was favorable and seemed to be summed up by India, which asserted the United Nations was fully within its rights to act. The United States backed this view.

The Soviet-led bloc of nations, hostile equally to Hammarskjold and to Tshombe, remained cannily quiet, although there was no doubt that Moscow was pleased at the setback both Tshombe and Hammarskjold seemed likely to receive.

The strongest expressions of concern came from Salisbury, Brussels and London, where the governments were interested broadly in seeing Tshombe's *power* preserved, whether inside or outside a Congolese state. One of their fears was that if Tshombe's regime was swept away there would be little or nothing to prevent all Katanga, with its resources, falling under the influence if not the control of the Lumumbists, and through them the Communists.

In Salisbury, Welensky alerted all Federal forces and sped troops, armor and airplanes to the border because of what he termed "the serious threat" to Rhodesian security. He told Parliament that "nothing so disgraceful in the whole history of international organizations" had happened ever before. He pledged all aid "to anyone from Katanga who is endangered because of his democratic beliefs." He lashed out in particular at O'Brien, allegedly for inspiring false rumors.

In Brussels, the Belgian Catholic newspaper *La Libre Belgique*, which often reflects official thinking, described the events as "a premeditated crime." It charged O.N.U.C. with massacring "the only prosperous and vigorous province" in the Congo. Another newspaper, the liberal *La Dernière Heure*, compared O.N.U.C.'s and O'Brien's actions and methods with those used by the Nazis in the 1940–1944 occupation of Belgium.

In London, the Foreign Office expressed Britain's "deep concern," and ordered Ambassador Derek Riches in Leopoldville to demand an immediate explanation from Hammarskjold personally. Foreign Under-Secretary Lord Lansdowne stood by to fly next day, Thursday, for talks with Hammarskjold and others on the crisis. Pro-Government newspapers branded the U.N. action variously as "aggression," "an outrage" and "a crime."

The Rhodesian, Belgian and British nightmare fear of a Red-run Katanga was shared by other countries, including France, South Africa and Portugal. To all of them the specter of a Congo under Communist influence meant only one thing: all of Black Africa would soon become exposed to Moscow's teachings. They wanted Tshombe's authority and power untouched, in order to buy the time they needed to transform the Congo, even with Katanga in it, into a buffer against northern and Red pressures. If, then, Katanga was to be reunited with the rest of the country the process must be carried out peacefully. Tshombe was a man they could work with. Tshombe was prepared to work with them.

One of the most embittered criticisms came from Portugal, which itself was deeply engaged in a grinding battle to crush an independence movement in the West African colony of Angola, south of the Congo.

The Lisbon newspaper *Diario Popular* accused Hammarskjold of having a "personal interest" in Katanga. It asserted his eldest brother presided over a Swedish-American firm with heavy investments in the region. Other pro-Katangan newspapers across Europe printed similar stories with variations. The general theme was that this newly formed Swedish-American company had mining interests in the Congo and that one of its representatives recently had visited Katanga to recruit Union Minière technicians.

There was, of course, no truth in the smear.

Hammarskjold's eldest brother Bo, onetime governor of the Swedish province of Sodermanland, did at one time serve as chairman of Trafikactiebolaget Grangesberg-Oxelosund (TGO). TGO is an iron-ore company with state capital in it, and with interests in North Sweden and Liberia. Bo Hammarskjold's chairmanship in fact was no more than a sinecure post awarded to a former civil servant, and it carried a token annuity.

These facts, provided by Swedish Government officials, were easily ascertainable. Nonetheless the false story was reproduced on September 28, 1961, ten days after Hammarskjold died, in *Congo-*

Africa. The fortnightly bulletin produced in the interests of Union Minière and its associated companies did mention that TGO had denied the report. But *Congo-Africa* also added: "Mr. [Bo] Hammarskjold, who is a good deal older than his brother, has so far refrained from any statement."

The reason why Bo Hammarskjold "refrained from any statement" was that he considered it beneath his dignity, in the midst of his sorrow over Hammarskjold's death, to grace an unchecked rumor with a denial.

The reason why some publications printed or reprinted the rumor was to spread the impression that Dag Hammarskjold had engaged the United Nations against Tshombe's forces in order to promote his brother's financial interests.

The United States, in contrast with some of its European allies, came out at once in support of the U.N. action.

"We believe that unity of that [Congolese] nation is essential to economic progress and stability," said the State Department. "The United States has, of course, been concerned particularly about the threat of civil war in the Congo as a result of separatist movements. A principal mission of the United Nations there has been to prevent this threat from materializing. The U.N. force has been operating in general support of the Central Government since its establishment."

Generally the Americans shared the same objectives as their friends who wanted to keep Communism at bay in Africa. Like India and other key neutral nations, they were convinced that the best hope of achieving this lay in a policy of wholly supporting the U.N. mission. Unlike Britain, France and other African powers, their attitude was not colored primarily by a need to safeguard prized territories where immeasurable human and material resources had been invested.

The policy-makers of Washington reasoned that a cooperative Tshombe could take his place in the Central Government and there counter the extremism of Gizenga and other Lumumbists. His separatism, in fact, was only strengthening Lumumbist influence. In that sense Tshombe seemed to be helping to create the very Frankenstein monster he said he had set out to destroy.

President Kennedy's Administration was convinced of the need to resist any drift toward a "Balkan-type" situation in Africa. All the demands of modern political, industrial and social organization called for ever-wider national and regional groupings. The continent and its peoples were far enough behind the rest of the world as it was. They simply could not afford the time or the energy that would have to be squandered in the kind of splintered, inward-looking tribe-states that had slowed the progress of nineteenth-century Europe. That was why the acknowledged political and intellectual leadership of African lands looked on Tshombe as something of a renegade to the cause of African nationalism.

The Americans were haunted by another anxiety, and day after day in friendly capitals their diplomats tried to get the message across. If Katanga's separatism was not discouraged how could the West stop the Russians from promoting a break-away movement in some other Congolese province—perhaps Gizenga's? If the mercenaries were not thrown out of Katanga how could the Russians or Chinese be stopped from pouring their own volunteers into another part of the country one day? Here lay one real American dread. A collapse of the U.N. mission in the Congo could suck the Communists from Russia or elsewhere into the vacuum. This would confront the United States with the challenge of intervening itself. It was a challenge Washington knew in advance it could not duck.

All these and many other dangerous implications of the push-and-pull Katangan struggle were clear to all, but each country looked at the situation through the spectacles of its own national interests.

Hammarskjold himself tried to get it all into focus through the telescope of the United Nations' future.

His main preoccupation, even during the sedate talks with Congolese leaders over the Linner dinner table, was with the perils of the Battle of Katanga. The manner and mood of Adoula and his friends during the evening merely underlined his misgivings. The Congolese were mightily pleased with the developments. To them it looked as if Tshombe, their current arch-foe, was taking a beating.

But Hammarskjold knew the pleasure of Tshombe's foes would be more than matched by the ferocity of Tshombe's friends. Rightly or wrongly they would see the U.N. operations as an attempt to impose a political settlement. They would shut their eyes to the plight of U.N. troops and to the provocations they had endured. They would be bound to assert the world body had exceeded its authority by displaying and using force.

Warning signals of the gathering political storm already were being flashed into the U.N. network from distant capitals. The British Embassy had telephoned a request from Ambassador Derek Riches for an urgent meeting with Hammarskjold. A late session for that night was arranged.

The word from the Secretariat in New York was that a lot of diplomatic fuss was being fastened onto a statement attributed, earlier in the day, to O'Brien, who had met with newsmen. The U.N. political chief in Katanga was being widely quoted as saying, "Katanga is now a Congolese province run by the Central Government in Leopoldville."

It was a short cut from that purported statement to the assumption that the U.N. action had been designed to oust Tshombe.

In fact there was some dispute over whether O'Brien made the statement. The Irishman denied it. Several newsmen insisted he was correctly reported.

Yet even if O'Brien was misrepresented—and misrepresentations were a dime a dozen in the affairs of the Congo—there could be little doubt that correspondents were reporting something well-enough known. Most U.N. authorities, in their heart of hearts, really did hope the expulsion of the mercenaries would end the Tshombe era. They loved his regime as little as the regime loved them. U.N. men for months had been swallowing insults and humiliations in silence.

And if, on the other hand, the ebullient O'Brien was faithfully reported, his remark was a statement of what seemed obvious to many at the time. It looked then to independent newsmen as well as to U.N. authorities as if the U.N. action *was* succeeding and as if Tshombe *had* fled. Later events, of course, provided their own reprimand to anyone who might have prematurely forecast a Katangan defeat.

As the Congolese guests took their leave to make way for Ambassador Riches there was no doubt at all that Hammarskjold was confronted with a major political and personal crisis.

Riches drove up to Linner's home in a British Embassy car, accompanied by his Head of Chancery. The aide was John Powell-Jones, a taciturn, handsome, aesthetic-looking young diplomat. The pair were in highly serious mood.

Hammarskjold received them in the company of his senior advisers, who were anxious to hear his latest thoughts on the crisis.

Riches had arrived at his post only a few days before. The cabled instructions he brought from Foreign Secretary Lord Home represented the first major assignment of his new mission.

The British envoy got to the point at once. He told Hammarskjold that news of the U.N. action, indicating a resort to force, had been received with a sense of deep shock, concern and horror by the British Government and said he was under orders to ask for an explanation of the day's operations in Elizabethville. He asked in particular how Hammarskjold envisaged the development of U.N. policy in Katanga, and he demanded to know how the use of force could be justified on the basis of authority so far given by the Security Council.

The envoy acknowledged that London did not then have its own firsthand information from Elizabethville. He drew attention to news despatches quoting O'Brien as saying the U.N. action had been taken to head off civil war between the Katangans and the Central Government forces.

If O'Brien really did say this, Riches went on, an explanation was all the more essential. He argued that if a civil war seemed in fact imminent, it would have been more appropriate for U.N. forces to have acted against the potential attackers, rather than against the intended victim of attack.

Hammarskjold's eyes flickered at this.

Some months later aides recalled he had been irritated by the argument. For he remembered that the same view had been rejected by the Government of ex-Premier Sir Anthony Eden (later Lord Avon) in 1956 when British and French forces landed in the Suez area. At that time the British claimed they were attacking the Egyptians to protect the Suez Canal against damage. The threat of damage came from the fighting that followed Israel's invasion of Egypt.

The rustling of Riches' papers pulled Hammarskjold back to the present.

The ambassador began to read with care a compelling passage in his instructions. Hammarskjold's aides leaned forward to listen more intently. The sense of what they heard amounted to just this:

Her Majesty's Government was serving notice, with the greatest emphasis at its command, that Britain would have to consider withdrawing *all* support from O.N.U.C.'s mission unless:

1. Hammarskjold could provide an acceptable explanation for what had happened in Katanga; or
2. Hammarskjold could provide an assurance that the fighting would swiftly be ended.

There was a hush in the room. Outside the eternal crickets chirruped. The U.N. chiefs alongside Hammarskjold pondered the true meaning of the British warning

Politically, it was clear at once that a British withdrawal would cripple, if not finish, O.N.U.C., which already was limping along for want of greater support. It was not just a matter of the $10 million worth of funds contributed by Britain. It also was a matter of another great power ranging alongside Russia in a display of "no confidence" in the Secretary-General. Could Hammarskjold survive opposition on this scale?

Militarily, it was plain also that a British withdrawal could be a damaging, if not a fatal, setback to the entire operation. Commonwealth contingents like the Nigerians, Malayans and Ghanaians had for months depended on the help of R.A.F. transport planes for their supplies.

The threat that Riches had brought pointed like a dagger at the heart of the world body itself.

The Secretary-General betrayed no hint of what may have been his true feelings at that moment.

He had been sitting with thumb and forefinger supporting his chin.

Now he moved forward to answer Riches.

Speaking briskly, without a document before him, he gave a crystal-clear presentation of the rationale behind the thoughts and acts of the U.N. mission in the Congo and Katanga.

His backgrounding, his recital of the legal justification, his narrative of the way the whites of Katanga had built up their "hate campaign" against U.N. forces, were so orderly and logical that Linner used them as the basis of his official report. (At that time the report had not been prepared.)

Hammarskjold also took time out to deal with specific points raised by Riches. He clarified, for instance, O'Brien's reference to the peril of civil war. He denied that O'Brien had suggested Central Government forces were then about to invade Katanga. The danger of civil war, he insisted, was a local danger within Katanga, where leaders of the regime, and the mercenaries, seemed by their actions to be deliberately spreading panic among the Baluba. Already U.N. refugee camps were bursting with 35,000 Baluba fearful of massacre by Lunda and other tribal foes.

Hammarskjold's voice—listeners reported later—rose fractionally when he talked about the activities of the mercenaries. It was clear that he regarded the soldiers of fortune with the deepest contempt. It had become the inescapable duty of the United Nations to chase them out once the Central Government had formally decreed it and had called for O.N.U.C.'s help in doing so. These foreigners were conspiring against U.N. chiefs, attacking the troops, threatening the peace and re-creating a powerful underground movement.

Hammarskjold at that point said something that seemed to surprise several of his audience.

The British delegate at U.N. headquarters in New York—Sir Patrick Dean—among others had been given advance notice of U.N. resolve to deal with the mercenaries with the greatest firmness; Hammarskjold said he had himself given that advance notice to Dean.

Hammarskjold paused before turning to the day's military flare-up. He spelled out the reasons why specific precautionary action had to be taken to control the post office, Radio Katanga and other public installations. All had the common purpose of preserving that law, order and security for which the United Nations Command was responsible.

As for the use of force. . . .

Again he paused.

U.N. troops had gone about their operations in as unprovocative a manner as possible. The cooperation of the gendarmerie had been requested, and was given to some extent, until it was ruined by the intervention of the soldiers of fortune and others.

The shooting?

First shots were fired, he said, in the post office area, and they came from gun nests seen in the building that housed the Belgian Consulate. (The Belgian Government later denied this in a statement from Brussels.)

Hammarskjold ended his explanations. The British diplomats collected their papers. They left without giving any indication of whether they had been impressed.

It emerged some time later that several senior British officials regretted that Hammarskjold's account of the U.N. position—or something like it—had not been made public immediately. They felt it might have helped to avoid the great international outcry that followed.

Riches and Powell-Jones left Linner's home around midnight. But Hammarskjold was far from finished with his day's work. He was driven to an office prepared for him at the U.N. headquarters building, Le Royal, a crudely converted apartment block. The senior advisers accompanied him.

For three hours, at Le Royal, they examined all aspects of the Katangan situation on the basis of O'Brien's reports. They discussed at length the significance of the British warning. And they talked about the sort of instructions to be sent to O'Brien on the conduct of the operations. Some of these orders had to be sent off at once in response to specific ideas and requests he had put in. One of O'Brien's recommendations was that a three-week-old plea by Brigadier Rajah for air support be approved immediately.

In these exchanges the top authorities of the United Nations were by no means united in their views. One group, which included McKeown, Khiari and Fabry, argued the case for rushing reinforcements into Katanga to boost O'Brien's power. They also favoured a less passive military strategy for U.N. troops.

But Hammarskjold overruled the idea of tougher U.N. action, perhaps in order to gain time and to see how events in the battle zone developed.

The Secretary-General instead outlined the sort of directives that were to go back to O'Brien, and insisted on checking their contents personally.

The broad line running through the messages was the emphasis, time and again, that U.N. troops never fire unless in self-defense and that any new operations were to be cleared in advance with Leopoldville. They also spelled out the importance of seizing any chance for a truce that might present itself.

A certain remoteness marked their note. The famous Hammarskjold iciness began to spread its chill.

Once they had taken care of Elizabethville's needs Hammarskjold, Linner, Khiari, Fabry and some of the others turned to the precise terms of the official report that had to be sent early next day to New York.

Shortly before 3 a.m. Hammarskjold released his weary staff. An automobile flying the U.N. flag swept Linner and him back home through the deserted Leopoldville streets. Hammarskjold retired to his room and went to bed.

7 | The Thursday

Hammarskjold arose Thursday morning convinced the United Nations must not win the Battle of Katanga—yet dared not lose it.

As he saw it, that was the logic of Britain's warning the previous night and of the Afro-Asian attitude that had been conveyed to him in New York.

His interpretation of the situation, according to his colleagues, ran roughly like this:

1. The British had set a price on the eviction of Tshombe's regime. The price was nothing less than their withdrawal from U.N. operations in the Congo. A British pull-out probably would kill the mission, weaken the general U.N. peacemaking role and perhaps irreparably damage U.N. prestige and authority. Whether the British were right or wrong did not matter at this stage. What did matter was the probable effect of a fight-to-the-finish policy in Katanga. The inescapable conclusion seemed to be that Tshombe must not be beaten and U.N. troops therefore would have to be held back.
2. The Afro-Asians, on the other hand, had begun grumbling in New York over what they took to be his kid-glove treatment of Katangan separatism. Tshombe's defiance of Security Council resolutions appeared to the Afro-Asians to have the support of the African colonial powers. Welensky's white-supremacy government seemed to be thumbing its nose at the world body. This must not be allowed to go on. O.N.U.C. had to reassert itself and produce results. Otherwise, willy-nilly, it might be difficult to prevent some Afro-Asian states from looking once again to the Soviet bloc for action.

Hammarskjold cared nothing for the personal threat implied by all this. But he did identify himself with the Afro-Asian sense of frustration over the flouting of U.N. decisions by the Katangans and their friends. And he knew O.N.U.C. dared not risk any sort of appeasement of Tshombe. If the battle against him could not be won, equally it must not be lost.

The Secretary-General had slept little more than three hours. Yet he seemed refreshed when he went down to his usual breakfast of fruit, corn flakes and coffee.

This pattern of intense, driving, sleepless activity was something that distinguished Hammarskjold at times of crises. His body was like tempered steel. He rarely went sick, and even common colds irritated him. During the Suez crisis of 1956, for weeks at a time he would work twenty or twenty-one hours a day and sleep no more than three or four.

The harder he worked—or played, during vacations—the less rest he found he needed. He seemed to be sustained by an insatiable need to talk, argue, listen or read—on art, politics, music, books, writers—and these were the activities that shaped his life and his few deep friendships. More than one quarrel ensued with old companions over his blank refusal to go to bed until deep into the night.

But conflict and uncertainty worried and depressed him. He had had his painful share of these in the preceding months, when Soviet attacks on him had reached their crescendo. He was sensitive to criticism of his fair-mindedness and impartiality, and the strain told on him. There were times during those hapless last hours when his voice sharpened and his eyes narrowed.

Before setting out that day on his round of official engagements Hammarskjold and Linner checked through the latest reports of the spreading Katanga battle. O'Brien and Rajah made it clear that most of the firing—at least in Elizabethville—came from white civilians in ordinary buildings. They wanted authority to hit back hard, and asked for swift ground reinforcements. The whole operation could be settled decisively within two or three days, they said, if only the U.N. command was permitted to abandon its defensive, one-handed role.

Hammarskjold was not prepared to contemplate this. He had been shocked, as he had indicated to his colleagues at the staff meeting the previous day, by their evident ignorance of the power of Tshombe's fighting machine. He recognized, and Linner could not disagree, that if U.N. troops at this stage were to be allowed to clean up the snipers and machine gun posts there might well be something of a massacre. Passions among the Swedes, Irish and Gurkhas were high. They had been insulted and spat upon long enough. They were not likely to try too hard to distinguish between attackers with guns and those who merely loathed the blue and white U.N. helmets.

Then and there Hammarskjold resolved that a firm and stern order must be sent to O'Brien rejecting suggestions for an offensive strategy. For the security of the U.N. position reinforcements would go in, but not to force a decision.

The message later sent reminded O'Brien in cold terms yet again that U.N. men shoot only in self-defense.

The grim telegram from Hammarskjold was only one of many O'Brien and his colleagues received on Thursday and the days that followed. Plainly, some deep misunderstanding had arisen between them and their chief. The true depth emerged weeks later. O'Brien was to discover that Hammarskjold did not know the main elements of the directive that Khiari—according to the Irishman—had brought to Elizabethville.

O'Brien related in *The Observer* (December 10, 1961) that "a curious hesitancy, much in contrast with previous instructions, had crept into the cables from Leopoldville," and he went on:

> Not only was there no tendency to urge us on, but any suggestion for new initiatives was met with sharp refusal. The word "not" was much in evidence in the telegrams reaching us and the bleak phrase "not without prior authority" occurred in one of them. Statements we made to the press and on the radio, in explanation and pursuance of the policy directives

which had been enjoined on us, were met with harsh reprimands.

Knowing that everything we had done was under precise and explicit instructions from ONUC headquarters in Leopoldville, and knowing Mr. Hammarskjold's staunchness in defense of subordinates who came under fire while carrying out their instructions, I could not understand the cold current of the telegrams. . . .

The pitiful little war, meanwhile, ground on.

Through the long Thursday the battle raged in three main areas of Katanga. At Kamina there was a surprise turnabout by a Baluba chieftain with a group of mercenaries at his elbow. In Jadotville U.N. men talked darkly about an ugly Belgian-British-French betrayal. And plain bitterness blanketed the Elizabethville scene.

One of the most poignant aspects of the savage duel was that neither side seemed to know quite how to end it. U.N. attempts to trace the missing Tshombe failed. A meeting between O'Brien and the Katangan leader was announced by Tombelaine over Radio Katanga, but it never came off. Tshombe's Finance Minister Kibwe broadcast a truce order that went unheeded.

In the military base at Kamina, the U.N. holding force suddenly was attacked by 1,000 Baluba tribesmen, whose Chief Kasongo Niembo had switched allegiance to Tshombe. His force was under the command of a mercenary group and supported by well-handled armored cars. Parts of the big base 250 miles northwest of the capital had to be evacuated by the U.N. troops, who temporarily lost radio contact with their headquarters.

An Irish company at Jadotville, 75 miles northwest of Elizabethville, also was surrounded by a vastly superior force of white-led Katangan gendarmerie. The Irish were bombed by the Lone Ranger. Relief columns racing to their rescue were stopped at a blown bridge by Katangans using automatic weapons and mortars. The town, neighboring the famed Shinkolobwe uranium mine, accommodated the biggest white community in Katanga outside

Elizabethville. It also was the main base of the Katangan gendarmerie, and about two thousand men were stationed there.

The Irish had been sent there on August 29 at the insistent request of the Belgian, British and French consuls. They argued that, after the mass round-up of foreigners the previous day, the white settlers were in danger of massacre, with the discipline of the mercenaries removed. It was the U.N.'s duty to provide quick protection.

But, as O'Brien related in the above-mentioned article in *The Observer*, "The European population at Jadotville, who were in no danger whatever, had greeted the arrival of their protectors with hoots, jeers and missiles and had done their best to whip up the hostility of the African population against the Irish."

And in a letter to the same newspaper a fortnight later he claimed:

> The idea [of the consuls] was to insure that the placing of the company at Jadotville should be permanent and to obtain if possible the placing of similar detached garrisons elsewhere, for example at Kolwezi and near the hydroelectric station at Le Marinel. As it happened, all these garrisons would have been fairly easily mopped up in the event of hostility. . . .
>
> The local military command strongly objected to the placing of the company at Jadotville and, after it had been placed there, asked for its withdrawal. The military were overruled for political reasons, among the strongest of which was the insistent demand for the dispersal of U.N. troops, ostensibly for the sole purpose of protecting European lives and property.

O'Brien's suspicion unmistakably was that the Belgian-British-French aim was to secure, for their own reasons, the dispersal—and therefore the weakening—of the U.N. forces. In the event, the Irish were cut off, and prospects for relieving them were bleak. Their fate became a major preoccupation of the U.N. leadership from Hammarskjold down.

Meanwhile, in Elizabethville, violent Katangan counterattacks against U.N. positions were repelled. The camp housing Baluba and other refugees was fired on with mortars and machine guns. Early U.N. hopes of a swift coup vanished for good. The capital itself was split between the U.N. forces, controlling the eastern part, and the Katangans, who held the west.

A sense of futility and a cold hatred between the contenders loaded the general atmosphere.

At one point a Swedish company was assigned to capture the Katangan radio transmitter, if possible without inflicting casualties. The troops met with fierce resistance, and so merely returned to base. Undoubtedly the major factor in the situation was the leadership provided to the Katangans by the white mercenaries and resident Belgian "ultras." Calm and quiet pervaded the African quarters, but in the white areas shooting subsided only when U.N. patrols appeared. Official U.N. reports claimed whites had been observed either firing or directing Katangan operations at all the main centers of fighting. The downtown building housing the Belgian Consulate, where expelled Belgian officers were accommodated, also harbored a Bren gun post, according to U.N. statements.

David Halberstam of the *New York Times* later graphically related an incident that took place in Elizabethville shortly before the second Battle of Katanga flared up in December. It was a measure of the passion that stalked the scene after those nightmarish September days. Halberstam recounts: "Three Swedes were shot going through a Katangese roadblock. One Swede lay dying and the other two were badly injured. Just then two Belgian women passed by. One of the wounded Swedes shouted to the women for help to get them to a hospital. Instead one of the women spat at them and said: 'You got what you deserved, you swine.' "

Although the U.N. operations had been widely forecast, their actual execution staggered the whites of Katanga, who previously had been accustomed to refer contemptuously to the U.N. troops as cowards who would quit the minute shooting started. Now their hatred deepened with each blaze of gunfire.

The pro-Katangans had their own ready catalogues of atrocities and villains and heroes. Visiting newsmen were bombarded with horror stories about the U.N., and notably the Indian, troops.

They were accused, among other things, of shooting at Red Cross ambulances picking up wounded. Reporters who expressed doubt, or disbelief, courted danger, and more than one was threatened with violence. Topping the list of U.N. "villains" were men like Hammarskjold himself, O'Brien and Rajah, all of whom to the Katangan whites were "Communists." Radio Katanga filled the air with exhortations to its listeners to do their duty by killing at least "one Swede, one Irishman and one Indian" each.

Sir Roy Welensky was the great white hope of the Katangan settler community. Many of them were convinced Rhodesian Federal troops would arrive in a sort of miraculous rescue operation. Perhaps the wishful thought had been inspired by Kimba's announcement on September 12 that talks were under way with the Rhodesians for the despatch of men and materials to Elizabethville. Welensky, on Thursday, took time out in the Salisbury Parliament to deny the idea as a "canard." He offered Tshombe safe refuge in Rhodesia if he should have to flee. And he asserted that the atrocities committed in Katanga—meaning U.N. atrocities—were worse than "those in Budapest" in 1956, when the Russians crushed the Hungarian uprising.

Hammarskjold's official day began at 9 a.m. with a call on Kasavubu in the Presidential palace overlooking the Congo. For an hour they ranged over the entire political canvas, speaking in French. Hammarskjold's relations with Kasavubu were correct but cool. His regard for that one-time arch-foe of the Belgians had drooped somewhat when the President connived in handing over Lumumba to the Katangans and to what he must have known would be a violent death.

A meeting of all U.N. departmental heads awaited Hammarskjold next, at 10:15 in Le Royal's conference room. Linner, McKeown, Khiari, Wieschoff and Ranallo were among those who attended.

Katanga, of course, was on everyone's mind. There was a mood of growing gloom. It was only too clear that the U.N. force was not equipped for an extended military action, was not prepared for resistance so fierce, was not above a military buffeting. Equally cheerless were the political perils that loomed ahead in the event of victory, defeat or stalemate.

Hammarskjold was in the chair. By all accounts there was no inquest of any sort into the Katangan affair. Nor was there any report by Khiari or Fabry of the instructions O'Brien said he had received from them on September 10. The political and military situation in Tshombe's province was examined in its broadest sense.

One decision of importance was approved by Hammarskjold at the urgent request of O'Brien and Rajah, down in Elizabethville, and on the advice of McKeown, at his side: to scour supporting countries in the region for swift air reinforcements. The Lone Ranger—and a second Air Katanga Fouga jet fighter thought to be operating—seemed likely to sway the whole course of the campaign. They had to be neutralized—and quickly.

The military men figured the mere appearance of U.N. air striking power—even if it went unused—was essential to the righting of the tactical balance. Accordingly, urgent requests for jet fighters were sent, with Hammarskjold's authority, to several countries, including Ethiopia. Replies were expected with twenty-four hours. Hammarskjold, frankly, did not like the idea of sending offensive weapons into Katanga, but he recognized the psychological need to counter the presence of the Fougas.

Talk turned to some of the main issues that had brought Hammarskjold to the Congo. Brief reports were submitted on the general U.N. policies to be followed in long-term economic and technical planning. These related to future aid priorities, the training of Congolese specialists, and the supply of field experts from abroad to help the rebuilding program. Hammarskjold's over-riding interest, of course, related to policy matters. But his fiscal and economic training in Sweden had given him a quick grasp of the complex problems of planning. Some of his detailed questions found his advisers thinking and talking fast.

The Secretary-General's detailed talks with Adoula and his ministers began after lunch at the Premier's residence, where once the Governors-General of a bygone Belgian world had lived. Here in the stately riverside home, standing in its own gardens, the ill-fated Lumumba had sometimes slept. Hammarskjold, Adoula and their advisers spent the afternoon in one of the ground-level reception rooms, austerely furnished and with chairs as hard as they were uncomfortable. Iced drinks and coffee were served toward the end of the long afternoon of dry business.

The meeting broke up in the early evening to allow the participants the time they needed to dress for a government dinner in Hammarskjold's honor. The dinner was held in one of Leopoldville's best restaurants, in the grounds of the city zoo. Amid the night noises of sleeping and sleepless birds and beasts of Africa, they ate—and talked about the storm in Katanga.

The man at the center of the Katanga storm, who came to symbolize to local whites all that was hateful about the United Nations, was the forty-four-year-old Dubliner, Conor Cruise O'Brien.

Hammarskjold had personally selected this erudite writer-diplomat for the trouble-shooting job in Katanga, which he took up in mid-1961. O'Brien was engaged on a two-year contract. He was to spend six months in Katanga and then take over as Director and Deputy to the Under-Secretary in the Department of Political and Security Council Affairs, a job held most recently by Heinz Wieschhoff (who died with Hammarskjold aboard the *Albertina*). Wieschhoff, a German-born anthropologist who left Nazi Germany for the United States in the 1930s, was a member of Hammarskjold's inner circle, and the fact that O'Brien was chosen to take over his key post indicated the esteem with which the Irishman was regarded.

O'Brien has related why Hammarskjold picked him rather than anyone else for the thankless Katanga assignment: "He happened to have read a book of mine. This book, 'Maria Cross,' had appeared some years earlier not under my own name. It had nothing whatever to do with the U.N., Africa, politics or diplomacy. It was a collection of critical essays on a group of French and English Catholic writers. Mr. Hammarskjold was one of the very few people who had read it, and he liked it."

Maria Cross was the sort of book that would have appealed to a man of Hammarskjold's intelligence. It was as much a creative work of social and political inquiry as it was of literary criticism. With insight O'Brien examined the writings of men like Graham Greene, Evelyn Waugh, Paul Claudel, François Mauriac and Georges Bernanos for a pattern of unity. In the book O'Brien talked of the pitiless nature of tomorrow's world, and predicted: "We shall have an intelligible and practical code; desire that which is desirable, hate your enemies, repair or destroy the sick, admire your leader, obey the sanitary laws. . . . Man is perfectible provided he sets his own standards of perfection."

The book was O'Brien's best published work, and it established him as a creative author in his own right. For years his essays, articles and critiques had been appearing under the pen name Donat O'Donnell in Irish, American and British journals, including the leftwing *New Statesman* and the middle-of-the-road *Spectator*.

"I like to have a foot in each grave," he explained.

The lure of the wider world of international diplomacy had taken him into the Irish Foreign Ministry in 1944. For several years he had served abroad, but without finding much scope for his eloquence or his classical talents. Then in 1955 Ireland had joined the United Nations, and he had been called upon to help build an active, new role in world affairs for his neutralist country. A dry humor, an independent judgment on some of the big issues, and a gift for clear, analytic thinking soon marked him as a man worth hearing when he rose to speak in the debating chambers of the East River glass house. A career of promise stretched ahead.

The Irishman's deft touch was noticed particularly in the active and friendly relations he developed with the Afro-Asians during General Assembly sessions. Also, his knowledge of Russian once enabled him to catch a translation error in an important Soviet resolution—and when the Soviet sponsors were quietly told of it, they were grateful. Once or twice in General Assembly speeches he reminded British listeners of the partition of Ireland with pun and pointed shaft. He favored disengagement for Europe, greater liberalism for his homeland, an evolutionary advance to statehood for the dependent Afro-Asians.

Certainly there was nothing very radical in all this. Straightforward conformism was manifest too in his upper-middle-class upbringing as the only son of a Roman Catholic family, including a Quaker school, modern literature and history at Trinity College, and the Civil Service, with writing as the outlet for his restless, energetic ambition.

Yet, by the very nature of his assignment as Hammarskjold's man in Katanga, he found himself drawn into an incessant duel of words with Tshombe and his friends for the duration of the crisis. And the controversy over his own role was to extend far beyond his half-year of office.

It was not long after his arrival that the Katangans recognized O'Brien as a man who meant to carry out his assigned task. Dag Hammarskjold had entrusted him with a crucial mission: to implement the terms of the Security Council resolution ordering the expulsion of all unauthorized foreigners—political and military advisers and mercenaries—from Katanga. For months U.N. men had sought by conciliation and negotiation to do the job. For months they had failed.

The hatchets were out for O'Brien in real earnest after the August action, in which more than two hundred mercenaries were arrested. Some of the Elizabethville consuls arranged the subsequent suspension of the action in the name of "conciliation and negotiation." In reality the fateful pause was used by the Katangans and their friends to achieve four seemingly separate, but actually inter-related, objectives:

1. The regroupment of the mercenaries to fight another day.
2. The redeployment of U.N. troops, as displayed by the despatch of the Irish to Jadotville on the appeal of the consuls.
3. The replacement of O'Brien, on grounds that Katangans no longer trusted him and he no longer could deal with Tshombe. (The governments that pressed these demands on Hammarskjold

in New York may have felt that by "personalizing" the Katanga difficulties around the head of O'Brien they might somehow induce a change of U.N. policy.)

4. The revival of a vicious anti-United Nations hate and terror campaign, which almost compelled some form of retaliation or reassertion of authority.

But, at the time, Hammarskjold dismissed the Belgian-French-British criticisms of the Irishman. He was pleased even with the partial success of the August operation. He joined with all the members of the "Congo Club"—the group of nations that helped to formulate U.N. policy—in hailing the work of the Elizabethville team.

"Il a du cran!" he commented on O'Brien's performance. "He has pluck!"

Not surprisingly, quite opposite reactions came from the slogan-masters of Katanga.

"O'Brien au poteau!" they demanded on public walls. "O'Brien to the gallows!" They called him the "Gauleiter of Elizabethville" and "ce maudit Hitler." Some even discovered in him a real or imagined facial likeness to Der Fuehrer. A Belgian newspaper solemnly concluded he would take a deserved place in "the gallery of felons in the museums of the future."

His life was in constant danger from the mercenaries, the plastic-bomb plotters and others. Yet these were physical hazards, and robust men of red blood entering the Congo game were ready for them, perhaps even relished with some zest the element of peril that threaded their days.

But the Congo game did not, by any means, end at the Congo's frontiers. It was being played out in faraway foreign ministries and parliaments, in board rooms and in newspaper offices.

In distant capitals the Katanga lobbyists used the sledgehammer of scorn in their propaganda against O'Brien, as if the U.N. policy they hated began and ended with him. When his name came up the more subtle diplomats would shrug wearily, raise their eyebrows or refer crushingly to his cleverness as if it was something un-nice. Darkly, politicians accused him of waging a punitive war against the innocent Katangans. For the Britain-firsters of some London newspapers the Irishman was easy meat. To them he seemed to be one of those diplomats who did not quite conform. Several of his forebears had been prominent in Ireland's unforgotten struggle against England. His Catholicism was diluted by a marriage to a Presbyterian wife. When that marriage broke up after twenty-two years it only appeared to emphasize his liberation from timeworn social taboos. He almost invited the headlines, in the circumstances of the time, when his bride-to-be, Maire, the daughter of Irish Vice-Premier Sean MacEntee, visited Katanga. He augmented his French and Spanish with conversational Russian. For a diplomat he was an enthusiastic partygoer and a tireless talker in the salons of the cities he served in.

All this made it easy, if not exactly truthful, for critics to portray him as an England-hating, Irish nationalist, unstable, radical, perhaps even something of a Red sympathizer. O'Brien was none of these things. His courage, intelligence and honesty were undisputed. When he set out to indict those powers that he asserted were impeding U.N. policies he knew he was kissing diplomacy good-by. His main arguments were never directly answered by the British, French or Belgian governments the Congo policies of which he denounced. Instead he was counteraccused of being melodramatic, temperamental, "Irish," romantically involved.

The tall, intense Irishman did not emerge altogether blameless himself from the hell's kitchen of Katanga. As civilian chief he could not be faulted for the evident misjudgment of the military situation, or the failure to prepare adequately for setbacks, at a time when the luxury of mistakes could not be afforded. But the orders he received—legitimate or illegitimate—amounted virtually to the arrest of a "government." Rajah, surely, could not have objected if O'Brien had wished to satisfy himself that U.N. forces were fully capable of carrying out that mission. Perhaps, being new to Africa, especially that part of Africa at that time, O'Brien took Khiari's orders too literally. Perhaps he was awaiting too eagerly Khiari's particular set of instructions because they contemplated, as O'Brien has said he himself contemplated, an end to Katangan separatism.

All these things are speculations. One undeniable truth is that O'Brien was taken to town, given the treatment, scorned and harassed and pilloried by some powerful newspapers in Britain, Belgium and France, the moment he showed himself determined to fight the baneful influence of the mercenaries and other foreigners in Katanga. The forces he faced were big and rich, and they certainly included governments. If, then, he expected any mercy after the failure of a U.N. operation, he was being naïve. He should have known, therefore, that there could be no valid justification for underestimating the resources and ruthlessness of the enemies of the United Nations.

In Katanga, 1961, risks that did not succeed could not be condoned. And those who associated themselves with a gamble —knowingly or otherwise—had to expect to be held accountable along with the men who gave them their orders.

Back in Leopoldville, Hammarskjold returned to Le Royal from the Government dinner party about eleven o'clock. With the faithful Linner and his wilting senior staff officers, he sifted the latest reports from O'Brien and Rajah in Katanga—and those from his New York headquarters, summarizing world reactions.

O'Brien still was pressing for permission and for reinforcements that would enable him to undertake operations that might restore the situation of the hard-pressed U.N. forces. But Hammarskjold and his advisers composed discouraging messages, which only reaffirmed the need, as they saw it, for continued caution, restraint and defensiveness.

Perhaps the thing that upset Hammarskjold most that night was the substance of some public statements being issued in Elizabethville by O'Brien and his staff about the nature of U.N. objectives. Tombelaine, for example, had announced on Radio Katanga that the United Nations meant resolutely to continue the operations it had launched in order "to end the secession of Katanga."

Hammarskjold was infuriated by this. He had never conceded

that the function or purpose of the United Nations was to end Tshombe's separatism. He sent off a scorching message to Elizabethville, reprimanding all concerned for suggesting that U.N. troops were seeking to impose a political settlement. That message, addressed to O'Brien, was probably the most blistering of all his many hot communications in the period.

O'Brien and his staff, inevitably, were astonished. In the context of their instructions from Khiari they figured their public declarations not only conformed with what they took to be U.N. policy but also had received prior clearance from the Secretary-General. They could not know then that the Secretary-General was totally unaware of the details, and indeed probably of the general outline too, of the orders they had been given. Misunderstanding, therefore, appeared to be complete.

Word came in from London, meantime, that the British Government had made a slight tactical shift in its public position of extreme hostility toward the use of U.N. force. No change in Britain's basic position was indicated, but the Foreign Office now was saying that Britain was concerned more with controlling the Katangan incident than with conducting a post-mortem into its origins. This to Hammarskjold was not an unwelcome contrast with the fire-eating British mood of the previous day. It was reported also that Lansdowne had flown by air from London and would be in Leopoldville next morning.

Once again around 3 a.m. the Secretary-General left his desk for home. Once again he went back to the consoling, simple, honest, other-worldly wisdom of à Kempis. . . .

8 | The Friday

That black Friday Dag Hammarskjold approached the Rubicon he never thought he would have to cross.

The world saw him only as the machinelike administrator with the apparatus of a great international organization at his command.

Yet, through a day that seemed as if it would never end, Hammarskjold was the loneliest man on earth, facing a choice that he knew he and only he could make. And there seemed to be nobody he could talk to about his own personal conflict.

The choice before him was between all-out offensive action in Katanga by the United Nations—and a dubious cease-fire that would leave proud Tshombe's power propped up still by foreigners.

Intellectually, Hammarskjold calculated ruthless use of force would rock and maybe wreck the United Nations. It would require the swift, substantial reinforcement of the 5,000 Indian, Swedish, Irish and Gurkha troops with air power and heavy ground weapons. Just that sort of course was being urged by some of his advisers. Hammarskjold himself shrank from the notion. He abhorred violence in others and rejected its use by nation-states as an instrument of policy. How, then, could he rationalize the exercise of force by the United Nations, with its first article of faith being to underpin peace? A little war to prevent a bigger war? Where would the process end? In any case, the world was not yet ready for a concept of catharsis so sophisticated. Britain already had clearly shown that. The little war very likely would prevent a bigger war, but history might record the international organization itself as the chief casualty.

Emotionally, Hammarskjold felt anger and resentment at the immorality of having to compromise with men he thought to be guilty. It was, of course, Tshombe's own business if he wanted to tear the Katangan rump from the Congolese body. But it became the world's business when that process, inspired from the outside, threatened to suck in big powers already poised for a new scramble in the very heart of Africa. The guilt of the Katangan leadership seemed to him to lie not only in its defiance of the words of the Security Council but also in its wanton shedding of the blood of those troops whose orders—cast-iron ones—were to fire only in self-defense.

Yet if all-out war was excluded, nothing else remained but to renew efforts for a cease-fire. At least this would allow the United Nations the chance to fulfill its mission of removing the trouble-makers later on.

One thing was clear in this context: it would have to be he —Hammarskjold, the man—who met Tshombe. Only the Secretary-General could take on the responsibility of signing a truce that part of the world would consider to be an appeasement, almost a surrender.

This, then, was his mood when he attended the morning meeting of the U.N. staff and right away made clear his intention of postponing the flight back to New York scheduled for early next day.

Overnight developments were as cheerless as his thoughts.

In Katanga blood still flowed. The position of the Irish at Jadotville was worsening. The Ethiopian and Swedish governments promised to provide the needed jet fighters, but it would take time to hustle them to the scene.

As if to cap everything, a taunting messsage had come into U.N. headquarters from Brazzaville, the capital of the (French) Congo Republic, just across the river.

Abbé Fulbert Youlou, President of the Congo Republic, sent to Hammarskjold through his Deputy Chief of State Jacques Opongo a message that amounted to just about this: "I do not think it would be wise for you, Mr. Secretary-General, to try to pick up your plane for New York at Brazzaville Airport, as you have been planning to do. My Government feels it would be unable to guarantee your personal safety in view of the effervescences provoked by the events in Katanga."

Youlou's public advice was designed to underline his sympathy with Tshombe. Hammarskjold was not at all bothered, because he recognized it for the political gesture it was. It was well enough known that if he did pick up a plane in Brazzaville he would not need protection. A U.N. helicopter would take him directly from Le Royal to the well-guarded airport.

The real meaning of Youlou's message did not, however, go unnoticed at U.N. headquarters. That priest-turned-politician plainly was turning the heat on Hammarskjold. As subtly as a head of state could, without overstepping the bounds of protocol, Youlou brought into the open for the first time the idea that Hammarskjold might be assassinated. In itself, coming from a man whose government actively and loudly supported Tshombe, the warning would have had little significance. But U.N. diplomats knew that what President de Gaulle of France said, Youlou invariably shouted. The incident was a reminder to Hammarskjold and his staff of the forces and the feelings ranging up against the United Nations and its policies.

If they needed another reminder one was offered the same morning by Lord Lansdowne. The British diplomat, on arrival in Leopoldville, pointedly told newsmen: "We have had certain explanations from Mr. Hammarskjold of the recent events, many of which have come as a great shock and surprise to us in the United Kingdom."

As the day wore on, surprisingly the issues clarified for Hammarskjold.

The pattern of his actions and decisions began to show that his plan was to launch a personal cease-fire initiative. He canceled a news conference due that afternoon. Since his arrival foreign correspondents had been pressing to talk with him, but he had turned them down. Understandably, they would have wanted to grill him on all the lurid inside details of the Katanga affair. But, for Hammarskjold, this was not the time for a catechism or an inquest. A word from him out of place might only deepen the crisis and imperil the prospects for quiet diplomacy.

He took another decision. The Ethiopians had offered to lend three jet fighters for use in Katanga. They had a treaty with the British providing for mutual over-flying facilities in Africa. But advance notice and permission were needed in special cases. To get to Katanga the Ethiopians would have to cross British East African territories. As all Congo-bound war material had to be funneled through O.N.U.C., it was necessary for the United Nations to endorse the Ethiopian request for over-flying facilities. Hammarskjold ordered that a formal U.N. request urging the cooperation of the British be addressed and sent to them through the Secretariat in New York.

Over lunch that day McKeown gave Hammarskjold a rundown on the Katangan military outlook. They agreed to throw in whatever reinforcements could be spared from outside, firstly to help out the hard-pressed garrisons, secondly to improve the U.N. position in advance of any truce talks, and thirdly to demonstrate to Tshombe something of the power he faced. A Tshombe confident of survival obviously would be more difficult to cope with in a negotiation than a Tshombe on the defensive. Hammarskjold also asked the Military Commander to hurry down to Katanga to see for himself if there were other ways in which the U.N. situation could be improved. The relief of the Irish had, of course, a priority rating.

If anything, the U.N. plight in Katanga worsened on Friday.

About the only gleam of light came when Kibwe arranged for Tshombe and O'Brien to meet that night at Dunnett's Consulate. But the rendezvous—called for 7 p.m.—was never kept by the Katangans. Dunnett later reported Kibwe told him Tshombe had been "prevented from attending by his military advisers."

The main military developments of the day were:

The Fouga, using bombs, machine guns and rockets, made altogether five raids on Elizabethville, Jadotville and Kamina. One of the attacks was an obvious attempt to blow up O'Brien in his home, and another was aimed at the Lido Hotel, where U.N. troops were quartered.

The Fouga fired rockets as it streaked low across Elizabethville Airport, where U.N. transportation planes were lined up on the apron. As the jet climbed away the pilot radioed the control tower in English: "I'll be back, boys."

In Elizabethville itself U.N. troops held firm in all their positions, but one mobile detachment was surprised and badly mauled by the Katangans, who claimed to have captured twenty-three men. Several hours later Munongo sent a messenger to O'Brien with a warning that he personally was holding two Irish officers captured in the action. They would be shot, he was quoted by the U.N. Command as saying, unless two Belgian officers taken at Jadotville were freed at once. Munongo's threat was taken seriously. His father had been chief of the Bayake, once a cannibal tribe, to whom lives were cheap.

In Jadotville the Irish, according to the U.N. Command, rejected two surrender ultimatums and battled valiantly on despite heavy losses. Tshombe, however, claimed during Friday night that the company had been routed. Radio Katanga triumphantly announced fifty-seven Irish dead and ninety hostages. The radio warned that prisoners would be shot in groups of ten for every Katangan killed in captivity.

In Kamina U.N. troops restored radio contact with headquarters. They evacuated twenty-one Belgian officers and mercenaries by air to Leopoldville. Afterward attacks on their position subsided.

Newspapers around the world reported Hammarskjold was looking "tired and worried" that day. It would have been surprising if he were not. The responsibility for the crisis in Katanga would in itself have weighed heavily on most men. But Hammarskjold had a lot more to wear him down. His schedule for the day, after three hours or so of fitful sleep, packed in an early morning and late night staff conference; separate meetings with two or three ambassadors, including Edmund A. Gullion of the United States; a long afternoon working session with the Congolese ministers on economic and political affairs; a crowded U.N. reception in the evening; and a state banquet in his honor. All the time he was talking, listening, concentrating, analyzing and pondering the situation, in its global sense as well as in its local meaning.

The evening reception was held at La Deveniere, a swank restaurant built by the Belgians on one of the hills overlooking the city. Most of the big names of Leopoldville were there. The guests spilled out of the restaurant itself onto the terraces and into the garden. A Nigerian band attached to the U.N. forces played light music in the fairyland setting.

There were touches of a political wonderland too about the scene. Early on, Kasavubu strode in through the cocktail haze. Behind him marched Adoula and Gizenga, arm in arm. For those who had followed the painful Congo saga from the start, this was a spectacle that they would not have thought possible even a few months before. Suddenly outsiders became conscious of the quiet hope among the national leaders that the unity of the land still would be restored. The Battle of Katanga could yet chronicle its own unplanned joys for the agonized Congolese.

The guest of honor, Hammarskjold, did not look as if anything joyful had crossed his mind for some time past. He withdrew from the chattering groups for low-voiced talk with a few serious-faced Swedes. In his hand was a glass—perhaps the last Manhattan he was ever to sip.

Soon a newspaperman approached him. It was Andrew Wilson, the correspondent of a British national Sunday newspaper, *The Observer*. They were together briefly and the Secretary-General talked earnestly.

Nine days later, on September 24, *The Observer* published a report by Wilson under the title "Dag's Last Interview" that said in part:

> Shortly before his last flight from Leopoldville Mr. Hammarskjold spoke to me at length about the United Nations' aims in the Congo as he saw them. It was an off-the-record talk—a "seminar exercise" he called it. But his death has changed the circumstances, and the present perilous situation

seems to justify revealing as much of the conversation as may help to a better understanding of the U.N. position by the west.

Mr. Hammarskjold's policy was based on three convictions:

1. That the continued presence of foreign elements in Katanga was a threat to the peace not only of the Congo but of the world.

2. That the U.N. must never become the "hammer" of the Central Government in a war to bring Katanga to heel.

3. That its aims should be achieved without bloodshed. . . .

He divided the whole Congo operation into two phases—the phase before the formation of a legally recognized Government last August [1961], and the phase that followed.

During the first phase the U.N. was obliged to rely on negotiations and persuasion in its efforts to reunite the opposing factions of Leopoldville, Stanleyville and Katanga. As between Leopoldville and Stanleyville, it succeeded.

With the formation of the Adoula Government, the U.N.'s duty to evict the Katanga mercenaries . . . became "inescapable."

What were the means by which the Secretary-General intended to achieve this? My conclusion from our conversation was that they amounted to a swift and painless presentation of force, strictly to the end laid down by the Security Council and no further. Everything possible was to be done to avoid combat—even with the mercenaries themselves, who, in his one phrase of anger Mr. Hammarskjold described as the "residue of adventurers left over from Algeria."

His shock when he reached Leopoldville and heard of the Katanga fighting was great. Not once did he offer anything which could be construed as criticism of any member of his staff and he implicitly accepted that the battle was caused by the firing of mercenaries on U.N. forces. But he must have been profoundly exercised by the poor preparations for the U.N. action, as they subsequently revealed themselves from the military side. . . .

After Hammarskjold broke away from Wilson, Lord Lansdowne was brought along to be introduced to him. There was little chance for serious talk in the milling throng. Curious guests crowded and craned to see the distinguished visitor at close range. There were flapping ears as well as prying eyes.

The Swede and the Britisher—the one as fair as the other was dark—talked quickly and quietly about a meeting Lansdowne had requested for next day. It was arranged Lansdowne should call on Hammarskjold only after he had completed a round of official visits to leaders of the Congolese Government.

Soon they parted, each to drive back to change for the Presidential banquet they were attending that night.

Kasavubu and his big, buxom wife were waiting to greet the guests arriving for the very formal occasion in his riverside residence. High-ups in the Government and the U.N. mission came along. Lansdowne was the only foreign guest outside the officials of the United Nations.

Hammarskjold was seated on Kasavubu's right during the slow-moving dinner. Lansdowne found himself opposite the Secretary-General. Occasionally, as the table talk ebbed and flowed over the difficulties of the Congo and the Katanga situation, the two men addressed each other directly, openly, in a fashion that in no way excluded the other guests. It was during these exchanges that Hammarskjold made the observation Lansdowne was later to cite publicly, in support of the British Government's criticism of U.N. actions in Katanga.

"You know," Hammarskjold said, "this work of an international agency is only in its infancy. There is still so much that we all have to learn."

At another point during dinner that night Lansdowne asked Hammarskjold if it was absolutely essential for him to attend the opening of the coming week's General Assembly session in New York.

It was not essential, Hammarskjold replied. Then he added: "We are not yet through here."

During the evening a member of Hammarskjold's staff from Le Royal brought in a closed envelope a message that was later communicated to him.

The message from U.N. headquarters said in effect: "Radio Katanga announced tonight that the Irish Company at Jadotville has surrendered—fifty-seven claimed dead and ninety held as hostages." This claim was premature for Jadotville only fell on Saturday.

After the banquet things at Le Royal began to hum a bit.

There was a signal from Dublin that Irish Foreign Minister Frank Aiken would be flying next day to Elizabethville to assess for himself the precise position of the Irish contingent. At the same time Irish Premier Sean Lemass seemed to voice concern over the U.N. action, in a statement saying the Irish troops had gone to the Congo to preserve peace, not to impose any particular solution. There was mounting anxiety in Ireland over the fate of the trapped company.

A message from the Secretariat in New York also reported fears among member-delegations over what looked to some like a major setback for the United Nations. Feeling was building up toward crisis dimensions over future handling of the situation. Russia and her Communist friends were thought likely to demand even greater powers to enable the United Nations to crush Tshombe. The Western nations appeared split on the issue whether U.N. operations were permissible in the first place. The Afro-Asians tended to favor the tough line attributed to Moscow.

The news from O'Brien was equally discouraging: Tshombe had failed to turn up for the cease-fire rendezvous at the British Consulate.

To Hammarskjold, Tshombe's absence meant only one thing. The African could not easily shake himself free from the grip of those who surrounded him. It was becoming ever more important, therefore, that Tshombe be drawn out of Elizabethville, preferably out of Katanga, if effective truce talks were to be held.

Hammarskjold knew Tshombe would not come to Leopoldville; only that Tuesday he had refused to do so. Tshombe was terribly afraid of being taken prisoner again, perhaps even to suffer the fate he had helped to create for Lumumba. Only very good luck—or the frailty of man—had given Tshombe back his freedom from captivity in Coquilhatville during the spring.

Hammarskjold knew the story. When the Katangan was beginning to despair of ever being released, something of a transaction had been arranged, partly through people and offices in Brazzaville. A considerable sum of money (reputedly more than $250,000) had been moved by the Katangan authorities to a bank in Geneva. The bank in Geneva had transferred the funds to a Congolese politician in Leopoldville. Two days later Tshombe's detention had come to an end.

From his soundings with Government leaders Hammarskjold was equally sure Adoula would not and could not agree to meet Tshombe outside Leopoldville. Gizenga and his Lumumbists would not stand for the idea, even if Adoula were tempted to play with it, and there were no signs of that.

The bare essentials of the situation, as Hammarskjold and some of his advisers saw things, amounted that night to something like this:

On the U.N. side: It had to be recognized there could be no military victory or defeat. Security nevertheless had to be restored. The only politically conceivable way to do so was by way of a cease-fire. The Secretary-General himself would have to undertake the truce initiative. Tshombe would find it hard to toy with him or to defy his personal authority. The negotiations would be held neither in Leopoldville nor in Elizabethville. The most obvious "neutral" meeting place was Addis Ababa, Ethiopia, where the United Nations had a permanent mission and all the facilities that went with it. But Addis Ababa was a long way off, and some nearer site might be preferable because of pressing time factors. If the talks proceeded reasonably well they would open the way to a wider settlement.

On the Katangan side: Tshombe's interest in, and need for, a truce had been demonstrated by Kibwe only that day. Katanga could not indefinitely maintain its fight against the world organization. A parley inside Elizabethville, even within the sanctum of the British Consulate, had already been proved difficult to arrange amid the boom and bitterness of battle. Yet talks in Leopoldville seemed out of the question. A meeting outside Congo territory would suit Tshombe best.

It seemed to Hammarskjold and some of his advisers that there was an area of common ground between the two positions. The legal experts got down to work on the draft of a message to Tshombe. Hammarskjold directed that the message be firm and polite in tone, yet touched with a promise of conciliation. It was not to be sent out of the blue but to be held until an opening occurred. The essence would be to explain where and why the United Nations considered itself right in the current feud, and Tshombe wrong.

Deep into the night they worked once again, and only when the draft was completed, many times amended and many times checked did they go home to rest.

9 | The Saturday

The trail of mysteries that led Dag Hammarskjold and his companions to their death near Ndola seemed to begin on Saturday.

Only historians in the distant future, with all the diplomatic secrets at their disposal, will be able to determine the precise starting point of the tragic journey. At the time, those who chose to judge arrived inevitably at predisposed conclusions colored by their political fancies and personal problems. Communist powers, for instance, found it hard to abandon suspicion of Britain's complicity in what they saw as Hammarskjold's murder. Afro-Asians also felt unable completely to acquit the British and their friends of blame for his death. The pro-Katangans, plausibly, traced everything back to the U.N. men themselves, who, they said, had started the Battle of Katanga. All the protagonists, in argument, tended to ignore their own share of responsibility.

One key to the mystery that will linger for years lay in a highly significant meeting during the morning between Hammarskjold and Lansdowne. Few people know exactly what transpired. For a while the two men were quite alone. One of them was soon to die. The records of all their exchanges are closely guarded secrets. Yet even so, in the political post-mortem that followed, a conflict of evidence was revealed over several crucial issues, including the question of who suggested Ndola as a site for the projected truce talks.

A day packed with drama also brought:

An arrogant proposal from Tshombe for an armistice on the condition that U.N. troops quit Katanga. The alternative would be "total war," he warned.

A suggestion from the Katangan for truce talks in Rhodesia, which O'Brien felt was unacceptable.

A demonstration of Sir Roy Welensky's solidarity with Tshombe.

Renewed attacks on U.N. positions throughout Katanga.

A British move to prevent air warfare between Katangan and U.N. forces. It had the effect of delaying permission for the Ethiopian jets to over-fly British East Africa.

Hammarskjold's personal intervention in the Katanga crisis. It took the form of an offer to meet Tshombe in Ndola for cease-fire talks outside the framework of U.N. operations in the Congo.

Early in the morning McKeown flew off to Elizabethville in the *Albertina* to look over the military situation. He arranged to send the airplane back in case it was needed by Hammarskjold.

In the Leopoldville Parliament, meanwhile, Congolese deputies passed a resolution calling on the army to help U.N. forces in Katanga. Gizenga offered to take personal command of an invasion force. Both Mobutu and General Victor Lundula, who led Gizenga's troops, came out in favor of the proposed expedition.

Far away to the southeast, two of Tshombe's trusted ministers slipped into Northern Rhodesia at a lonely border crossing. They were met by senior officials of the Federal Government. Evariste Kimba, the Foreign Minister, and Alphonse Kiela, Communications Minister, then were flown to Salisbury for an unannounced meeting with Welensky.

Hammarskjold himself began the day with a close discussion of the Katanga situation, in all its aspects, with his advisers at a staff meeting. There were expectations that some sort of peace initiative was near. The order went out that U.N. positions were to be consolidated where possible, but not in a way that might impede the work of the diplomats.

The first foreign caller received by the Secretary-General that day was Lord Lansdowne. More than fifty years before, his grandfather, Foreign Secretary from 1900 to 1905, had felt compelled to denounce old King Leopold's way of running and ruining the lives of the Congolese. Lansdowne was accompanied by Ambassador Riches. Linner was alongside Hammarskjold.

Britain's envoy, as is usual, opened the conversation. He made a general statement expressing the horror of his government and people at the news of the fighting in Katanga, and he repeated the warning Riches had delivered on Wednesday—that unless U.N. actions could be satisfactorily explained, or the fighting ended, Britain would have to consider quitting the entire U.N. operation in the Congo.

In his response Hammarskjold, of course, offered the same accounting of the U.N. actions of August 28 and September 13 that he had given Riches. Then he said he regarded the most important immediate task as being to arrange a cease-fire. The two men began ranging over the past, present and future developments of the struggle. At one point, by arrangement, the advisers withdrew and the principals were left on their own, freely, frankly and with no punches pulled to say what they thought.

A great deal of history was to flow from the fascinating encounter between Hammarskjold and Lansdowne at Le Royal on that 16th day of September, 1961, and statesmen of the future may well consider that it profoundly influenced the course of affairs not only in Africa but also in the United Nations and, consequently, in the wider world.

There are three versions of what went on between the two men.

Hammarskjold's account is locked away at his old New York headquarters. Nobody has admitted publicly or privately to having seen it. Under U.N. arrangements it cannot be disclosed for twenty-five years.

The Lansdowne version, in all its details, is safe and sound in the secret files of the Foreign Office. By British rules it need not be divulged in this century, and even after fifty years its contents can be withheld. The British minister gave only a glimpse of the proceedings in a carefully worded statement to the House of Lords on October 18, one month later.

There is, finally, the unofficial story. It was heard in the lobbies and lounges of the U.N. skyscraper in New York. High-ranking statesmen, ministers and officials discussed it in low voices in key world capitals for months afterward. There were whispers of it in Leopoldville, Paris, London, Washington and indeed any place where diplomats with an eye on Africa assembled. Essentially, though, it was a story that was second-hand. It may have been embellished, as tales told twice, thrice, many times, often are. Even those who said they believed it could not be absolutely sure of its truth.

This is the account Lansdowne presented to the House of Lords during a foreign affairs debate:

> From my talk with Mr. Adoula I went straight to see Mr. Hammarskjold on the morning of September 16. I went, as your Lordships can imagine, with two main purposes in mind: first, to try to get from Mr. Hammarskjold personally a more precise account of the events of August 28 and September 13; and, secondly, to explain to him how shocked Her Majesty's Government were at the trend of events since September 13.
>
> I was therefore very pleased when Mr. Hammarskjold said to me straight away that he thought that the most important thing was to achieve a cease-fire. He showed me a message which he had drafted for transmission to Mr. Tshombe proposing a meeting, and he told me that he had reached the conclusion that Ndola was the most suitable place to meet.
>
> I told him at once that I was sure Her Majesty's Government would entirely support his decision and that I would seek early approval for the use of Ndola both from Her Majesty's Government and from the Federal Government. Mr. Hammarskjold's plan did not envisage that Mr. Adoula should participate in that meeting. I asked the Secretary-General whether he thought there was still not a chance that Mr. Adoula might also be brought in from the start. Mr. Hammarskjold did not think that this would be possible, but undertook to discuss it with the Congolese Prime Minister before his message was despatched to Mr. Tshombe.
>
> Mr. Hammarskjold then explained to me the origins of the United Nations actions on September 13. He said that in the opinion of his officers on the spot it was necessary to act

urgently against the remaining foreign mercenaries in the Katanga. The operation of August 28 which had been endorsed by Mr. Tshombe had only been partially successful. Intimidation against the United Nations had been increasing and there had been instances of arson, stone throwing and incitement to violence. There was a danger that with the assistance of these foreigners an organized underground movement might be built up. Mr. Hammarskjold made it very clear to me that the object of the action of September 13 was to complete the work of August 28 and that no further instruction had therefore been required from him.

Now I must tell your Lordships that in both my long conversations with Mr. Hammarskjold (the second conversation took place next day) I spoke with absolute frankness and it is my conviction that he spoke with equal frankness to me. Although he did not disagree with my views that his officers had made a quite erroneous appreciation of the resistance that they would encounter, he fully accepted responsibility for the action that they had taken.

As the noble Earl the Foreign Secretary [Lord Home] told your Lordships yesterday, and it was certainly my impression also, mistakes were made; and I believe that Mr. Hammarskjold also shared this view.

I emphasized, however, that Her Majesty's Government were not so much concerned with the past as with the achievement of a peaceful reconciliation between Mr. Tshombe and the central Government.

I said that I had reluctantly formed the impression that there was an insufficient desire among certain of his officers to bring about the cease-fire. They seemed to me to be carrying out a punitive war, rather than a precautionary police operation.

I also felt obliged to draw the Secretary-General's attention to certain inconsistencies, as I saw them, between his account of the events in the Katanga and the reports which we had had from Elizabethville. There were press and radio statements attributed to United Nations officers in charge of operations in the Katanga which seemed to me to run directly counter to what he himself had stated to me was the position of the United Nations *vis-à-vis* the Central Government. Also they had said that the United Nations action was begun at the request of the Central Government, which the Secretary-

> General had denied. In order to be precise, I undertook to prepare for the Secretary-General a document setting out in detail the points which had worried me.
>
> At the end of this meeting I had formed the impression that many of the apparently more outrageous aspects of the United Nations action as we had seen them from London were inaccurate or exaggerated. I thought that there had been a gross miscalculation of the effect of the United Nations action, and that this was due to ineptitude and bad judgment. When I left Mr. Hammarskjold it was in the knowledge that he would be asking Mr. Adoula and his Cabinet for their acquiescence to the despatch of his message to Mr. Tshombe. . . .*

There were important differences in emphasis between the unofficial version of the meeting and that given out by Lansdowne.

The British diplomat portrayed a Hammarskjold somewhat on the defensive, worried if not actually apologetic over what had happened. Other accounts indicated Hammarskjold did some very straight talking himself, complaining notably he was entitled to expect greater loyalty to Security Council resolutions than some great powers in fact had displayed.

Lansdowne left no doubt in his public report that he had expressed British misgivings and objections with great force. But nowhere did he suggest that he had warned or threatened or in any other way pressured Hammarskjold.

U.N. men have insisted that he bluntly asked Hammarskjold how many permanent members of the Security Council he felt he could offend. The implication of this inquiry—if Lansdowne made it—was startling. Moscow had broken with Hammarskjold. Paris had quarreled with him. Nationalist China cut little ice. He had only Washington's unqualified support. And now here was Britain, in so many words, telling him not to count on her if current U.N. policy in the Congo continued. Even if Hammarskjold was not overly concerned about his personal future, he was acutely aware

---

* Hansard Official Report of House of Lords Debate, Wednesday, October 18, 1961, Columns 447–449.

that his post and the United Nations itself had become identified.

In his speech Lansdowne made plain that the British Government had lost confidence in O'Brien. He did not mention what has become generally known, that he called directly for the Irishman's dismissal. The secret letter he sent Hammarskjold was a catalogue of inconsistencies that he said existed between the reported statements of U.N. men in Elizabethville and the explanations offered by Hammarskjold himself. He also told Hammarskjold of instances when he felt O'Brien had failed to use chances for negotiations and for a truce. And he asserted O'Brien had erred grievously over the timing and method of his September attempt to complete the arrest of the mercenaries.

Whatever may have been his own true feelings, Hammarskjold, of course, displayed no lack of confidence in O'Brien or in any other member of his staff. Characteristically he was staunch in their defense and insisted that the responsibility for what had happened was his and his alone. He went no further than to undertake to look at the letter Lansdowne offered to send.

Two other elements of Hammarskjold's talk with Lansdowne —the unofficial account—were packed with political dynamite.

The first element suggested:

Lansdowne, not Hammarskjold, suggested Ndola as the site for the cease-fire. O'Brien made the assertion three times in *The Observer* of December 10 and 24, 1961, and quoted Linner as his source. He was doing more than accuse Lansdowne of not telling the truth. He was implying the Britisher was partly responsible for a journey that ended in disaster. From the very day of the crash of the *Albertina*, British Government statements stressed that it had been Hammarskjold's own idea to set up the meeting at Ndola. The British version was that although Lansdowne had warmly welcomed Hammarskjold's peace initiative when the two were together, he also had expressed surprise over the choice of Ndola and had said he assumed Hammarskjold had carefully pondered all the implications. Lansdowne also was represented as having told Hammarskjold he was prepared to set up all the necessary arrangements on his own initiative in case clearance did not come through in time from London and Salisbury, and he was quoted as offering the comment: "After all, as a junior Minister, I am expendable." The British story goes that Hammarskjold came back with the observation: "So am I."

The second element asserted:

Lansdowne warned Hammarskjold that the struggle to preserve Katangan integrity would go on indefinitely from Rhodesian territory even if U.N. troops scored what seemed to be a decisive victory. This version was persistent among Afro-Asian and other powers for a long time. It was given an impetus in December, 1961, when Lord Home and other British spokesmen expressed grave fears that the Katangan war might go on for years and ultimately destroy the United Nations. The plain implication of Lansdowne's warning—if he made it or said anything like it—was that Britain would find it difficult to prevent a grinding underground guerrilla struggle waged by whites and non-whites alike who associated themselves with Tshombe's cause. In such a situation Britain, with her hand on her heart, could claim to be in the clear. The Rhodesian Federation did not belong to the United Nations. It was British territory, true, but Britain controlled only its external and defense affairs and not its internal security.

To Hammarskjold the perils of such a prospect must have been plain. The Katangan incident could turn into an international conflict, an undeclared war against the United Nations, and like any colonial power the world body might find it impossible to confine the campaign to a localized region of Central Africa. And he, the Secretary-General, would be held partly to blame.

Nobody on the outside could be sure if Lansdowne in fact spoke to Hammarskjold in terms so stark.

Equally nobody on the outside could doubt that the events of the next few hours actually did raise the specter of positive Rhodesian involvement in Katanga's struggle for autonomy.

Several rapid-fire developments followed the Hammarskjold-

Lansdowne meeting, as if to remind Hammarskjold of the alternative to a truce:

1. After a long meeting with Kimba and Kiela—Tshombe's two men who had slipped across the frontier—Welensky announced he would send food and medical supplies to Katanga, regardless of what Britain or anyone else might think. Asked at a news conference how the Federation would be placed by helping foes of the United Nations, Welensky replied: "I don't know how it places us. I don't really care. If I get a request from starving people I am prepared to help them."
2. About the same time Tshombe had a message smuggled across the border and telephoned to Welensky, who released it to reporters. The proclamation ordered, in Tshombe's name, "all-out, total war" against the United Nations. It offered an armistice only if U.N. troops evacuated Katanga.
3. Troops of the Rhodesian Light Infantry and Selous Scouts, with armored cars, moved up to the frontier, and a concentration of jet fighters and Canberra bombers was reported at Ndola Airport.

All these expressions of an active Katangan-Rhodesian alliance may, of course, at a later stage, have produced the story of Lansdowne's warning. In subsequent months other indications of at least unofficial Rhodesian military aid for Tshombe came to light. Federal territory, for example, was freely used by mercenaries, although not necessarily with the actual consent of the authorities. Instances of gun-running were listed by U.N. officials, and their accusations were widely believed despite the vehement denials of Welensky himself.

But, undoubtedly, on that Saturday the Rhodesian moves appeared designed to bring home to Hammarskjold the probable consequences of further fighting in Katanga.

The thing that then seemed to matter most—looking back on the scene through the eyes of some of Hammarskjold's closest associates—was that the Secretary-General was under maximum pressure to come to terms quickly with the ambitious leader of an African province

In Katanga, meantime, attacks continued on U.N. positions in Elizabethville, Jadotville and Kamina.

The Lone Ranger, still unchallenged, hit a U.N. DC-3 ambulance plane heading for Leopoldville from Kamina. The Fouga also bombed besieged garrisons at Kamina and Jadotville. And through the day it streaked over and around Elizabethville Airport to discourage the landing of reinforcements and supplies.

On the whole, Elizabethville was quiet except for sniping and mortar attacks that cost U.N. troops several casualties.

The most dramatic action took place around Jadotville. Two relief columns, including Gurkhas, tried in vain to cross the Lufira River, 15 miles short of the town. They run into intense small arms and mortar fire, and the Lone Ranger dive-bombed them. In the town itself the 150-strong Irish company saw the 2,000 Katangans close in on their camp area. U.N. helicopters flew in urgently needed food, ammunition and water supplies. Shortly before 2 p.m. the garrison radioed Elizabethville "We are still holding on."

Then the radio went dead.

Later in the day the Katangans claimed the Irish had given in. Linner's headquarters put out a different version:

> . . . In the late afternoon, the Congolese soldiers in Jadotville refused to obey their foreign officers and stopped attacking U.N. troops.
>
> A cease-fire was agreed upon, including a provision that the jet fighter would be grounded and the road-blocks set up by the gendarmerie on the Elisabethville-Jadotville road removed. U.N. troops were provided by the Congolese soldiers with fresh food and other commodities. . . .

But it became clear during the night that the U.N. account was not correct. Failure of the relief columns to break through to the town shattered the last faint hopes that the Irish would indeed hang on. They were overwhelmed after a mortar bombardment and, soon afterward, they surrendered.

The garrison of 450 Swedes, Irish and Malays at Kamina also was under heavy attack from the Fouga and from mortar and small-arms fire. Some of the tribesmen encircling the U.N. force, huddled in a small perimeter around the airport control tower, had begun systematically to loot the huge stores and supply depots built by the Belgians. Millions of dollars worth of equipment were stock-piled in the great Kamina base area, which the United States had helped the Belgians develop.

Echoes of the Katanga war were heard in London Saturday night.

Irish Foreign Minister Frank Aiken, on his way to see his hard-pressed countrymen in Katanga, told airport newsmen: "I have no complaints about the way Irish troops have been used in the Congo. There are no plans for withdrawing Irish troops." (As some British newspapers had suggested.)

One reporter asked Aiken if the Government of Ireland had been warned its troops would be going to Katanga.

"I really forget," Aiken retorted.

The Minister's reply demonstrated his country's loyalty to the United Nations, despite the widespread abuse of O'Brien and the dangers facing the Irish troops in the field.

Meanwhile, the calm of autumn was hanging over the Foreign Office in Whitehall when a message came into the cipher room from Sir Patrick Dean in New York. It outlined the U.N. request for over-flying facilities that would allow Ethiopian jets to reach Katanga quickly.

The message was passed to a departmental head, who saw quickly that the issue was one requiring a ministerial decision. Lord Home was telephoned. In turn he consulted Prime Minister Macmillan. Both at once recognized that the introduction of U.N. air power would transform the military—and political—situation in Katanga. And so they urgently signaled Lansdowne in Leopold-ville to discuss the matter with Hammarskjold. They suggested the Secretary-General perhaps could be dissuaded from pressing the request, especially if Tshombe would agree to ground the Fouga.

And for the time being the British Government withheld permission for the Ethiopian jets to pass over the East African colonies.

Tshombe's triumph at Jadotville brought an immediate political sequel.

The Katangan leader, elated by the sweet smell of success, made contact with Dunnett toward midnight and asked the Consul to advice O'Brien of his "wish" for a meeting. He said he was "prepared" to see the U.N. representative at 11:30 next morning in the Northern Rhodesian border town of Bancroft. It seemed very much like a victorious general's summons to a defeated foe.

O'Brien flashed the news to Hammarskjold in Leopoldville but urged that the proposal be turned down. A meeting any place in Katanga would be fine, he said, but a conference in Rhodesian territory would look like accepting "the mediation and even the arbitration" of Sir Roy Welensky.

Tshombe's move, though, provided Hammarskjold with the chance he had been waiting for. He paused only to amend his own already-formulated message so as to make it refer to, and conform with, the Katangan leader's request for a meeting.

Earlier in the day Hammarskjold had shown the draft of that message to the American ambassador, Edmund Gullion, and to Adoula himself, as he had promised Lansdowne he would do. Gullion had been able to assure him of broad U.S. support for the peace project, and Adoula raised no valid objection. Adoula made it clear, though, that there could be no question of the Central Government's joining the talks.

With all speed, then, Hammarskjold shot back to Tshombe his own counterproposal for a personal confrontation—the two of them, with advisers, to meet in Ndola at the earliest possible time. The letter was sent over the teleprinter network to O'Brien in Elizabethville for transmission to the Katangan.

The message read like a patient schoolmaster's lecture to a pupil. In clear, cool terms Hammarskjold traced the story of the U.N. mission in Katanga and then appealed to Tshombe's sense of logic by arguing the case for an unconditional cease-fire.

Here is what Hammarskjold's letter said:

(1) The mandate of the United Nations force in the Congo is, broadly speaking, to help maintain public order. The resolution of 21 February defined further two aspects of this mandate which are binding on the Organization and on all Member States and their nationals. I quote the two relevant paragraphs:

"1. *Urges* that the United Nations take immediately all appropriate measures to prevent the occurrence of civil war in the Congo, including arrangements for cease-fire, the halting of all military operations, the prevention of clashes, and the use of force, if necessary, in the last resort;

"2. *Urges* that measures be taken for the immediate withdrawal and evacuation from the Congo of all Belgian and other foreign military and para-military personnel and political advisers not under the United Nations Command, and mercenaries."

(2) In the same resolution the Security Council declares that it is convinced that the solution of the problem of the Congo lies in the hands of the Congolese people themselves without any interference from outside and that there can be no solution without conciliation. The Council adds that it is convinced further that the imposition of any solution not based on genuine conciliation would, far from settling any issues, greatly enhance the dangers of conflict within the Congo and the threat to international peace and security.

(3) A principle of the United Nations which is absolutely binding upon all is the maintenance of peace and, to that end and in order to protect human life, they are bound to cease all hostilities and to seek solutions to the conflict by means of negotiation, mediation and conciliation.

(4) You have yourself accepted the objectives of the United Nations mission as defined in paragraph (1), that is to say, the maintenance of public order, the prevention of civil war and the evacuation of all the personnel referred to by the Security Council. There should therefore be no difference of opinion between the Organization and you as to the framework within which ways must be sought of putting an end to the present armed conflict.

(5) As regards the idea that a solution to the problem of the Congo should be sought through reconciliation—which would naturally have to be achieved within the framework of the Constitution of the Republic—you have several times

given us clear indications that you also accepted this point of view. I am therefore convinced that you do not share the opinion of certain elements who reject the idea of reconciliation, which leads me to the conclusion that your views and those of the United Nations are identical with respect to the principles on which the attempt to find a solution to the political problem should be based.

(6) On the morning of 13 September, you yourself requested a cease-fire and I understand that you made efforts to bring it about. Since the United Nations desires without reservation to avoid hostilities and the shedding of blood, your request was accepted in advance, on condition, of course, that you could establish an effective cease-fire on your side. In so doing, you would remain faithful to the position you have taken, which I mentioned in paragraph (4) and (5) above. The efforts to bring about a cease-fire have failed for reasons which we do not know, but which seem to derive from the opposition of certain of those responsible for military operations in Katanga. We have unceasingly sought to make contact with you and you even promised us that you would meet United Nations representatives for discussions on Friday evening, but you did not come to the meeting place chosen by common consent.

The United Nations, faithful to its principles, still wishes to see established, without delay, the cease-fire which you yourself requested and which it should be possible for you to achieve, given your position of principle as I have described it.

(7) I have been informed of the message received by Mr. O'Brien from Mr. Dunnett, the British Consul, inviting him to meet you tomorrow at 11:30 at Bancroft in Northern Rhodesia. I suggest that I should meet you personally, so that together we can try to find peaceful methods of resolving the present conflict, thus opening the way to a solution of the Katanga problem within the framework of the Congo. The proposed meeting obviously requires that orders should be given beforehand for an immediate and effective cease-fire. I therefore propose to you that such a cease-fire should be firmly imposed by both sides, so as to make a meeting possible and to come nearer to a solution of the present conflict within the framework established by the Security Council and already accepted by you. As I shall have to go to the meeting place by air, I suggest that the meeting should be at Ndola. I am de-

pendent on our transport facilities and for this reason the hour which you propose is impossible for me. I shall inform you as early as possible tomorrow morning of my time of arrival, allowing for the fact that before I leave I must have your reply to this message, including your decision regarding the cease-fire. The cease-fire will occur automatically on the United Nations side, in view of the fact that according to the instructions given and the rules followed by the Organization, it only opens fire in self-defense.

(8) I am awaiting your urgent reply to this proposal for a meeting and for an immediate cease-fire.

(*signed*) DAG HAMMARSKJOLD

Hammarskjold's move, of course, stunned O'Brien and his colleagues, who found it almost impossible to believe. In the first place Hammarskjold had completely disregarded the advice of his Irish chief of operations in Katanga not to meet in Rhodesian territory. In the second place the Secretary-General had intervened without in any way providing, as far as could be seen then, for bringing his own delegates from Katanga into the negotiation. It seemed to be a monumental display of "no confidence" and in O'Brien's own words the whole thing "took our breath away" and "to me seemed absolutely inconceivable."

O'Brien in the article published December 10, 1961, in *The Observer* went on to relate:

It seemed to me essential that I should see Mr. Hammarskjold. I wanted to beg him not to go to Ndola. I wanted to explain to him the full situation in Elisabethville and answer his questions. And personally I wanted very badly to clear away the thunderous cloud of disapproval which I knew was over me in Mr. Hammarskjold's mind.

I knew that when he had picked me for Elisabethville he had picked me for the key post in the U.N.'s most crucial operation. And I knew, from the tone of the telegrams, that he thought I had let him down. I know now—though I would certainly not have so expressed it at the time—that I felt then somewhat as a son feels if he is under the displeasure, for reasons unknown and inexplicable to him, of a revered father. I was rebellious, uneasy and sick at heart. But, whatever I felt,

I knew it was wrong for Mr. Hammarskjold to go to Ndola to meet Mr. Tshombe. That had to be stopped.

I knew there was no point in cabling. My cabled advice, which would not have been ignored before September 13, would be ignored now. I cabled proposing that the Secretary-General's plane should touch down at Kamina Base, that I should join him there and go on with him to Ndola. On the way I could explain to him—officially—the situation in Elisabethville and—privately—I could find out what on earth was wrong.

The cable came in a bad time. Lord Lansdowne had been hard at work in Leopoldville and Mr. Hammarskjold, most imperfectly informed (if indeed he had been informed at all) of the instructions conveyed to us, could not defend me effectively against Lord Lansdowne's charges and his insistence on my elimination. To include me in the party would have been a red rag to the people who were pressing—the word is a weak one—the Secretary-General to go to Ndola. There could be no question of it.

The answer came back, polite and cool. The Secretary-General proposed to deal with this matter outside the framework of O.N.U.C. There was no need, therefore, for the Representative in Elisabethville to join the flight to Ndola.

There was little more that could be done at Le Royal after Hammarskjold sent off his fateful message.

He and Linner went over some of the arrangements for the Ndola meeting—travel plans, the choice of officials to accompany him, security matters and so on.

Linner asked Hammarskjold if he would take one of his American aides, Vladimir Fabry, along with him. Fabry had been working himself to a standstill lately, Linner explained. He deserved the honor and experience. After Ndola he could go on to take a vacation. Hammarskjold agreed.

The very special honor and experience he conferred on Fabry were to haunt the nights of Sture Linner for a long time to come.

Well after midnight the two old friends drove home. Hammarskjold went up to his room.

10 | The Sunday

That Sunday the tidy life of Dag Hammarskjold moved forward to fiasco with all the inevitable doom of a Greek tragedy.

He was out of bed as usual by about 6 a.m. and, before going down to breakfast, he packed a briefcase with clothes and a few belongings needed for the one or two nights he expected to stop over in Ndola.

For a methodical and normally unforgetful man he left behind —inexplicably, it seems—several very personal articles.

One was his checkbook. Another was his wallet, which contained highly important political papers that, in history's good time, may yet surprise the world. It was almost as if the compulsion of some inner awareness prevented him from risking their destruction.

On his bedside table lay the *Imitation of Christ.*

Inside, facing page 119, was a plain card bookmark with some typescript on it.

The words were the oath sworn by Secretaries-General of the United Nations on assuming their high office.

The oath on Hammarskjold's card read:

> I, Dag Hammarskjold, solemnly swear to exercise in all loyalty, discretion and conscience, the functions entrusted to me as Secretary-General of the United Nations, to discharge these functions and regulate my conduct with the interests of the United Nations only in view, and not to seek or accept instructions in regard to the performance of my duties from any government or other authority external to the Organization.

On the page facing the bookmark the central passage started off: "Les coups mêmes et les châtiments qui nous viennent de cette main paternelle nous doivent être doux; puis qu'il ne permet jamais qu'aucun mal nous arrive que pour notre bien et notre salut."

The analagous, extended passage evokes an impression of the wise, old, ineffably tender à Kempis conveying his compassion and his calm to the tormented Swede:

> Son, suffer Me to do with thee what I will; I know what is expedient for thee.
>
> Thou thinkest as man; thou judgest in many things as human affection suggesteth.
>
> Lord, what Thou sayest is true. Greater is Thy care for me than all the care I can take of myself.
>
> For at too great a hazard doth he stand, who casteth not his whole care on Thee.
>
> Lord, provided that my will remain true and firm towards Thee, do with me whatsoever it shall please Thee.
>
> For it cannot but be good, whatever Thou shalt do with me.
>
> If Thou wilt have me to be in darkness, be Thou blessed; and if Thou wilt have me to be in light, be Thou again blessed; if Thou vouchshafe to comfort me, be Thou blessed; and if it be Thy will I should be afflicted, be Thou still equally blessed.
>
> Son, thus must thou stand affected, if thou desire to walk with Me.
>
> Thou must be as ready to suffer as to rejoice; thou must be as glad to be poor and needy as to be full and rich.
>
> Lord, I will suffer willingly for Thee whatsoever Thou are pleased should befall me.
>
> I am willing indifferently to receive from Thy hand good and evil, sweet and bitter, joy and sorrow, and give Thee thanks for all that happeneth to me.
>
> Keep me from all sin, and I will fear neither death nor hell.
>
> So that Thou cast me not off for ever, nor blot me out of the book of life, what tribulation soever befalleth me shall not hurt me.*

---

* Everyman's Library edition (London and New York: J. M. Dent and Sons, 1960).

Hammarskjold and Linner whizzed through breakfast and hurried to Le Royal, where Lansdowne was due for another conference at 9:30.

The British minister, accompanied by Ambasssador Riches, was shown into Hammarskjold's sixth-floor office exactly on time. He already knew that the message to Tshombe had gone off. But he had not heard from London whether all arrangements at Ndola were complete.

Two main topics dominated the discussion. The first was the problem of the Ethiopian jets, and the second related to the arrangements for the talks in Ndola.

Lansdowne's instructions from London were to ask Hammarskjold to keep the jet fighters out of Katanga. The British feared that the consequences of air warfare might be far-reaching. In their view it could wreck peace prospects, start an air-arms race and generally add a new dimension to the contest. Very probably too some authorities in London felt the Katangans, whose mastery of the skies had until then given them a tremendous advantage, would come off second-best if U.N. air power was introduced. Lansdowne, accordingly, asked Hammarskjold if he really wanted to risk an air war at the very time truce talks were being organized. Britain for her part would try at once to persuade Tshombe to ground his Fouga.

Hammarskjold's advisers, if not the Secretary-General himself, later professed surprise at the British proposal. They saw it as an intrusion on Tshombe's behalf. If the British were so concerned to prevent aerial warfare why had they not intervened earlier, when the Lone Ranger first took to the skies? Anyway, did London think newly acquired air power would be used by the United Nations if a truce was arranged and if the Fouga ceased its offensive?

In the talk that followed Hammarskjold displayed close agreement with his staff and insisted he could not possibly accept the proposal, or bargain, Lansdowne had outlined. The Ethiopian jets were considered by the most senior members of his military and political staff to be essential for the defense—and he stressed the word defense—of U.N. troops, and it would be irresponsible to disregard their viewpoint.

Lansdowne saw it was pointless to press the matter further. In his report to London later in the day he said Hammarskjold was standing pat on the request for over-flying rights, and he recommended they be granted. In the event, Macmillan and Lord Home agreed. The United Nations were informed on Monday that the Ethiopian airplanes were free to fly over British East African territory. They did so five days later. Certain equipment had to be installed in the jets before they could leave, at the insistence of air authorities on the route. By the time they arrived, it was somewhat late. The *Albertina* had crashed. The Battle of Katanga had ended.

The two men turned next to the Ndola meeting. At the time Lansdowne still was waiting for London's word that all the arrangements for the parley were in order. In case that clearance did not come through, he said, he would be happy to ride along in Hammarskjold's plane. Time was short. As a British minister, obviously he would be able to facilitate the discussions if any on-the-spot help was required.

Hammarskjold's response was negative. In a situation so delicate it would do no good at all—indeed it would be positively embarrassing—if the impression got around that the United Nations was working closely with an outside government as interested in the outcome as Britain. He would not even consider a suggestion that Lansdowne should go along with him as a secret passenger. That sort of thing never worked, Hammarskjold said. Someone would be sure to recognize the secret passenger, and the situation would become more complicated still.

Hammarskjold came up with a countersuggestion. Lansdowne could go on ahead of him just to see that all was ready for the meeting. But the British diplomat must promise neither to interfere in the negotiations with Tshombe nor even to remain on the scene. If that was acceptable an aircraft of the U.N. fleet would be loaned to him and he could leave at once. Hammarskjold himself said he would be ready to take off the moment Tshombe's acceptance of the truce talks came in.

Lansdowne agreed. He undertook not even to meet with Tshombe. He promised also to leave Ndola for Salisbury—where he was due to go anyway—before Hammarskjold's arrival.

They parted then, for good.

The *Albertina*, meanwhile, had touched down safely at Ndjili Airport after a hazardous run to and from Elizabethville.

To Aahreus, Litton and other members of its crew the journey's attendant perils had become almost part of the everyday job that flying in the Congo then was. To outsiders the risks appeared enormous.

The previous day the *Albertina* had taken McKeown to the Katangan capital. It was dark, there were two possible landing runways—one held by U.N. troops, the other by Katangans—there were no landing lights, the plane had to fly in a wide arc from Luluabourg to avoid the Fouga, using dead reckoning despite two cross winds—and the crew did not know for sure if Elizabethville was expecting them. In fact, coming in to land at the wrong runway, the *Albertina* was shot at, and thereby found out its true position in the darkness. This was the machine carrying the U.N. Force Commander. Later the pilot confessed there had been about one chance in ten that they would make it.

Again, on take-off that morning, antiaircraft guns had fired at the departing *Albertina*, and a bullet had pierced the exhaust pipes of one of the engines. The damage had been discovered at Ndjili. Engineers of Swedish Transair thereupon had carried out a tip-to-tail check in case of further damage. They could find none. And so the *Albertina* was pronounced flight-worthy. The Air Transport Officer and Le Royal headquarters were so advised.

At Le Royal, Hammarskjold was holding his last staff meeting. With his top intelligence, security, political and military advisers he prepared himself for the crucial truce negotiations. They also went over the arrangements for the journey to Ndola.

The political strategy he intended to follow in the encounter with Tshombe was straightforward enough. He had spelled it out in the letter he had sent the previous day. The twofold purpose he had in mind was, firstly, to achieve a truce and, secondly, to open the way for a reconciliation between Tshombe and Adoula. His advisers knew he was hoping to promote that second aim by persuading Tshombe to display some gesture of good faith that would impress Adoula, for instance, to agree to cooperate in the evacuation of foreign elements.

As for the flight, it was necessary to work on take-off and touch-down times, on routing, the flight plan, the aircraft to be used and overall security precautions. Everyone attending that staff conference at Le Royal was conscious of the need for extraordinary safety measures. Everyone was equally aware that some risks were inevitable because certain hazards were built into the situation.

The need to avoid the Katanga battle zone was one obvious precaution to be taken. The idea of using escorts was considered but discarded; Hammarskjold himself showed no interest in having his plane escorted either inside Congolese or Rhodesian territory. Perhaps that seemed to him to be too dramatic. His principal preoccupation was with secrecy.

Dag Hammarskjold was not a man who flinched from danger. Nor was he a person disposed normally to recklessness. The precise role he played in the arrangements for the flight has still to be disclosed. But that Sunday he undoubtedly lent himself to a decision —and indeed seemed almost obsessed with a wish—to shroud his coming journey in circumstances of secrecy.

An elaborate arrangement was made whereby his pilot was ordered to observe radio silence. O.N.U.C. headquarters radio station was alerted to maintain a listening watch on a predetermined wave length throughout the period of the *Albertina*'s flight—but under strict instructions to initiate no contact. Indeed, O.N.U.C. later was to report that it had heard no calls made to, or from, the DC-6B. The Ndola authorities were not given an advance estimate of his arrival time, except by Hallonquist himself from the air. It was agreed that the commander of the aircraft would file a dummy flight plan. (Aviation control officials later asserted this decoy plan endangered almost every plane flying in that part of Africa that day, because no airfield knew for sure where the Secretary-General was heading.) And finally, Hammarskjold made it known he would be following Lansdowne—disregarding, or unaware of, the fact that the British minister's take-off plans had not been firmly fixed.

Hammarskjold's staff accepted all this without obvious uneasiness. There seemed to be another factor at play among them, one that may have been transmitted by the Secretary-General himself: to his subordinates there was something godlike about Hammarskjold. Their view of him verged on awe.

"His aim was the creation of a center of international moral authority, rising out of a chaos of nationalisms and clashing ideologies, to defend the human cause of peace and justice," O'Brien once wrote. "He himself in the eyes of many people, and in my own eyes, incarnated this authority."

Few of his staff would have described him as lovable. He was not warm. He did not himself display a capacity to express love for others. But he was a man who commanded tremendous respect. In intellect, energy and insight he seemed to those who knew him to be almost superhuman. He was one who consorted with kings and presidents and premiers. All this gave him an aura of omnipotence. If he recognized this illusion of himself in others he did little to dispel it.

And so it came to be accepted, unspokenly, that mortal dangers which beset mortal man just could not touch Hammarskjold. Hammarskjold die in an ordinary airplane crash? The idea was unthinkable.

In Elizabethville Sunday morning, soon after Lansdowne left Hammarskjold, O'Brien received Tshombe's reply to the cease-fire proposal. It arrived through Dunnett and it amounted to a conditional acceptance of Hammarskjold's offer.

Tshombe said in his message to the Secretary-General:

> (a.) The President and the Government [of Katanga] agree on the principle of an immediate cease-fire.
>
> (b.) He requests that U.N. troops be confined to their camps.
>
> (c.) He requests that the U.N. stop troop movements and the sending of reinforcements by land and air.

(d.) The President agrees to go to Ndola and requests transportation by light plane capable of landing and taking off from the Rhodesian airport of Kipushi.

Tshombe added he would be accompanied by Kibwe, Kimba and his Minister of State for the Common Market, Mwenda Odilon.

Firing in Katanga did not cease while these exchanges over the truce conference were going on.

There was a noticeable abatement in the capital itself, although the Gurkha camp had come under heavy mortar fire during the night.

The Lone Ranger made two bombing attacks on the Kamina air base. In the early morning he tried to destroy the control tower and at noon he struck at U.N. planes and flyers on the ground.

The U.N. Command at midday finally confirmed that the Irish garrison in Jadotville had been overwhelmed.

"There was a sudden change [in the town]," a communiqué announced. "At noon on 17 September a message was received from the Irish company commander [Major Pat Quinlan] indicating that they were being held as hostages by the gendarmerie."

During the uneasy truce period that was to follow the Katangans were as good as their word, and used the hostage Irish to extract advantages from the United Nations.

Tshombe's conditional agreement to attend the Ndola talks came in shortly before lunch, and it annoyed Hammarskjold. He found Tshombe's terms quite unacceptable and with some impatience told him so. He sent off an instruction to O'Brien saying:

> *Kindly inform Tshombe that the Secretary-General finds it impossible to accept the conditions for a cease-fire and a meeting which have been conveyed to him.*
>
> According to the terms of the letter from the Secretary-General (Para (7)), in the existing circumstances, there can be no question of anything but an unconditional cease-fire on both sides and an agreement to meet together, all other modalities obviously to be discussed in the course of the meeting. *The Secretary-General cannot agree to meet Tshombe unless*

> *this preliminary agreement, which is fully in accord with normal practice, is accepted.*
>
> The Secretary-General regrets that by introducing conditions, Mr. Tshombe has delayed the taking of measures to protect human life. He sincerely hopes that a favorable reply to his observations by Mr. Tshombe will make possible a meeting without further delay.
>
> As regards military movements and maintaining the positions of the various military groups, the cease-fire order should naturally be interpreted as having no effect on the *Status quo*, which is to be maintained in all respects throughout the period during which an agreement is being sought.

The British Embassy telephoned Hammarskjold's office after the message to Tshombe went off. Word had come in from London that all was ready in Ndola for the conference. On the face of things it seemed to cancel the need for Lansdowne's journey to the Rhodesian town.

But Hammarskjold later telephoned Lansdowne back and told him to go on ahead anyway. Perhaps he figured Lansdowne's flight would divert attention from his own. Hammarskjold also described the terms of Tshombe's reply and said they were unsatisfactory. But he said he intended nonetheless to go through with his mission. Finally, he mentioned that he had received and had studied Lansdowne's personal letter—which had come in overnight—listing the British complaints against O'Brien.

"The Secretary-General informed me that he had taken note of my personal letter to him," Lansdowne told his fellow peers in the House of Lords in his speech of October 18. "As he wished to investigate himself the points which I had raised there would be some delay in his reply."*

It was just about then during their telephone talk that the take-off times for Lansdowne's and consequently for Hammarskjold's planes were finally settled. Shortly after lunch, the Air

---

* Hansard Official Report of House of Lords Debate, Wednesday, October 18, 1961, Column 450.

Transport Office at Ndjili advised Hallonquist and his tired co-pilots of the departure arrangements. Under the hot sky, perspiring ground-staff men completed the loading of the *Albertina* with cases of beer and Coca-Cola, containers with sandwiches and some small arms and ammunition. Hawk-eyed security officials were on the alert for suspicious-looking parcels. They spotted none.

Hammarskjold's last message stressing there could be no truce talks unless Tshombe dropped his preconditions was ignored by the Katangan leaders. O'Brien asked Dunnett just after lunch to pass Hammarskjold's communication on to Tshombe, but he got the reply: "President Tshombe has already made plans to travel with his group to Ndola at 1500 hours [1 p.m., G.M.T.] and has already chartered a plane for this journey."

The wording of Dunnett's reply—as reported by the United Nations—suggested the Consul was not all that keen to transmit at so late a stage a message that could upset the delicately planned meeting. It was possible that he felt the main thing was to get the two men together in the same place at the same time, and that then difficulties about terms and so on could be settled swiftly.

In fact Tshombe was given a look at Hammarskjold's curt warning. But he studiously avoided answering it.

Hammarskjold, back in Leopoldville, was at a loss for a while over the significance of Tshombe's failure to respond. Was the British Consul truly out of touch with him? Could this be a new act of defiance? Would the Katangan show up at Ndola and so imply an acceptance of the unconditional cease-fire, or would he seek deliberately to stage a headline-raising snub to the servant of the United Nations?

Hammarskjold resolved to go on being conciliatory. He chose to go back on his own words of a few hours earlier, when he had said he could "not agree to meet Tshombe" unless Tshombe dropped all his conditions. He meant to go forward to Ndola in pursuit of peace.

Lansdowne, appearing five months later before U.N. investigators in Geneva, recalled his last telephone conversation on the subject as follows:

> He [Hammarskjold] told me he had received a reply from Mr. Tshombe. That reply, alas, was not satisfactory.
>
> Nonetheless he proposed to proceed to Ndola on the basis of the [first] message he had sent to Mr. Tshombe.
>
> I took it from that he was absolutely determined to go to Ndola and to have this meeting with Mr. Tshombe . . . almost at any price. . . .

So it was just after 3 p.m. that a weary Hammarskjold drove with Linner to Ndjili. It was stiflingly hot, and they turned down the windows of the automobile to catch the breeze. The watchful newsmen were waiting at the far side of the airport. Despite all the security precautions the journalists had learned, as journalists usually do, where he was heading.

Hammarskjold, serious-faced and with really nothing to say, refused to talk to them.

At Ndjili, shortly after 3:30, Hammarskjold's personal aide, Bill Ranallo, with Julien and a team of security officials made a final check of the cabin of the *Albertina* for plastic bombs and other tools of the saboteur.

They gave Hallonquist the all-clear.

In the cabin Dag Hammarskjold said a Swedish good-bye—"Adjo"—to his good friend Linner and settled back for the journey.

Part Three The Riddles of Dola Hill

11 | The Man

What sort of man was it who flew off to meet destiny aboard the *Albertina*?

"Fate is what we make it," Dag Hammarskjold observed in 1953 when he took up his lonely post as servant of the world. "I hope I survive."

The Swede had mastered his personal affairs in a career of meteoric brilliance. Then, as if to show that society too was perfectible, he had set out to transform the United Nations into a true parliament of man.

Dreamer, statesman, adventurer—it does not really matter how, in the end, history classifies him. In reality, the powers, if not the peoples, were unready for him.

Few would say that the age-old vision of world government—the vision to which his thoughts had turned—moved any nearer fulfillment through his stewardship. The last fifteen months of his life slipped by in a crescendo of controversy over the role of the organization he led. He drew stinging personal charges—ranging from "murderer" to "megalomaniac"—for the way in which he interpreted his tasks.

Yet the death of this quiet and gentle man left countless millions of ordinary people with a sense of deep personal grief. To little men and women everywhere, the United Nations was Dag Hammarskjold. He became known to newspaper readers the world over simply as "Dag," "Mr. H." or "Mr. U.N." And if this was a way of helping to get around a name too long for the headline writers, it also, in time, came to reflect the affection with which he was almost universally regarded.

What did they see in the face of the lost leader? Where did his greatness lie?

"Mr. H." embodied the yearnings of men for peace and international order. He never felt a need to declaim his love of humanity, but his actions showed he cared. His patience was balm in an age of violence. Through dangerous years his poised wisdom restored balance to feuding powers. At a crucial moment in world history he not only personalized the neutralism of his homeland but transformed that neutralism from a passive to an active doctrine, by giving it the catalytic properties of compromise and conciliation. Therein lay the source of his genius. And destruction.

Toward the end of his time a certain passion began to lace his altruism. He seemed to be a man with a mission—to foster a living internationalism. It was not chance alone that led him, more than once, to quote the question of the English "Corn Law Rhymer," Ebenezer Elliott:

> When wilt Thou save the people?
> Great God of battles—when?
> The people, Lord, the people.
> Not crowns or thrones, but men.*

Shadows of war darkened the life of Dag Hjalmar Agne Carl Hammarskjold from the day he was born at Jönköping on July 29, 1905.

At that time Sweden was in crisis over Norwegian demands to end the union binding the two countries. Appropriately, Hammarskjold's own father, Hjalmar, then a Judge-President of one of Sweden's three Appeal Courts, was among the peacemakers who fashioned a settlement.

Hammarskjold's brothers Bo, Ake and Sten were fourteen, ten and five when he was born. Bo became Governor of Sodermanland Province. Ake, whom Hammarskjold resembled most in talent, intellect and temperament, shone at law, and became Sweden's nominee at the International Court of Justice at The Hague. He was only forty-two when he died at his post, of rheumatic fever. Sten served on Sweden's National Housing Board.

* "The People's Anthem," *Corn Law Rhymes* (1831).

Old Hjalmar Hammarskjold was a patriarch of a man, who drew pride from his family's long tradition of service to the nation. With an occasional man of letters among them, his ancestors had been soldiers or statesmen for three centuries since an ancestor, Peder Hammarskjold, a Swedish knight, was honoured with this surname in 1610 by King Charles IX. The award was in recognition of the first Hammarskjold's bravery in helping to defend the Baltic island of Oeland against the Danes. "The name is exactly what it means in English," the Secretary-General once explained, "hammer-shield." His own name of "Dag" means "day." Hjalmar, trained in law, was Sweden's Minister of Justice at the turn of the century. King Gustaf V called on him to form a Government at the beginning of World War I, and, for the greater part of the war, he was Swedish Prime Minister. He followed a policy that, if anything, was to the right of the Conservatives.

Hammarskjold's mother was as tender as her husband seemed cold, as exuberant as he was controlled, as warm and sympathetic toward people as he was remote. Agnes Almquist to the end remained close to her youngest son, and his own attraction to, and for, all kinds and classes came clearly from her influence. Agnes's father was the step-brother of Carl Jonas Almquist, one of Sweden's most revered nineteenth-century poets and playwrights. A love of literature and writing was, therefore, part of Hammarskjold's heritage, and to the end he found solace in studying, interpreting and translating the work of poets he admired.

From the start, circumstances sentenced Hammarskjold to a solitary life. It was not only that he was set apart, the son of a national figure who reared his family in palaces and castles; it was also that in his formative years he lacked the companionship of brothers close in age and interests. A need to win the approval of a demanding father drove him to emulate the others. He seemed able to communicate deeply only with his mother. These were some of the factors that shaped his future. He was affectionate with a few very old friends but had no intense personal relationships. The result was to accentuate his withdrawal. The more aloof he became, the harder he worked. The harder he worked, the higher he climbed. Those who knew him well have said Hammarskjold was fully conscious of his involvement in the giddy process of climbing, ever climbing, in the affairs of men. Once, at least, he confided that he wondered sometimes where it would all end. Yet he maintained that he was at peace in the things he was doing. A sense of mission became detectable, as his role and personality developed in the United Nations. He looked upon his years as Secretary-General as the finest period of his life—possibly because his capacity for work and feeling for people were fulfilled in a cause that gripped him.

Hammarskjold rose to be a non-party specialist Minister without Portfolio in Sweden's Socialist cabinet (in the period immediately before taking on his high U.N. office). But throughout his career he avoided the entanglements of classical political alignments. From the Almquists he had inherited "a belief that, in the very radical sense of the Gospels, all men were equals as children of God," as he once wrote.

This principle of neutrality he carried to the depths of his personal life. He never married, and there were those who wondered why. First in Uppsala, then in Stockholm (where the family moved in 1930), he would shun the young ladies of the neighbourhood whom his mother would discreetly invite to parties. Some time after his mother's death in 1940, a friend and fellow economist, Bertil Ohlin, who was to become leader of the Swedish Liberals, tried to play the role of matchmaker between Hammarskjold and a certain very pretty girl, the daughter of a Swedish financier and a Ph.D. But the intended romance, with all its apparent ingredients of success, fizzled. When Ohlin was asked to explain why, he shrugged: "Dag said she didn't like T. S. Eliot."

Another time, in London during an official visit, Queen Elizabeth is said to have asked Hammarskjold why he had remained a bachelor. He explained he felt he could not give his wife the sort of life she should expect and yet himself be able freely to carry on with his work. He had seen, he said, the effect on his mother of Hjalmar's official commitments, and he could never bring himself to make another woman endure the same sort of suffering. Yet when Hammarskjold was at a marrying age he had not yet become the captive of his work. It may have been that at some stage in his growing-up period Hammarskjold consciously thought the thing through and then decided coldly that career must come first. Close friends, however, felt it was not so simple as that. As they saw it, once Hammarskjold plunged into his work a momentum built up, developing a logic of its own. First he had to master the big posts to which he was appointed so young. Then the great social problems of the 1930's immersed him. World War II came next. Finally, there was the period of reconstruction. Hammarskjold was neck-deep in it all.

Without necessarily realizing it, he had betrothed himself, for better or for worse, to the service of his people.

For a man born to be great there could have been few settings finer than Uppsala. The ancient seat of kings, scholars and churchmen had soaked up much that was best of Europe. It reached down the centuries for its traditions. And in the ashes of those dead yesterdays were the sparks to kindle new flames of creation among the intellectuals who thronged the cobbled streets of the university town during the 1920's. One of those so fired to create in the service of men was the young Hammarskjold.

He excelled at school and university. As a measure of his versatility, his formal university achievements included degrees in law, economics and the humanities. The intensity of his intellectual pursuits did not lead him to neglect his body. Gymnastics had a special appeal for its demands of grace, skill and coordination of thought and movement. He was fluent in English, French and German, and could understand other languages, including some Russian.

When he was twenty-five, Hammarskjold moved with his family to the Swedish capital, there to meet and mingle with the group of progressive economists who came to be known as the "Stockholm School." The group evolved a middle way between the liberalism of John Maynard Keynes and the radicalism of Karl Marx. Characteristically Swedish, their solution combined elements of free enterprise and rigid socialism, and it became the theoretical base of the world's trail-blazing welfare state. Those were times of changing political landmarks and shifting social patterns throughout Europe, and it was another pointer toward the shape of things to come for Dag Hammarskjold that his brilliant gifts were swiftly recognized, even among the talents of his distinguished contemporaries: he was made Secretary of a Royal Commission on Unemployment. There he was, barely out of university, in the mainstream of policy-making on issues that were shaking loose the old orders and making way for a new one.

Hammarskjold was also in the mainstream of Swedish intellectual thought. His work brought him into intimate contact not only with fellow economists but also with politicians, administrators, sociologists and labor union leaders—the nation's managers. But for his restless, groping, searching mind even that was not enough. People were his passion. And if he was too shy or reticent to seek them out for the therapy of their companionship, he would settle for the next best thing, which was to read and think and hear and talk about them.

So began his untiring quest for the company of writers, artists, musicians and actors. When he was not at work he was reading, or looking at paintings, or listening to music, or watching some play or film. Nothing living bored him. The motives of men fed his need to *know.* He was fascinated by the social behavior of pagans and Parisians and Polynesians. His memory was prodigious. Steeped in the classics of all the arts, he yet found time to keep up with the moderns: The symphonies of Brahms, Beethoven, Bach, Vivaldi, Tchaikovsky, Mahler, Schubert. The language of Shelley, Auden, Eliot, Spender, Buber, St.-John Perse. The symmetry of Thomas Mann, Faulkner, Wolfe, Lagerkvist, Hesse, Steinbeck, Hemingway, Jean Genet, James Baldwin, Salinger. The color and form of Matisse, Picasso, Gris, Fritz Glarner, Braque, Fernand Leger. In each he found something to appeal to his universality.

He collected—and never lost—many friends who helped his development. At Uppsala they included Axel Hagerstrom, professor of jurisprudence, Jon Olof Soderblom, son of the Archbishop of Uppsala, and Gunnar Haggloff, for long the *doyen* of the diplomatic corps in London.

In Stockholm there were Sven Stolpe, Gunnar and Alva Myrdal (the economist and sociologist), and several members of the "Stockholm School," among them Erik Lundberg, Alfred Johansson, Professor Karen Kock (who became Sweden's first woman cabinet minister), and Ivar Rooth of the Riksbank. The man who, in a career sense, influenced Hammarskjold perhaps more than anyone else—always excepting father Hjalmar—was Ernest Wigforss, who served as a sort of keeper of the conscience of Swedish Socialism. In 1936 Wigforss was reappointed as Finance Minister, and brought Hammarskjold in as Permanent Under-Secretary of his ministry. Thus, at thirty-one Hammarskjold became the youngest man ever to be appointed Under-Secretary of Finance, a post in which he stayed on until the end of World War II.

The ascent to the peaks had begun formally for Hammarskjold, with his work on the Unemployment Commission. Somehow he simultaneously fitted in a programme of research for his doctoral thesis which dealt with the theory of the business cycle. A year at Cambridge. A teaching post at Stockholm University. All this by 1936, when he waved farewell to the world of scholarship and entered the policy-making echelons of the State. There followed a succession of big posts inside and outside the country. Each was performed with distinction; all added to his stature as a person and as a negotiator. The British and Americans got to know something of his skills when he negotiated Sweden's first postwar trade agreements with them. He commanded the attention of officialdom in other parts of non-Communist Europe for his bridge-building and his qualities of conciliation within the Marshall Plan. And he conveyed traces of his toughness to the Russians during the tense summer of 1952 when Soviet fighters shot down two Swedish planes over the Baltic; at the time he was in charge of the Foreign Ministry.

By 1953, when he was summoned to be the world's top civil

servant, Dag Hammarskjold had already joined the cabinet of Europe's strongest neutral—a nation that has practiced the art of peace by staying out of wars for 150 years.

The Security Council named Hammarskjold as Secretary-General without first asking him, because his French and British sponsors were sure he would say no.

They were right. To him the job seemed an impossible one. He did not consider himself capable of performing it. When journalists called him with the news on the night of March 31, 1953, he said he thought it must be a premature April Fool's prank.

About the first person he consulted was Hjalmar. Then 91, the old man was as spry and commanding as ever. Dag had come to terms with him in the years after his mother died. The advice he gave Dag was to accept the offer.

Hammarskjold took over the Secretary-Generalship at a time of crisis for the office. In the United States the era of Joseph McCarthy and the hunt for suspected Communists were at their height. The Russians had broken relations with Trygve Lie since the Korean war, making him increasingly dependent on American support, and, as a result, Lie had buckled under Washington's pressure and purged the U.N. Secretariat of several American officials thought to be Reds or fellow travelers. These firings had shaken the morale of the U.N. staff. Thus Hammarskjold was faced at the outset with the task of restoring the confidence of the Secretariat, a job that took nearly a year. He got the General Assembly to approve a new code of conduct, which reaffirmed the international character of the Secretariat and the freedom of its members from national influence.

At the same time, through a combination of firmness and tact, Hammarskjold evolved a system for balancing American anxieties over security with the need to establish the United Nations as master in its own house.

The Swede did more to drive out the gloom from the big U.N. Secretariat building. One of his first acts was to throw a party for the nearly four thousand employees. Among the entertainers were

Danny Kaye and Marian Anderson. By the end of the evening the Secretary-General and the comedian were calling each other "Danny" and "Hammy." After that, Hammarskjold attended similar staff get-togethers before the opening of each General Assembly session.

There was a certain informality about the slim, sandy-haired statesman that emphasized his identification with those around him. He would appear occasionally in the cafeteria queue carrying his own lunch tray. An elevator reserved for his personal use in the Secretariat building was, on his orders, made available to the whole U.N. staff. On his arrival he asked to be introduced individually to the thousands of employees, and in two weeks he had shaken them all by the hand. When on U.N. business, he invariably flew tourist class.

Hammarskjold had his office on the thirty-ninth—and top—floor of the Secretariat building. Outside the polished wood door a single sentry in the blue and gold uniform of the U.N. Security Force stood guard. The room was not large. Hammarskjold liked to catch the sound of riverboat whistles while he worked. The view from the window took in the towers and peaks of Manhattan. Simple, fresh, clean austerity marked the décor. Examples of his taste were on view: a La Fresnaye still life, a sculptured oriental head bowed in sad contemplation. In a nearby conference room hung one of Hammarskjold's best-prized photographs—a Himalayan peak. An occasional Picasso—on loan from the Museum of Modern Art—caught the eye.

It was not long before a series of big political assignments fell to Hammarskjold. In December, 1954, the General Assembly asked him to work for the release of eleven American airmen held by Red China on spying charges. He flew at once to Peking for talks with Premier Chou En-lai. The flyers were freed during the summer. It was an important personal success in an operation made delicate by the Assembly's criticism of Chinese behavior over the Korean truce.

In the spring of 1956 tensions were rising in the Middle East, and the Security Council sent him to strengthen the Arab-Israeli armistice agreements. For a few months after that there was a lull. Then, in July, President Gamal Abdul Nasser of Egypt nationalized the Suez Canal and touched off one of the most hectic periods in the stormy diplomatic aftermath of the war. Prolonged attempts at a negotiated settlement came to nothing. Then Israel, followed by Britain and France, invaded Egypt. Vetoes blocked action by the Security Council. The Assembly stepped in and ordered a cease-fire, and, on later instructions, Hammarskjold organized in forty-eight hours a U.N. Emergency Force; its task was to keep a watch on the Israeli-Egyptian frontier while the invaders withdrew. During that period the ferocity of Hammarskjold's attack on the Israelis, British and French surprised many people. London and Paris, which had sponsored his nomination, were unprepared for the positive new role he had assumed.

About the same time as Suez, the Soviet Union was taking care of the Hungarian uprising, with the help of tanks and other tools of war. Again the Assembly sought to intervene, and U.N. representatives were assigned to Budapest. But, despite ten Assembly resolutions, the Communists refused them entry. Hammarskjold had to abandon the mission.

Out of these experiences he fashioned his own brand of "private diplomacy," which he explained in a speech at Ohio University, Athens, Ohio, on February 5, 1958:

> The legislative process in the United Nations serves its purpose only when it helps to arrive at agreements between the national states concerned.
>
> It is diplomacy, not speeches and votes, that continues to have the last word in the process of peacemaking....
>
> The office of the Secretary-General, by its very nature under the Charter, must practice private diplomacy on almost all occasions until results are reached.

In that same year Hammarskjold began to put his concepts into action. Without orders he reinforced a military observer group in Lebanon. He submitted a program for conciliating the opposing Arab factions. In 1959 he brought the Laos crisis to the attention of the Security Council—and then went ahead and established a

U.N. "presence" in the kingdom, stressing the country's economic rather than political troubles. The effect was to build a window through which the United Nations could watch a situation that threatened to become a focal point of East-West conflict.

To Hammarskjold the concept of the U.N. "presence" meant giving the world body a role resembling that of "an ambassador . . . . exercising 'good offices' or operating as a negotiating party." But he recognized that the moment it became necessary for the U.N. "presence" to take military form, the authority of the world body would be endangered. He confided to associates in early July, 1960, that the despatch of U.N. troops to the Congo would in the end be judged "a sign of weakness."

In 1958 Hammarskjold was unanimously elected to a second five-year term as Secretary-General. He took the occasion to stress his resolve to maintain the office as an independent force and to go on acting as he judged best, without political dictation from anyone.

Both by circumstance and by his own personality he had greatly extended the prestige of his office and the influence of the United Nations. He had achieved this without the help of the big powers —who had picked him essentially in the hope that he would be the efficient administrator, content to keep out of trouble. But his role did not go unchallenged. The British and French were deeply displeased with his performance during the Suez crisis, although formally they buried the hatchet. The Russians began in 1958 to criticize his independent action. His position became ever more delicate as he strove to hold the balance between the conflicting claims of the great power blocs.

The real storm burst around his head—and implicitly around the United Nations—when the Congo exploded. While the fortunes of the contenders ebbed and flowed, controversy raged over the nature of the U.N. operations. As a by-product of the Congo crisis, came the Soviet charge that he was not neutral and that the Secretariat-General should have three heads.

The abuse that was heaped upon him—mainly by the Russians—might have been considered by less sensitive men as an inevitable hazard of action. If he had chosen a less conscientious interpretation of his office, he probably would have escaped the assaults. But in all honesty he could do no such thing. His roots in a small and neutral country aroused in him instinctive sympathies for the efforts of the newer and smaller states to preserve their neutrality and indeed their independence.

"It is not the Soviet Union or indeed any of the other Big Powers who need the United Nations for their protection," he said with quiet dignity in his own defense when answering Khrushchev's onslaught in the fall of 1960. "It is all the others. In this sense the organization is their organization and I deeply believe in the wisdom with which they will be able to use and guide it."

Russia's denunciations of Hammarskjold as a tool of "colonialists" had left many U.N. delegates shocked. But now, hearing him, the smaller countries responded with a standing ovation. It was their way of answering his cool offer to quit any time they wished.

The calm and patience of his bearing nonetheless masked deep pain—the pain of a man who had prided himself on his detachment and ability truly to steer a middle course. To friends he confessed that the episode had in parts been "nightmarish."

Others put it more starkly. The U.S. delegate, Adlai Stevenson, was quoted as saying there were times during the fifteenth session of the General Assembly that made him "yearn for the simple brutalities of American party politics."

The two faces of Dag Hammarskjold were as different as they were difficult to understand.

His public image was that of the quiet diplomat, managing the affairs of the nations and discouraging all attempts to personalize him. In private he was the erudite aesthete, liking nothing better than to quit the feverish contact of crowds.

The world saw him as the complete political sophisticate, companion of kings, world traveler, lover of good food and fine wines. On his own, he was rarely happier than when stoking a fire on some river bank or mountain slope to prepare a breakfast of bacon, canned beans and coffee.

When he became Secretary-General, Hammarskjold refused to discuss his personal affairs. "The private man should disappear and the international public servant should take his place," he said. He took his words literally. Whenever the world allowed it he would retreat to his country hideaway near Brewster, New York, or to his native Scandinavian haunts. There, either alone or with some old friends, he would often set out before dawn on long treks, to restore and refresh himself for the new challenges that always lay ahead. And yet, although he sometimes yearned to break loose from the chains of protocol and formality, always he came back, with new zest and some gladness, to his chaining duties.

A countryman, Olof G. Landberg, has told how Hammarskjold was "lost to the world" when the Suez crisis broke in 1956. "He had walked off into the wilderness of Mount Kebnekaise, and planes and Lapps had to be sent out to find him in order to take him back to civilization and the hectic General Assembly in New York," Landberg recalled. "They found him after 36 hours, with his rucksack and stick, walking alone with his map in his hand."

At times of crisis Hammarskjold's working hours would stretch almost around the clock, and often he would stay overnight in the suite set aside for his personal use, alongside his Secretariat office. He declined as many social invitations as he safely could without giving offense but entertained graciously himself, usually at select and intimate dinner parties.

His apartment mirrored a fragment of his mind and some of his interests. Austere simplicity marked its Scandinavian-style furnishings. Pastel shades glowed under soft lights. His treasury of books spanned centuries, peoples and the gamut of endeavor and imagination. A prized souvenir in the living room was the ice axe given him in Nepal by the Sherpa Tenzing Norkey, who had helped guide the New Zealander Sir Edmund Hillary to Everest's peak. Elegant ceramics from Sweden, paintings from Paris, and some of his own photographs lined the walls.

Late at night, before retiring, Hammarskjold would read for an hour or two, but when he needed peace, rather than mental exercise, he would turn to his record player.

When he was young, Hammarskjold had wavered for a while between creative writing and public service as a career. Perhaps the indecision reflected the differing influences of his mother and father.

He chose, in the end, to serve, clearly because he considered that this would satisfy him more. But he also wrote. And he took excellent photographs. He published no original literary work of his own, and there is no record to suggest that he produced any. He did, however, display a poet's talent in the brilliant translations he made of the writings of others with whom he could identify.

By combining the best of both worlds he fashioned a compromise that expressed his personality. The very act of reconciling two compelling needs—to create *and* to serve—was the sort of fulfillment that gave his whole life meaning. The form his creativeness took also suggested a resistance to exposing his innermost self, as any writer must: with his camera, he could reproduce reality objectively, even while relating the part with the whole, the detail with the totality.

When his father died, Hammarskjold took over his vacant seat in the Swedish Academy, the eighteen members of which make the annual award of the Nobel Prize for literature. It was the first time a son had been called upon to succeed his father since the Academy was formed, in the late eighteenth century. Hammarskjold threw himself into the task. And, on two occasions at least, it appeared as if his personal influence lay behind the selection of the winners.

In 1960 he backed the claims of St.-John Perse, who had given up a diplomat's career to become a poet. That was not the only reason why Hammarskjold developed a special feeling for Perse: his poetry so affected Hammarskjold that in 1960 he translated a volume, entitled *Chronique*, from the French into Swedish. Some critics acclaimed the translation as a poetic work in its own right.

Two years earlier Hammarskjold had, by all accounts, backed the selection of Boris Pasternak for the 1958 Nobel Prize, and had helped draft the citation of the Russian poet's literary merits. Pasternak's *Dr. Zhivago*, with its overtones of criticism toward the

Soviet system, had provoked something of a political uproar in Russia, culminating with the disgrace of the author. What it was about *Dr. Zhivago* that impressed Hammarskjold so much has never emerged clearly. The literary merit of both the book and its poems is arguable, and few have maintained that in itself it could have been the reason for the award. The likelihood is that Hammarskjold probably was moved more by Pasternak's theme of anti-violence and his conscious defiance of the pressures against free expression in the Soviet Union.

Joseph P. Lash, in his first-rate biography of Hammarskjold, tells how he raised the issue of the Nobel Prize award to Pasternak in his meetings with Khrushchev and other Soviet leaders in 1959. Evidently the Secretary-General surmised that the Russians might have resented the backing he had given Pasternak. Lash relates:

> To clear the air he [Hammarskjold] himself at his first dinner with the Soviet leaders brought up the fact that he had been a member of the committee which had awarded the prize to Pasternak. There was a moment of startled silence which [Deputy Premier Anastas] Mikoyan broke by asking how the Secretary-General of the U.N. could identify himself with a book like *Dr. Zhivago* which voiced reactionary views, and Mikoyan cited one or two offending passages.
>
> Not the least abashed, Hammarskjold recalled that on a previous occasion Mikoyan had sung the praises of Dostoevsky. Did that mean Mikoyan approved of the killing of old ladies, he asked in a reference to *Crime and Punishment*. Khrushchev roared with laughter. Hammarskjold had made his point that art was something different from propaganda.*

Hammarskjold wrote his own speeches, making them sound like the dry, mechanical report of a businessman addressing his stockholders.

He deliberately chose flat, rather gray words and phrases so as to defy black-and-white interpretations. Even on great issues—as when pleading for the future of the United Nations—his voice never varied in tone, his face remained expressionless.

One trick of his occasionally betrayed his feelings to those who

* Joseph P. Lash, *Dag Hammarskjold* (London: Cassell, 1962).

knew him well. He would sit motionless with a pencil held between his forefingers, as if measuring its length. An American journalist, who had been watching him go through the performance for years, commented once to a colleague: "There goes old Dag again, flipping his top."

Hammarskjold could, when he wanted, flip his top in the most elegant fashion. He was guest of honor at a luncheon in London in late 1957, after the full fury of the Suez storm had been spent. Prime Minister Macmillan loaded a nice speech of welcome with the observation that everybody was so happy to see the Secretary-General, particularly as this happened to be the first time he had made an official visit to Great Britain. In his reply, Hammarskjold said he shared the Prime Minister's regret to be making his first official visit to Britain so long after his appointment. But, he said, it was only fair to add that this happened to be the first time he had been officially invited. Macmillan pulled thoughtfully at his cigar.

Dag Hammarskjold was a forward-looking man, who reached into the past for lessons only to help shape the future.

He drew comfort from the warm friendships he had preserved, which, in some cases, stretched back to his childhood. Personal suffering, acts of violence, unexpected deaths—all moved him deeply, and though he succeeded in concealing his feelings most of the time, on occasion they did show through. Always he tried to spend Christmas with U.N. troops on duty in the Middle East before going back to his brothers and friends in Stockholm. When President de Gaulle in July, 1961, rebuffed his offer to help settle the flash Franco-Tunisian dispute over Bizerta, he was hurt, not for himself but for the United Nations.

But Hammarskjold bore no grudges. He accepted Spinoza's advice: "Do not laugh and do not cry, but try to understand."

In a rare moment of personal confession in mid-1961, he gave as his favorite motto: ". . . to hope 'till Hope creates From its own wreck the thing it contemplates."

Perhaps Hammarskjold found all the power and splendor of Shelley's poetic drama embodied in that one poignant line. The symbolism of *Prometheus Unbound* needs no stretching. Lesser leaders than he may well have identified with the captive Prometheus, friend of man, chained in the mountain fastness by Zeus.

When Hammarskjold was fourteen or fifteen someone introduced him to the works of Maurice Maeterlinck, including *The Life of the White Ant.* At once he became fascinated by the organized life of animals.

It was a short step to an active interest in human relations—not in any "Brave New World" sense, but in that of the structure of societies and social orders.

From that chance encounter the trail of Dag Hammarskjold's life wound onward through the affairs of men until, in ironic symmetry, it came to an end near Ndola, in Rhodesia, on an anthill.

12 The Investigation: *Possible Causes of the Crash*

On that clear and windless Sunday night, about one minute after passing west over Ndola, the DC-6B began its wide, descending procedure turn to the *right* before coming in to land.

The pilot, with the lights of the town behind him and bush ahead, was over a "black hole." Then, evidently intending a visual landing, he swung around to the left for a full turn that would enable him to double back on his tracks and complete his shallow descent to the critical height of the runway.

Before completing its full left turn to course, the *Albertina* was very nearly skimming the trees of the forest—anything from 200 to 500 feet lower than it should have been—with the airport lights obscured by an intervening ridge of high ground.

In all respects other than its height, the aircraft seemed to be in a normal approach position. The landing wheels were lowered and locked. Engines seem to have been working under normal approach power, with no signs of excessive speed. The flaps were in an intermediate (30 degrees) position, usual for that stage of approach. The landing lights were not turned on, but need not have been if the pilot thought he had 500 feet or so to spare. The aircraft, still slightly banked to the left, had straightened out almost to level flight or to a very shallow angle of between 1 and 5 degrees.

Then something happened.

Moments later the propellers cut the treetops, leaving as imprints the rubber of the de-icing boots. Then the angle of descent began to increase, and with it, the list to the left. The wing tip was torn off, and, in the next few seconds, more and more of the wing was ripped away by the sturdy trees—as far inward, almost, as the number one engine.

Nearly eight hundred nightmare feet beyond the initial brush with the trees, the stub of the *Albertina*'s left wing hit the base of an anthill. The aircraft swung around, cartwheeling leftward until it came to fiery rest facing the way it had come. As it cut its swath through the forest the right wing disintegrated too, and the tanks spewed gasoline in all directions.

The fire that followed—flashing back nearly four hundred feet along the trail of petrol—lit up the Mufulira sky in a hopeless call for help.

That was how it happened.

Why did it happen?

The Rhodesian and U.N. investigating commissions have failed to give a definite answer.

In February, 1962, the report of the Federal Rhodesian commission expressed the view that "pilot error" was the probable cause. The Rhodesians reached that conclusion by eliminating—to their satisfaction—other possible explanations, including sabotage. The idea of a ground attack, or a strike by a pro-Katangan sky marauder, they dismissed. In a rare sally into the field of political appraisal the commission noted: "No reason was suggested, and we cannot think of one, why anyone should have wanted to attack it as it carried Mr. Hammarskjold on the mission he was then undertaking."

In May, 1962, however, the U.N. commission returned what amounted to an open verdict on almost all the various theories.

It brushed aside the suggestion of "pilot error" with the comment: "The Commission, while it cannot exclude this possibility, has found no indication that this was the probable cause of the crash." The group said sabotage "cannot be excluded." It noted that the *Albertina* had been unguarded at Ndjili, that access to it had been possible and that "there are many possible methods of sabotage." It declined, also, to rule out air or ground attack, or even some suddenly induced incapacity of the pilots. Many times over, the U.N. men stressed they could discover no evidence to justify the acceptance of one suggested cause in preference to others. "It was impossible," the report added, "to establish an order of priority among them [the causes]."

The two commissions agreed that Hallonquist had sacrificed some safety for the sake of security in preparing, and conducting, his flight.

The Rhodesian report noted:

> He flew over a large distance in Africa without any person, other than the crew, knowing what his route or intentions were; he did not take the precaution of filing a proper flight plan or even a proper passenger manifest; he undertook the flight in conditions of radio silence and with no apparent information on the weather conditions en route; he did not avail himself of any navigation aids en route which would have been available on request; he did not report his presence on the Nairobi Flight Information Region.

With studied dispassion the Rhodesians commented: "We express no opinion on whether security measures justified these actions."

And, just as pointedly, they added that Lansdowne's plane, which flew openly, directly and with full, forward radio contact, arrived at its destination "without incident."

The U.N. report accepted that the danger of attack by the Lone Ranger was a valid explanation for the decision to file no accurate flight plan or to advise Salisbury of departure time. It regretted that Hallonquist had given no advance outline of his route to O.N.U.C. But it asserted that Ambassador Riches' telegram to Lord Alport, stating as it had that "flight details will be notified direct from the aircraft," should have made it obvious to the Rhodesians not to expect a flight plan. Alport's failure to advise the Federal aviation authorities of the text of Riches' message was noted, but with a thundering lack of comment.

Technically, the precise task of the Rhodesian commission was to investigate "the cause of and circumstances surrounding the accident involving aircraft SE-BDY near Ndola during the night of 17th September, 1961, including any matter or circumstances relating to the preparation for and flight of the aircraft, the accident, the deaths of the occupants and the accident."

Sir John Clayden's group heard the evidence of 120 witnesses during public hearings at Ndola and Salisbury in January. It examined technical reports prepared by experts on various aspects of the flight and crash. The members of the commission inspected the scene of the tragedy on the ground and from the air. With great thoroughness they studied all the relevant factors of geography, weather, terrain, flight preparation, security and causes of death. In a thirty-two page report the commission also summarized and analyzed the evidence offered by thirty-one men and women classified as eyewitnesses.

Most of the groundwork had been carried out for the commission by Colonel Barber's Board of Inquiry, which had sat from September 19 to November 2, 1961. The Rhodesian specialists, in the full gaze of the international observers, checked and cross-checked almost every bit of material evidence and information that came their way. Some of their studies on specific technical aspects were repeated independently abroad, notably in the United States and Sweden.

The Rhodesians—through the offices of Great Britain—invited both the United Nations and the Swedish Government to be represented on the Clayden commission, but the invitations were very politely declined. The U.N. authorities, like the Swedes, would have preferred an international investigation from the start; as they did not get one, they considered the common interest of establishing the truth would be best served by keeping the two inquiries separate.

The U.N. team began work in New York in mid-December. It went on in January to Leopoldville, in February to Salisbury and Ndola, and it ended up in March—after another spell in Salisbury—in Geneva. Altogether eighty-eight witnesses appeared before it, and of these twenty-four had not given evidence to the Rhodesian commission.

The chairmen of the two investigating groups—Sir John Clayden and Rishikesh Shaha—consulted from time to time to dovetail their work and to arrange for the exchange of information, evidence and records, and for other forms of cooperation. They sought to avoid the ever-present possibilities of conflict—possibilities deriving from the nature of the tragedy. Rightly or wrongly, Hammarskjold—and the world body he represented—had become subjects of deep controversy, and the attitudes of some of those who had parts to play in the investigations inevitably were colored by political factors.

The waters therefore appeared deep and dark, and it was to the credit of the two investigating authorities that they managed to steer safely through the rocks that menaced them.

Nonetheless there were difficulties and differences aplenty.

One important problem related to the fact that witnesses who appeared before the U.N. commission in Federal territory were not protected by the laws of privilege. The Rhodesian Government pledged, without prejudging the legalities involved, that it would take no action against anyone by reason of his appearance or testimony before the international commission. This was a welcome assurance, but it did not protect witnesses from legal processes that might be instituted privately. Inevitably it was bound to be an inhibiting factor, and one the effects of which could not be measured.

Another difficulty concerned the tests carried out on some of the remains of the *Albertina*. The most important stemmed from the strong suspicion on the part of the Swedish Government and others that Hammarskjold's plane might have been shot down from the ground or in the air, or blown up by a time bomb or similar device. The Rhodesians first, then the U.N. commission, were asked during the inquiries to melt down the fused blocks of the debris of the *Albertina*—its wings and fuselage—in order to establish if any foreign bodies like bullets, shell fragments or other explosives were present. The Rhodesians refused to do this, on the grounds that they feared subsequent accusations of destroying evidence in the process. However, the U.N. commission agreed to undertake the laborious task, and after consultation with Acting Secretary-General U Thant, a Swiss forensic expert was brought in to perform the tests.

The nominee was Professor Max Frei-Sulzer, Chief of the Scientific Department of the Zurich police, and head of the science criminology faculty of the University of Zurich. Frei-Sulzer was invited to examine all the evidence gathered by both commissions and to give his own views on the possible causes of the crash in the light of his experience and his special studies of the debris. Many of his tests were carried out—with the help, and in the presence, of the Rhodesian authorities in Ndola, during the first two weeks in March.

The difference between the commissions—methodological and perhaps political—emerged in their reports assessing the possible causes of the crash that had killed Dag Hammarskjold.

Before turning to specific suggested causes, the two commissions offered several general observations regarding the search for an explanation for the crash. They maintained that all available evidence showed the *Albertina* had, in fact, meant to land at Ndola. The Rhodesians had considered that the path of the aircraft showed the pilot to have been making a visual descent—whereas the U.N. men noted that Transair pilots are under standing orders to make an instrument approach when using an airfield for the first time. Both considered the crew of the *Albertina* to be highly competent and in every way qualified to perform their mission, including a night landing at a strange airfield. The Rhodesians attached far less importance to the danger of an attack by the Lone Ranger than did the U.N. commission. Similarly, the opportunity for sabotage afforded by the lack of special security precautions at Ndjili worried the U.N. investigators more than it did the Rhodesians.

The words of Sergeant Julien were examined closely by both groups, but without much weight being given to them, because of his condition and the possibility of amnesia. His references to "the runway," "great speed" and, at one point, "an explosion" before the crash were dismissed as remembered impressions. The same explanation was advanced for Julien's suggestions that Hammarskjold had "changed his mind" or said "turn back." On this point the Rhodesian report said:

> It seems likely that the phrase "changed his mind" was the witness's interpretation from the words "turn back" or "go back." These words could not have been said after the crash for the evidence shows that Mr. Hammarskjold died instantaneously. So the words must have been said in the aircraft. On both versions given the words were said before the explosion.
>
> There is nothing to indicate that Mr. Hammarskjold, apart from anything connected with the crash, would be likely to have changed his plan to land. What seems likely is that the first impact with the tree tops gave the impression to Mr. Hammarskjold that there was some designed obstruction to his landing, and that he then shouted words such as "go back."

The two investigating commissions discussed twelve possible causes of the crash.

Damage at Elizabethville:

The exhaust pipe pierced by a bullet was replaced at Ndjili. Transair engineers satisfied both commissions that no other trace of damage was found; for example, from explosive bullets. A bullet hole in the cowling of number two port engine had done no harm. What had happened at Elizabethville had not, they concluded, contributed to the crash in any way.

Circumstances of the flight:

In themselves the security precautions did not cause the accident. The detour taken by Hallonquist was not difficult to fly. Even if Litton or Aahreus were tired, in a journey of six and a half hours they could have made use of the available sleeping accommodations. Hallonquist himself had had twenty-four hours of rest.

Sabotage:

According to the Rhodesian argument, sabotage action with Hammarskjold as the intended victim would have had to take place at Leopoldville. True, some sort of time bomb could have been placed in the undercarriage wells while the plane stood unguarded.

But nothing had showed up in the wreckage to suggest explosive damage to the undercarriage. The cabin had been checked before take-off. None of the occupants would willfully have taken a bomb aboard. If a bomb had been secreted in the personal luggage of an occupant, signs of an explosion would have been evident at some point short of the crash, or at the scene itself. Moreover, few unauthorized persons could have known Hammarskjold meant to be aboard, how long the flight would last or where the plane was heading. All this led the Federal commission to declare: "We find no grounds for attributing the crash to sabotage."

U.N. investigators recognized that chances for saboteurs did exist, and refused to rule out the suggestion. They took close account of three distinct possibilities: (a) interference with the plane's vital braking, rudder or undercarriage control mechanisms (b) use of a time bomb, and (c) skillful installation of an infernal machine linked with one or another of the control mechanisms, which, when operated, would detonate the bomb. Yet—the U.N. commission noted—each one of these methods might have been expected to leave some traces, even allowing for the fact that four-fifths of the material that went into the *Albertina* had been totally destroyed. No evidence came to light to support any one of these theories. Yet this lack of proof in itself did not eliminate sabotage as a factor.

Erroneous communication from Ndola:

Traffic Controller Martin's talks with the pilot had not been tape-recorded. The account he gave of the exchanges came from his memory and notes. He had been in a position to mislead the pilot by providing an incorrect altimeter check. But the Rhodesian commission reported the figure he said he gave corresponded with the readings on the *Albertina's* instruments, and was accurate. Martin had reported his conversations with the *Albertina* to Salisbury before it had been known that the plane had crashed; this report tallied with his evidence before the commission. "There is nothing to suggest that any but proper information was given to the aircraft," the Rhodesians ruled.

The U.N. commission expressed no opinion about the accuracy or otherwise of the information passed by Martin to the *Albertina.* It observed, however, that instrument approach charts for Ndola do not show terrain contours or elevation heights in the approach area. If Hallonquest had descended to 5,000 feet during his procedure turn, he might not, as a consequence, have realized that his safety margin was so small. The report commented: "The possibility cannot, therefore, be completely excluded that the disaster may have resulted indirectly from incomplete information supplied to the pilot for use at this most critical phase of his flight to Ndola."

Mechanical failure:

The Rhodesian and U.N. reports both noted the DC-6B was in very good condition, with its four Pratt & Whitney engines under power, at the time of the crash. Even with some degree of engine failure, the aircraft could have stayed aloft. There was plenty of fuel, and no sign of mechanical or structural defect; and even if there had been, the pilots probably would have had time to signal the control tower. All the investigators set aside this possibility as unlikely.

Defective altimeters:

All three altimeters in use were set approximately to the barometric reading given by Ndola Control. All were damaged in the crash. But checks by the United States Civil Aeronautics Board, and the Kollsman Instrument Corporation, which manufactured the instruments, failed to reveal any precrash defect. Neither commission considered this to be the cause.

Fire in flight:

Two hand fire-extinguishers found to be discharged were closely examined to establish if they had been used by hand or released by heat. No absolute certainty emerged on the point. Both commissions discounted the likelihood of an ordinary fire in flight, or one that might have been caused by a sudden explosion. Flames during flight would have left horizontal streaks on parts of the plane, and the treetops would have been scorched; but there were no signs of these. It was inconceivable that experienced pilots would have failed to take emergency action, such as alerting ground control, crash-landing, decompressing the cabin or retracting the undercarriage. And even a sudden explosion that knocked out the pilots would have left some evidence in the search area. None was found.

Pilot incapacity:

This idea was suggested as a possible explanation by Colonel Barber's specialists, but neither the Rhodesian nor the U.N. commission considered it likely on the basis of available evidence. The Rhodesians noted: "The chances of simultaneous incapacitation [of the three pilots] are, in our view, so remote that that possibility can be dismissed." The U.N. group also expressed its satisfaction that pilot fatigue could not have been a factor, because there were facilities for sleep if any of the crew was weary.

Use of wrong landing chart:

Barber's theory that Hallonquist somehow "may have got mixed up" between the approaches to *Ndola* and to *Ndolo* was rejected by both commissions after close examination. The one Jeppesen Manual that was found did not have the Ndola chart in it—but the very absence of the chart was taken as a strong indication that it was being used. Other Jeppesen Manuals in the plane, like the loose-leaf chart, may have been destroyed in the fire. One of the three U.S. Air Force manuals aboard was opened at the chart showing *Ndolo,* with *Ndola's* elevation and other information written on it in green ink, but the handwriting did not correspond to that of any of the pilots.

The Rhodesians did consider there was something more than coincidence in the discovery of these manuals lying about loose when, normally, pilots keep such aids in bags. But they recalled that Hallonquist, in private conversations, had shown himself aware of Ndola's altitude. And they were convinced a pilot of his experience would at once have been aware of the differences in approach procedures, especially as the direction of descent is to the east for *Ndolo* and to the west for *Ndola.* "We do not consider that the pilots were misled by an *Ndolo* chart but it may well be that there was no *Ndola* chart in the aircraft," the members of the commission said.

In the U.N. view, Hallonquist had shown he was aware of the *Ndola* approach procedure because, generally, he was following it. Other topographical features, such as the Congo River alongside Ndolo, would have made the chance of confusing the two airfields remote. The international group thought Hallonquist had most likely removed the Ndola chart and clipped it to his map board.

Action from the ground:

Neither the Rhodesians nor the U.N. investigators found evidence to support the theory that a ground attacker might have shot down the DC-6B. Any such action would have called for a concentration of fire, and there was no direct or indirect indication showing bullet damage, pilot injury or the presence of strangers in the bush.

The Rhodesians argued further that an attacker could not easily have anticipated the *Albertina* would be off-course—and therefore could not have been able to site his guns with precision. But to this the U.N. group replied that (a) most Ndola-bound aircraft use roughly the same approach route; (b) Hammarskjold's plane signaled its estimated arrival time about two hours in advance; and (c) this and other messages could have been intercepted. In the U.N. view, therefore, the possibility of ground attack could not be excluded.

Action by other aircraft:

The Federal commission flatly ruled out the idea that another plane might have shot or forced down the *Albertina*. Although the U.N. group cautiously declined to exclude the idea, it could find no substantial evidence to support the theory. Both investigated the possibility at length and reported their conclusions in detail. And both emphasized that very careful examination of the wreckage and bodies disclosed no marks, holes or wounds caused by bullets fired through rifled barrels or by rockets. Certain holes found in parts of the aircraft were proved to have been for rivets and not caused by bullets, as first suspected. One unexplained hole in the right-hand window frame of the cockpit was too small for a bullet, and later spectrographic examination of the metal yielded no traces of a foreign projectile.

The bullets in the bodies patently had not been fired but had come from ammunition carried by persons on the plane. And finally, it was established by specialists that no rocket or other projectile could have hit the *Albertina* without exploding. Yet nothing was found in the crash area to show that some part of the aircraft had blown off, or to suggest shell or rocket fragments.

The Rhodesians started out by offering the opinion that there was no obvious reason why an assassin should have wanted to attack Hammarskjold while he was engaged on a peace mission. They sought also to eliminate the possibility that any aircraft known to be in the area could have made the attack. Royal Rhodesian Air Force planes and one American military aircraft at Ndola had all been grounded that night. No Congolese plane outside Katanga was capable of offensive action. In Katanga itself, Delin's Lone Ranger, carrying two 7.62-mm. machine guns, was reported not to have left its Kolwezi base 230 miles from Ndola. The commission noted that the Fouga sometimes used a second airfield, which Delin said was still farther away from Ndola than Kolwezi. The effective range of the Fouga, allowing five minutes for attack, was given as 135 miles, and anyway, Kolwezi was not equipped for night operations. The commission said it had no reason to doubt the evidence voluntarily given by Delin, who presented himself for further questioning when certain information reached the court that cast doubt on his earlier testimony.

The U.N. commission observed however that, on the subject of the Lone Ranger, Delin's evidence was "not entirely conclusive," since he admitted having taken off once from an unpaved track. Evidently, then, there was nothing to have stopped his using a track within range of Ndola, even though his presence near Ndola on the night of the crash could not be established. The U.N. group dismissed the Rhodesian statement that no other plane could have been in the area at the time of the crash. Ndola had maintained no radar watch that night, the U.N. commission reported, and therefore the possibility of an unknown aircraft's having been in the air could not be discarded.

Seven witnesses did, in fact, tell the Rhodesian commission

of a second plane on the night of the tragedy. The Rhodesian report described one of the witnesses as unworthy of consideration, and three others gave times "which could have no references at all to the time of arrival and crash" of the *Albertina*. And the three charcoal-burners, who claimed to have seen a small and a large aircraft close together just before the explosions, were rejected by the Rhodesians as "unsatisfactory" witnesses, whose evidence was said to be contradictory, confused and improbable.

The U.N. report took a somewhat different view of these witnesses' evidence. In an attempt to get a clearer understanding of their testimony the commission visited with the witnesses the spots from which they said they had seen the two planes. The conclusion was that these people were sincere but mistaken in the accounts they had given of their observations. The U.N. report theorized that the red, flashing anticollision beacon on the DC-6B's high tail fin probably had been the smaller, second plane that several Africans claimed to have seen.

This possibility seems supported by testimony that the smaller "plane" flew above and behind the larger machine. It does not explain the claim of some witnesses that the small plane flew away after the crash. But, said the U.N. report, misinterpretations or memory lapses might account for the discrepancy. In addition, certain witnesses might have been moved by their feelings of political hostility toward the Welensky regime.

The Rhodesians advanced two further arguments to dispel the widely held suspicions of an air attack on the *Albertina*. Firstly, they noted that no signal had been made to ground control reporting what was going on. Unless both pilots were "instantaneously killed or the wireless put out of action," some sort of message should have been possible. The second argument related to the "extreme difficulty of interception at night." Any attacker would have had to know roughly when the *Albertina* was due, and then would have had to position himself at least ten minutes in advance. This operation would have had to be carried out in such a way as to attract no attention. Many Ndola authorities heard the *Albertina*, but did not hear a second plane. Moreover, if Hammarskjold's plane had been coming in at a normal approach height "interception would have been difficult enough." But coming in low as the *Albertina* was, "it would have been in an unexpected position and interception would have been all the more difficult." The Rhodesian report then added:

> When it did attack the attack has to be assumed to have been such that either both pilots were disabled, or the aircraft was so put out of control that no communication could be made or emergency action taken. And this had to be done in such a way that no part of the aircraft was blown off, and the aircraft came down apparently in normal descent and under power. Having regard to all these factors we consider that it is clear that the aircraft was not shot down in any way from the air.

The U.N. investigators, lacking proof to the contrary, seemed ready to accept the Rhodesian analysis. They took note of Bo Virving's theory that testimony about sky flashes might flow from the fact that the *Albertina* had been shot down by a rocket-firing plane. But the commission suggested there were more logical explanations for this testimony, and claimed that rocket experts attached to O.N.U.C. strongly doubted the possibility of a rocket attack. The U.N. report concluded: "Had the aircraft been shot down, its descent might have been expected to have been at a steeper angle than that indicated by the path of the crash. Had SE-BDY been attacked and evasive action attempted, the normal reaction of the pilot, if time permitted, would have been to retract the undercarriage and flaps and to apply full engine power. None of these measures was taken."

Pilot error:

The Rhodesians, after eliminating to their satisfaction, other theories, reached the conclusion that "pilot error" had caused the crash. The U.N. men acknowledged "pilot error" could not be excluded, but added at once they found no indication that it was in fact the probable cause. The international group clearly disliked the process of elimination used by the Rhodesians. The U.N.

report said that without proof, no possibility could be excluded and no order of priority set as among the various causes suggested. And there simply was not enough evidence definitely to support any one cause.

As the Federal commission saw it, the *Albertina* had not followed the course laid down for an instrument approach but instead had tried to make a visual descent. There was no reason why Hallonquist should not have done so, the Rhodesians observed. The night was clear. The airport lights had been seen. There was no other traffic.

The report went on to offer reasons for the theory of pilot error:

> The altitude of the aircraft as it crossed over the airport has been taken by us, on the evidence of eye-witnesses, to be about 6,000 feet above sea level. The absence of a report on reaching 6,000 feet, which was asked for, may well have been because the aircraft had reached that altitude when the request was made. It is as certain as can be that the aircraft started to descend soon after it had passed over the airport.
>
> In the country to the west of Ndola there is bush, and after the lights of Ndola were passed and as the descending turn was made to the right there would be blackness ahead. This is what is known in the language of the air as a "black hole."
>
> And if in the course of the turn the aircraft came far too low the slight rise in the ground between the place of the crash and the airport would obscure the lights of the runway, and of Ndola, as the aircraft came back to a course on which those lights might otherwise have been seen to port.
>
> Failure to recognize the dangerous altitude of the aircraft in relation to the airport elevation, and the slightly higher elevation of some of the country to the west, is unexplained in view of the apparent correct settings of the three altimeters and the fact, as far as can be determined, they would have been functioning properly.
>
> It has been strongly urged on us that we should not reach the conclusion that the accident was due to pilot error by considering first other possible causes, dismissing them, and so being left with a cause which can seldom be dismissed in an

> aircraft accident. Obviously suggested causes have to be dealt with in some order. We have given our reasons for saying that other suggested causes were not really possible. And we have given our reasons for concluding that the approach to the airport was made by a visual descending procedure in which the aircraft was brought too low. We cannot say whether that came about as a result of inattention to altimeters or misreading of altimeters. But the conclusion to which we are forced is that the aircraft was allowed by the pilots to descend too low so that it struck the trees and was brought to the ground.

The U.N. investigators were not bound by the rules of evidence of any particular legal system in their search for the truth. Broadly, though, they had to choose between requiring proof beyond reasonable doubt for any suggested explanation, and basing their conclusions on the balance of probabilities. The upshot was that they agreed generally to apply a standard of proof, and each possible cause of the crash was examined in this light. Consequently they declined to accept or reject the idea of pilot error just as, for lack of proof, they declined to accept or reject most of the other explanations.

Nevertheless their skepticism toward the Rhodesian findings emerged clearly in their breakdown of the various forms of pilot error. The group felt Hallonquist had had the correct landing chart before him, that most likely he had read the altimeters correctly and that if he had descended below the accepted 1,000-foot safety level, it probably had been a deliberate act. In plain terms, the international group did not agree with the Rhodesian conclusion of pilot error, and went as far as it felt it could to make this clear.

Professor Frei-Sulzer's fifteen-page appraisal (appended to the U.N. report) dismissed the theories that the *Albertina* might have been sabotaged, shot down, or in any way interfered with when it crashed. His careful examinations showed, he said, that every recognizable fragment recovered from the wreckage and from the remelting processes demonstrably had belonged to the plane or its load. He reported that 3,189 pounds of metal had—with the help of

Colonel Barber, Madders and other Rhodesians—been "cooked" down, checked and rechecked, and that no suspect matter had been found. (Frei-Sulzer insisted that any sort of foul play would certainly have left significant traces.) He added: "The total weight of evidence that speaks *against* sabotage is so overwhelming that this possibility can be eliminated."

Summing up the results of his brief mission—which, he said, had unearthed no new evidence—Frei-Sulzer observed:

> The reexamination of the wreckage in the hangar and the melting down of the fused parts of the wreckage allow to exclude the possibility of hostile actions from the air or from the ground and leave no room for the suggestion of sabotage.
>
> As no evidence of technical failure could be found and considering that the aircraft obviously made a perfectly normal approaching procedure turn and was normally trimmed in the moment of the first impact with the trees, the only abnormal fact was the dangerous low altitude of the aircraft in relation to the airport elevation, probably due to human failure.

13 The Investigation: *Search and Rescue*

The inferno of the *Albertina* raged through the sad September night before an audience of shadows in the silent forest.

Away from Dola Hill, the world for the most part moved serenely, passively, on, even while fears for the safety of the DC-6B were rising.

Ndola Control and Lansdowne's plane both tried, but failed, to speak to Hallonquist after his last radio call at 10:10. To the Rhodesians this suggested, as one senior official put it, that the pilot had "pushed off" somewhere else. To Lansdowne it suggested disaster.

Police near Ndola spotted the Mufulira flash. To them it warranted an investigation, which proved fruitless. To the aviation authorities it was not worth pursuing until daybreak, and even then they dallied.

Ndola initiated "overdue" action eighty-two minutes after the *Albertina* was expected to land—or fifty-two minutes later than the regulations prescribe.

Salisbury initiated a "distress" phase four hours and thirty-seven minutes after the plane was declared overdue.

Air search and rescue action began *more than eight hours after Hammarskjold's plane vanished and more than three hours after the "distress" phase began.*

Finally, it took another five hours or so to sight the wreckage.

What went wrong? Why did it all take so long?

The whole fantastic story of what happened behind the scenes of Rhodesia's air control system, both before and after the *Alber-*

tina vanished, was told in close detail by both investigating commissions.

Their reports, taken together, give an impression of muddle and political confusion in high places, and of buck-passing and inertia in lower ones.

One of the most remarkable features was the contrast between the testimonies of Lord Alport and Lord Lansdowne, who had talked together at Ndola while waiting for Hammarskjold to arrive. Alport told the Federal commission he had thought "something must have caused Mr. Hammarskjold to change his mind and to decide not to land at Ndola as previously intended." His speculations influenced the actions of Airport Manager Williams. Lansdowne emphasized to the U.N. group: "I am absolutely convinced in my own mind, from the conversations I had with the late Secretary-General, that he was determined to go to Ndola and to put himself at the disposal of Mr. Tshombe for the talks which he regarded as so important. . . . So far as I am concerned, this was a plan that the Secretary-General had made and that he was determined to carry out." Unlike Alport and the officials around him, Lansdowne became "extremely apprehensive" when he learned that contact had been lost with Hammarskjold's plane.

Both commissions lashed the Rhodesian authorities for their slow recognition that the DC-6B might have run into trouble, and for the fifteen hours it took them to locate the scene of the crash. They agreed Julien's life might have been saved and the riddle of the disaster thereby solved if Rhodesian responses had been quicker. But they differed over whether Hammarskjold's own life could have been prolonged. The Federal report said he had been killed outright. But the U.N. men drew attention to Swedish medical evidence suggesting he had lived a while longer and could have been helped.

In examining the reasons for the tardiness of the search and rescue action, the Rhodesian investigators pinpointed much of the blame on one man—Williams, who they said should have displayed greater initiative and urgency after the *Albertina*'s failure to land. All other Federal authorities—civil aviation, police and air force—were said to have acted as promptly as could have been expected in the circumstances.

The U.N. commission took another line. It criticized Williams' colleagues in Ndola and Salisbury, the Federal Department of Civil Aviation, and Alport. The slow start of search and rescue action was attributed to what the report called "shortcomings in liaison and cooperation" and to "lack of initiative and diligence" on the part of the aviation officials involved. The Department of Civil Aviation was blamed for the delay in launching an air search. And Alport's political reflections were regretted, because they had had the effect of diverting the authorities from their proper duty of immediately beginning a hunt.

The commissions outlined the three-phase procedure for search and rescue action supposed to operate in the Federation in any emergency involving a civil airplane.

The first, "Uncertainty Phase" (INCERFA), begins thirty minutes after an incoming plane fails to report "all's well" or fails to land at the time estimated.

The second, "Alert Phase" (ALERFA), applies when radio contact is lost, when trouble is reported, when a forced landing seems imminent or when a plane fails unaccountably to arrive five minutes after landing clearance has been given.

The third, "Distress Phase" (DETRESFA), follows ALERFA when the absence of news indicates danger, when a fuel shortage is suspected or when a forced landing seems probable.

One broad exception applies to each phase: when there is reasonable certainty that the plane and its occupants are safe, emergency action need not be taken. However, any suspicion of grave and imminent peril would demand immediate air and ground search. The whole scheme normally hinges on the cooperation of pilots, who are expected to file detailed flight plans in advance and to maintain regular radio contact with the traffic control authorities.

During the INCERFA phase a Civil Air Search Officer should be appointed. And when DETRESFA begins the Royal Rhodesian Air Force is supposed to be notified and asked to begin searching.

Differing accounts were given by the Rhodesian and U.N. commissions regarding the search and rescue action taken after Hammarskjold's plane disappeared. They are here set forth separately, in shortened form, to facilitate understanding of exactly what happened.

The Rhodesian Report:

Air Traffic Controller Martin was told to expect the arrival of Hammarskjold's plane by "responsible people on the ground," by the Salisbury Flight Information Center, and by Hallonquist himself. He was given estimated times of arrival ranging between 10:20 and 10:35. And the latest estimated landing time—10:20—seemed to be confirmed at 10:10 when the *Albertina* passed overhead.

Martin, therefore, would have been bound to issue the first INCERFA signal at about 10:50 unless, under the exception, he was sure the silent and missing *Albertina* was safe. In fact, he waited fifty-two minutes before doing so. The report explains why:

> He [Martin] was at all material times in contact with and under the instructions of the Airport Manager, Mr. J. H. Williams. Mr. Martin's personal impression at the time, that the aircraft had refrained from reporting termination of its authorized descent because it was purposely holding off to enable the Secretary-General to complete radio communication with a base outside Rhodesia, was genuinely held, and sufficiently explains why he found no reason to question the prevailing belief expressed to him by Mr. Williams that the aircraft was holding off or had proceeded to some other destination.

Williams himself had returned to Ndola from vacation September 16 and was due to report back for duty only on Monday morning. But he was called in on Sunday to help in the arrangements for the cease-fire talks, which were to have been held in his office. From mid-afternoon on Tshombe and Lord Alport were using that office. From their talk, Williams formed the impression they were doubtful whether Hammarskjold would come in at all.

Then Lansdowne arrived with the information that Hammarskjold was, after all, on his way and would land only after he, Lansdowne, had taken off.

Then the passage overhead of the *Albertina,* on a heading toward Leopoldville, was notified to Williams. He saw Lansdowne depart. Next he learned from Martin that the *Albertina* was not answering signals. He checked with Salisbury and Lusaka, while continuing to call Hammarskjold's plane. Later he asked Salisbury to contact Leopoldville for news. By 1:15 there still was no word, and so he decided to return to his hotel, leaving orders to be advised if anything became known. No thought of peril crossed his mind. He believed the nature of Hammarskjold's mission somehow explained the silence of the *Albertina.*

In that belief he was not alone. Lord Alport confessed he thought Hammarskjold had at the last moment abandoned the idea of meeting Tshombe because of some breach of the truce (which, in fact, had not yet begun). "This and other speculations Lord Alport told us he communicated to Mr. Williams," the commissioners said. "We can well understand that the possibility of accident did not, up to his departure from the aerodrome, present itself to the mind of Mr. Williams, and that the overdue action already initiated was adequate in the circumstances."

Meantime, a few minutes after the *Albertina* had flown over Ndola, a patrolling police officer saw a flash or glow in the northwestern sky. Assistant Inspector Marius Uranus van Wyk turned in a report of this to the Ndola police station. He did not at once associate it with the plane because bush fires and lightning flashes were common in the area at that time of the year. But later in the night another officer, Assistant Inspector Adrian Begg, thought the sky flash sufficiently important to report it to the airport. At 1:30 the duty communications man referred Begg to Williams at his hotel, after trying vainly to telephone the Airport Manager. Together with Assistant Inspector John Pennock, Begg called on Williams and told him of the flash.

Williams said he thought nothing could be done about this

until first light—two hours and ten minutes later. The police officers left, saying they would investigate further. A ground patrol was sent out to the area, but nothing was found.

"It was not until 0700 [7 a.m.] (over three hours after first light) that Mr. Williams resumed duty as Airport Manager at Ndola, to find that Flight Information Center, Salisbury, had originated the Distress Phase signal at 0445 [4:45 a.m.]," the report said.

> It is, we think, a matter for comment that Mr. Williams' implied intention to initiate action at first light was not carried into practice. Though Mr. Williams did not suggest that it affected his action we have taken into account the fact that his official return from leave did not require his attendance at the airport until his normal duty time on that morning, but his part in the arrangements on the previous day and his acceptance of the police report as properly made to him, imposed upon him, as we see the matter now, an obligation to accept as from the time of his actual return the responsibility normally borne by the Airport Manager during his duty times.

The commission said it felt Salisbury would at once have authorized the Royal Rhodesian Air Force to search for the vanished plane if at dawn Williams had reported fears for its safety, citing among other reasons the flash in the sky.

During the night too, a second clue to the fate of the *Albertina* was observed by police. Assistant Inspector Nigel Vaughan was on a car patrol heading from Mokambo to Mufulira, 10 miles away, when he saw a sudden light in the sky and what seemed to be a falling object. (This was about an hour after the crash, but he may have been looking at a bursting gas container during the fire.) Upon being told at Mufulira that a plane was overdue, Vaughan reported what he had seen. Two patrols were sent out at once toward the area, and a third made an extensive search next morning—but all without result.

The information provided by van Wyk and Vaughan was plotted on a map next day while an air search was being mounted. The map was used by Flying Officer Gerald Craxford when he took his Provost spotter up, about 12:45. He located the site of the crash twenty-five minutes later.

Summing up, the commission remarked that a call for an air search involves a big responsibility: it may result in a dispersal of planes on fruitless errands just when they are needed elsewhere for more pressing purposes. But it said the report from van Wyk came from a responsible officer and was considered by his superiors important enough to warrant a ground hunt. Ordinarily, what he had seen might reasonably have been attributed to a bush fire or to lightning. Yet the coincidence of its timing in relation to the silence of the *Albertina* seemed to the commission "to make it a clear warning that an urgent situation had arisen."

The commissioners continued:

> When to this is added the feature that a defined segmental area within a radius of only a few minutes of flight was required to be searched for investigation of the report we think that initiative on the part of so responsible an officer as an Airport Manager would have caused him to invite Rescue Coordination Center, Salisbury, to authorize one of the available Royal Rhodesian Air Force aircraft to undertake the task. Discovery of the crash site might then have been made some hours before it was and the living survivor been given succour before further exposure to the tropical sun had aggravated the burns sustained in the crash.

The U.N. Report:

The investigators found that delays took place in proclaiming the "uncertainty" and "distress" phases and in starting an air search.

They did not agree with the Rhodesian commission that these hold-ups were attributable solely to "the mind of Mr. Williams." Alport, in their view, shared the responsibility, for two reasons:

Firstly, Williams explained that his lack of concern over the *Albertina*'s silence flowed from the evident abnormality of its behavior, its failure to forward a flight plan and so on. The international group commented drily:

> At least some of the mystery which surrounded the flight of SE-BDY in the mind of the Airport Manager might have

> been dispelled if he had been adequately informed of the signal announcing the departure of the Secretary-General for Ndola addressed by Ambassador Riches to Lord Alport . . . It will be recalled that in this signal Ambassador Riches specifically stated that "flight details will be notified direct from the aircraft." However the actual text of the signal, and in particular the sentence quoted above, was not shown to the Department of Civil Aviation and to the aviation officials who in fact received the flight details from the aircraft.

Secondly, Williams was influenced in his actions by regrettable "impressions of a political nature" given by Alport. The High Commissioner had at more than one stage of the overdue period advanced his own theories to explain the *Albertina*'s failure to land. Alport's impression that Hammarskjold might have diverted was not only groundless but also in contradiction to Lansdowne's conviction that Hammarskjold was determined to land.

The commissioners argued that Salisbury's failure to issue the DETRESFA signal showed that "the attitude of mind" of Williams was shared by officials there as well. They said this was shown in statements by (a) the Airport Manager, who told Colonel Barber that at 11:20 p.m. SE-BDY had flown over Ndola and "pushed off again;" (b) the Duty Controller, who testified he had been told by Deputy High Commissioner Scott that "it was quite likely that the aircraft was returning to Leopoldville;" and (c) the Senior Air Traffic Controller, who said "had this been a normal flight . . . . I think we might have gone into the alert stage."

The evidence of Rhodesian officials was rejected by the U.N. group on other counts too. A claim that Hallonquist was unduly secretive about his intentions was declared baseless. The Rhodesian suggestion that other U.N. planes often violated safety rules was dismissed as irrelevant. It was also argued that DETRESFA should properly not have been issued until Leopoldville had confirmed Hammarskjold's failure to return. But this too was rejected as a groundless excuse.

The police report of the Mufulira flash reached Ndola Airport seven hours before the air search got going. The U.N. group agreed with the Rhodesian commissioners that the news should have been regarded by all concerned as a red flag signaling danger ahead. But it disagreed with the Rhodesians that Williams alone was to blame for failing to act on the warning: the Ndola Controller had advised Salisbury of the police report at 4:45 a.m.

Eight minutes later Salisbury put out the DETRESFA signal. At that point the Royal Rhodesian Air Force should have been asked to help in an air search. In fact, the request was made only three hours later.

"It is true that the Director of Civil Aviation testified that it was only at 0700 [7 a.m.] that he had been informed of the[Ndola] signal," the U.N. report commented. "This, however, in the Commission's view cannot absolve the Federal Department of Civil Aviation of the responsibility for the delay in the initiation of an air search."

Summing up the Rhodesian performance in carrying out search and rescue action, the U.N. commission said:

> Although SE-BDY crashed 9½ miles from an airfield on which eighteen military aircraft capable of carrying out an air search were stationed, the wreckage was located by the Rhodesian authorities only fifteen hours after the crash and more than nine hours after first light on 18 September, 1961.
>
> The Commission is fully aware of the difficulty of conducting an air search over an area covered with bush and forest. It believes, nevertheless, that in the present case the delay in commencing search and rescue operations was increased by shortcoming in liaison and cooperation between the aviation officials concerned, by lack of initiative and diligence on their part and by delay in applying the prescribed procedures.
>
> Undue weight appeared to be attached to the groundless impression that the Secretary-General had changed his mind after flying over Ndola and decided to land at another airport without informing the Ndola tower. Had that degree of diligence been shown which might have been expected in the circumstances, it is possible that the crash would have been discovered at an earlier hour and Sgt. Julien's chances of survival materially improved. Had he survived, not only would

one life have been saved but also a possible source of direct knowledge of the conditions and circumstances surrounding the tragedy.

The reports of both the Rhodesian and U.N. commissions were curiously silent about one unexplained episode of the search and rescue operations. Details of it came to light during both the private and public phases of the Rhodesian investigations, but neither commission seemed to attach much significance to them.

Colonel Ben Matlick, the American air attaché at Leopoldville who had been named searchmaster, flew into Ndola shortly after 10 a.m. Monday and placed all available U.S. Air Force planes at the disposal of the Rhodesians. (At the time there were three American pilots and their planes at Ndola; one had been there since the previous night.) However, Matlick's offer was not accepted by the commanding officer of the R.R.A.F., evidently because the Rhodesians felt no great wish to have foreign planes scouring their territory.

Matlick, incidentally, was among the first to arrive at the scene of the crash when it was located three hours after his arrival, and was also among those who helped to identify Hammarskjold.

This undercurrent of feeling toward the Americans was also revealed in the evidence given the U.N. commission by Squadron Leader Mussell, when he described the unusual atmosphere at Ndola Airport during September 17-18. The Royal Rhodesian Air Force officer spoke of "underhand things going on" at the time, "with strange aircraft coming in, planes without flight plans and so on." He added that "American Dakotas were sitting on the airfield with their engines running and, I should imagine, transmitting messages . . . ." Later he withdrew his use of the word "underhand."

14 | The Appraisal

Few people were surprised by the failure of the Rhodesian and U.N. investigators to shed new light on the mysterious death of Dag Hammarskjold.

The Rhodesian finding that, in some inexplicable way, the *Albertina* had crashed through pilot error had been foreshadowed officially and unofficially all along by the Federal authorities. Both before and during the judicial inquiry they had emphasized the haphazard nature of the flight, and the unusual behavior and evident disregard for basic safety rules of the *Albertina*'s crew.

Equally predictable was the inability of the U.N. commission to resolve the widely held suspicion of foul play, in the form of sabotage or other external interference. There was no proof, of course, that any such factor was the cause. But there also was no firm evidence ruling the possibility out.

In short, the final judgments of the two commissions were inconclusive, unproven, rating no higher than expressions of authoritative opinion. Some might say that that very inconclusiveness was a measure of the honesty of the investigators. But this would be beside the point. The honesty of the Rhodesian and U.N. commissions was not, strictly speaking, under examination. The whole truth about the cause of the crash was being pursued. And truth, like sleep, eludes the pursuer.

Rarely do events of political significance result in an identical interpretation by all the interested parties. The Rhodesian commission of enquiry and that set up by the U.N., probing basically the same set of circumstances, provided their own answer to the question. Each group came up with its own findings and interpretations, some similar, others conflicting.

There were several reasons for these differences.

In the first place, it seemed to onlookers as if Rhodesians generally were in a defensive position. The Welensky Government had a record of political hostility toward the United Nations. The mysterious circumstances of the crash would have been enough in themselves to embarrass any government in whose territory it took place.

Secondly, and in contrast, the U.N. mood appeared to be inquisitive, indignant, even suspicious. Undeniably some member states of the world body were only too ready to believe the worst of the hostile Welensky, with his pro-Tshombe sympathies and his rainbow-like political vocabulary.

Finally, some witnesses themselves made a distinction in their approach to the two commissions. Several Africans, for example, chose to appear before U.N. investigators only. The international body noted that certain evidence was laced with strong anti-Federation feelings, which suggested that political motives, rather than a wish for the truth, might have inspired those who testified.

The pity of it all was that the verdicts of the investigators proved nothing.

Over Dola Hill the dust and smoke had settled, but the gruesome political doubts loosed by the *Albertina* seemed likely to haunt the world for years.

One of the most awkward problems, pinpointed by Swedish critics, concerned the composition of the Rhodesian technical inquiry commission. Barber's board was checking into a situation and conditions for which they, as the competent aviation authorities, were themselves administratively responsible. "In principle [we] support this criticism," said the journal of the Swedish Airline Pilots' Association, *Flygposten*, in an editorial of January, 1962. "It is a criticism we have directed against our own Swedish arrangements." In Rhodesia as in Sweden—the magazine observed—the National Air Board is bound by law to investigate crashes under rules it has helped to create. The magazine insisted nothing personal was implied regarding the objectivity of the investigators. But the suggestion was that Swedes would have been happier if, from the outset, some completely independent national or international authority could have taken charge of the wreckage, the evidence and the subsequent inquiries.

Another problem emerged from the very fact that there were two commissions, one inevitably following in the footsteps of the other. This allowed scope for conflict not only in judgments but also in evidence.

To illustrate:

On February 9, 1962, the report of the Rhodesian commission appeared.

Three days later an African witness, Leonson Npinganjira, told the U.N. commission, sitting at Ndola, that he had seen a small plane flying over a big one just before the *Albertina* had crashed and exploded. Then two Land Rovers had dashed at "breakneck speed" toward the scene. The flames had increased. After a few minutes the Land Rovers had returned. The witness was asked why he had not told all this to the Rhodesians. He replied: "Because I do not trust them."

There were, in addition, several aspects of the Rhodesian report that were puzzling because seemingly inconsistent with previous information.

Some examples:

Stationmaster Noork was named by the United Nations as a member of the *Albertina*'s six-man crew. The Rhodesians listed a five-man crew and described Noork as one of Hammarskjold's fellow passengers.

The report said that the three charcoal-burners who stole from the wreckage had been jailed for taking a typewriter. Court reports at the time said they had stolen a coding machine.

The Rhodesian finding that the accident was due to pilot error rested largely on the theory that *"a visual descending procedure"* was being made. But on October 18, 1961, the Federal Government, quoting Barber's board, said "the position of the wreckage was at a point where an aircraft making *instrument approach* to runway 10 would be completing a procedure turn."

The Rhodesian commission timed moonset on September 17 at 10:24 p.m. But the Federal Government on October 18 said the moon had set at 10:17. The point could be decisively important. A pilot making a visual descent would be deprived of a great deal of light by a setting moon. Some fliers compare the difference to moving from a lighted room into a darkened one. Hallonquist was over Ndola at 10:10. It is just possible that his crash coincided with moonset.

Both the Rhodesian and U.N. commissions brushed aside the suggestion—attributed to Julien—that Hammarskjold might have changed his mind about landing. In the absence of other evidence their conclusion may well be correct. Yet can the possibility of a change of plan be excluded entirely? How would Hammarskjold have reacted if, at the last moment, he had learned from Fabry—Khiari's collaborator—just how the U.N. action in Katanga had come to be ordered? Is it conceivable that the Secretary-General may have felt a need to talk with O'Brien—who had asked to be taken along to Ndola—before seeing Tshombe?

There can be few stranger interludes in the diplomacy of the twentieth century than the story of the Congo, 1961.

The fate of the United Nations trembled on the actions of an ambitious Katangan politician propped up in power by a dubious coalition of freebooters, financiers and governments.

They were prepared to stop at nothing. Sometimes, when other methods failed, the gunmen took over.

From the start of the Congo operation repeated attempts were made to sabotage the activities and the equipment of U.N. authorities and to kill leading U.N. officials.

Before Hammarskjold died Conor O'Brien in Elizabethville several times was a target of attack.

Gunmen tried on three separate occasions to kill Sture Linner in Leopoldville, once in the December after Dag's death. U.N. officials have disclosed privately that then the would-be slayer got to Linner's office before he was overpowered. And his connections were traced back to a well-known French terrorist organization.

Neither the Rhodesian nor the U.N. commissioners investigated these things. If they had, they might have been able to detect if a pattern existed indicating the aims and origins of the attackers.

They also would have been able to evaluate the effectiveness of U.N. security measures in the light of the threats and pressures.

And so, in the absence of a thorough-going inquiry into all the conditions of the Congo at the time, there always will be a certain irrelevance in seeking to determine whether the crash of the *Albertina* was a pure accident or the result of a well-timed bomb in its belly.

The real point is not whether Hammarskjold was murdered in cold blood—and there is no evidence of that. It was that there were some who wanted him—and Linner and O'Brien—dead. Dag Hammarskjold and his delegates had become the symbols of a hated organization whose purpose was an ordered world.

A Pole serving with the Katangan mercenaries was asked how he and his companions had taken the news of Hammarskjold's death.

Simply, he replied: "We were delighted."

The reluctance of the investigators to face up to certain painful realities was displayed in the cursory treatment of the question whether Hammarskjold himself lived awhile after the crash.

Despite a curiously unexplained conflict of evidence the superficial signs suggest that in fact he did, as Swedish physicians said, live briefly and that he might have been helped if rescuers arrived earlier. He was the only one unscarred by fire. Some rescuers said he was found in a sitting position, others said he was prostrate. There were differing explanations as to why rigor mortis had not set in. In one hand leaves and grass were found in his clenched fist. And although his injuries appear clearly to have been so terrible as to have made eventual death inevitable, it seems possible that he could have crawled away from the fire himself.

All this underlines how pitiful it was that air and ground searches were not undertaken sooner and more extensively. The wreckage of the *Albertina,* less than ten miles from Ndola Air Control, was reached fifteen hours after the crash. That delay deafeningly tells its own story.

But there is another, broader, infinitely more depressing implication to be drawn from the tragic death of Dag Hammarskjold.

Not all the saboteurs of the 1960's use things that explode in the night. Lives and institutions and great dreams can be wrecked by the subtleties and strengths of diplomacy and by the acts and omissions of politics. These things can be achieved in the name of fine causes.

This was something that was emphasized in the embittered political post-mortem that followed the death of Hammarskjold. There was talk and countertalk of conspiracy, sabotage, bad faith.

In Salisbury, Premier Welensky asserted the U.N. force in Katanga was controlled by a clique of countries whose "plans did not stop at the Congo." He feared there would be U.N. intervention in Rhodesia as a step toward ousting his white-run Federal Government, and, in the early months of 1962, it seemed as if his fears had been justified.

In Stockholm, Foreign Minister Unden accused the mercenaries of Katanga and their backers of trying "to sabotage the U.N. work for peace" in the Congo.

In New York, after quitting his U.N. post, O'Brien charged the British, French and Belgians had been impeding U.N. operations in the Congo. He was publicly supported in his assertions by General McKeown. O'Brien also claimed he was the "victim of a plot" —and neither the first nor most distinguished victim—by which these powers had tried to thwart the decisions of the Security Council. He warned that the authority and very future of the United Nations were imperiled by these activities.

In London, a British Conservative politician—Lord Hinchingbrooke—wrote in the *Sunday Express* that the United Nations was menacing the future of the British Commonwealth. He added:

> It is no distance at all, for example, from Katanga to Northern Rhodesia, or Tanganyika, or Uganda. What now prevents a daemonic majority of small Powers in the United Nations, drunk with new nationhood, from voting for military measures against one faction or another in these countries, creating civil war and bringing to nought Britain's painstaking

> attempts at multiracial Commonwealth development? The United Nations, while it receives the unconditional support of our great cousin across the Atlantic, is fast becoming Britain's principal enemy.

In Philadelphia, a high State Department official suggested the Union Minière was behind a "clever, big-money campaign to convince Americans" to back Katangan secession. Deputy Assistant Secretary of State for Public Affairs Carl T. Rowan described the mining combine as "a classic example of the profitable side of colonialism" and said its profits were still running high despite the Congo's troubles: "Isn't it natural that those with financial interests in Union Minière would rather see Katanga as an easily-controlled 'separate nation' than as part of a larger Congo nation whose government might not be as friendly as Mr. Tshombe and his associates?"

Finally, in Elizabethville, Tshombe launched a major behind-the-scenes attempt to achieve a political union between Katanga and the Central African Federation. In a remarkably frank interview with Rene McColl of the London *Daily Express* on March 4, 1962, Welensky spoke of this:

> "Yes, of course Tshombe and I have been discussing the possibility of a union—and it is this possibility that scares the daylights out of UNO. Get this straight. I am not trying to pull Katanga into my own orbit, nothing of the kind. But if anyone wants to join us of their own accord, that is another matter. If I were to agree to this union it would mean signing Tshombe's death warrant. He would be killed within a matter of days. The Americans would come barging in and the Afro-Asian group, which nowadays seems to run UNO, would scream their heads off.

All this is only a glimpse of the conflict of interests that had swirled and eddied around the Secretary-General as he struggled to steer the United Nations away from the threatening reefs.

He had been in the grip of other currents too. The Russians were assailing him. The British were insisting on a truce with

Tshombe. The Afro-Asians were agitating for the sinking of the Katangan separatists.

On top of it all, in the last days of his life Hammarskjold had been distressed by what semed to be dereliction, or defiance of his policies, on the part of some of his subordinates.

If Dag Hammarskjold had not been under such intense pressures, would he have embarked upon that journey to Ndola? And would that journey have been arranged so hurriedly and so haphazardly, if he had been given a greater demonstration of support by his friends, including the Americans?

Halfheartedly backed, wholeheartedly attacked, Hammarskjold seemed to lose the cool poise and judgment that had distinguished him in past crises. He offered to meet Tshombe. Then he said he could not. Next he said he would. The Secretary-General was lost.

It may be that the mystery of Dag Hammarskjold's death will only be solved when we have answers to some of the profound political enigmas that surround the last flight of the *Albertina.*

Just who were the people who conspired—using Tshombe and his mercenaries—to defy and destroy the authority, if not the existence, of the United Nations in Katanga?

Just why did Khiari order the arrest of the Katangan leadership without—as O'Brien claimed—Hammarskjold's full knowledge?

Just what passed between Lansdowne and Hammarskjold in their secret talks that led some U.N. officials to believe their chief was under British pressure?

There were inadequacies in the investigations conducted by the Rhodesian and U.N. authorities. Some seemed to be constitutionally unavoidable. Others raised questions of fact and interpretation. Should the Rhodesians (ignoring for the moment the requirements of Rhodesian law) have conducted their investigations concurrently with—and, in some cases, prior to—the investigations made by the United Nations team? Was either investigating commission sufficiently free from political pressures and considerations? Would it not have been preferable if, as the Swedes suggested, some completely independent international authority could have taken charge of the wreckage, the evidence and the subsequent inquiries?

Dag Hammarskjold and his companions were not simply the victims of a pure, or induced, airplane crash isolated from wider political realities. They were casualties of the turmoil of the Congo and the forces that produced it. Therein lay the major inadequacy of the two commissions: through no fault of their own they were looking for the shadow, instead of the substance.

The unexplained death of the Secretary-General of the United Nations was not a matter of passing concern. It nearly wrecked the United Nations and may, indeed, have harmed the organization far more than anyone can assess now. The mysterious crash of the *Albertina* demanded—still demands—a total investigation of *all* the circumstances that forced Dag Hammarskjold into a controversial mission to end an unwanted war against a synthetic foe.

CHRONOLOGY

Wednesday, 13th Sept.

Morning: U.N. troops move at dawn to take over Elizabethville's radio station and post office as part of operation to round up mercenaries. Met with shots, they return fire and first Battle of Katanga is on. O'Brien and Tshombe discuss truce meeting over telephone but exchanges break down. Katanga cabinet disperses.

Afternoon: Dag Hammarskjold flies into Leopoldville from New York on four-day policy-making visit. Confers with Premier Adoula, Linner, is brought up-to-date with crisis in Katanga.

Evening: Adoula and top cabinet ministers dine with Hammarskjold at Linner's home where grave Congolese problems are discussed. Later Ambassador Riches calls to express Britain's shock at U.N. involvement in fighting and to threaten withdrawal of British support if shooting is not swiftly stopped. Hammarskjold explains origins and purposes of U.N. operations, which he defends.

Thursday, 14th Sept.

Morning: Hammarskjold meets Kasavubu, then senior U.N. officers. Approves an urgent request from U.N. military command for air support in Katanga where Tshombe has run of skies. O'Brien and Rajah are reminded U.N. troops shoot only in self-defence and therefore are barred from counter-attacking.

Afternoon: Secretary-General confers at length with Adoula. In battle zone white-led Katangan troops attack U.N. force at Kamina base, surround Irish garrison at Jadotville and hit U.N. positions and patrols in Elizabethville. Tshombe fails to turn up for prearranged truce meeting with O'Brien. A cease-fire order broadcast by one of Tshombe's aides is ignored by Katangans.

Evening: Hammarskjold attends a Congolese Government dinner in his honour, later hears that Michel Tombelaine, O'Brien's deputy, has publicly expressed U.N. resolve "to end the secession of Katanga". Sends stinging message to O'Brien rebuking him for allowing such statements to be made and insisting that U.N. has no mandate to impose political settlement.

Friday, 15th Sept.

Morning: Hammarskjold decides to postpone return to New York due on Saturday, receives Ethiopian offer of three jet-fighters for use in Katanga. Hears President Youlou's warning that he should stay out of nearby Brazzaville because his safety would be imperilled. Lord Lansdowne flies in from London.

Afternoon: Hammarskjold cancels scheduled news conference, asks Britain to allow Ethiopian jets to overfly East African territories. In

Katanga Tshombe's jet raids key U.N. positions, including O'Brien's home. The Irish in Jadotville reject two surrender ultimatums although Tshombe claims they have surrendered.

Evening: For third successive day Tshombe fails to appear for truce talk with O'Brien. Hammarskjold is guest of honour at U.N. reception where he meets Lansdowne informally. Then attends a banquet given him by Kasavubu. Later, he and his advisers prepare a message inviting Tshombe to a peace meeting outside Katanga—but the offer is to be held up until Tshombe provides an opening.

Saturday, 16th Sept.

Morning: Lansdowne calls on Hammarskjold, strongly presses Britain's demand for an end of the fighting and dismissal of O'Brien. Hammarskjold restates U.N. purposes, desire for swift ceasefire, and expresses his own readiness to meet Tshombe personally. Ndola is suggested as a meeting-place. Lansdowne offers full British support.

Afternoon: Tshombe threatens "total war" unless U.N. troops quit Katanga. Rhodesia makes plain her moral backing for Tshombe's cause. Katanga military pressure increases on all fronts. British withhold permission for Ethiopian jets to overfly East Africa.

Evening: Irish in Jadotville surrender. Elated, Tshombe invites O'Brien to truce meeting next day in Bancroft, Northern Rhodesia; but O'Brien recommends rejection of the projected venue. Then Hammarskjold intervenes personally, despatches to Tshombe the letter prepared on Friday and suggests ceasefire talks in Ndola on Sunday.

Sunday, 17th Sept.

Morning: Hammarskjold and staff prepare mission to Ndola. Lansdowne calls on Secretary-General again, urges U.N. keep Ethiopian jets out of Katanga, undertakes to persuade Tshombe to ground his own plane. But Hammarskjold rejects offer and Lansdowne decides to recommend British approval of overflying request. The two arrange that Lansdowne should precede Hammarskjold to Ndola in U.N. plane to insure conference arrangements are in order. Security precautions laid down for Hammarskjold's journey, aircraft checked and rechecked.

Afternoon: Tshombe conditionally accepts Hammarskjold's proposals for Ndola meeting. But Secretary-General replies that Tshombe's conditions are unacceptable, calls for quick, unequivocal acceptance. Tshombe ignores the message and flies to Ndola. Hammarskjold decides to proceed, takes off 15.51.

Evening: 22.13—Crash.

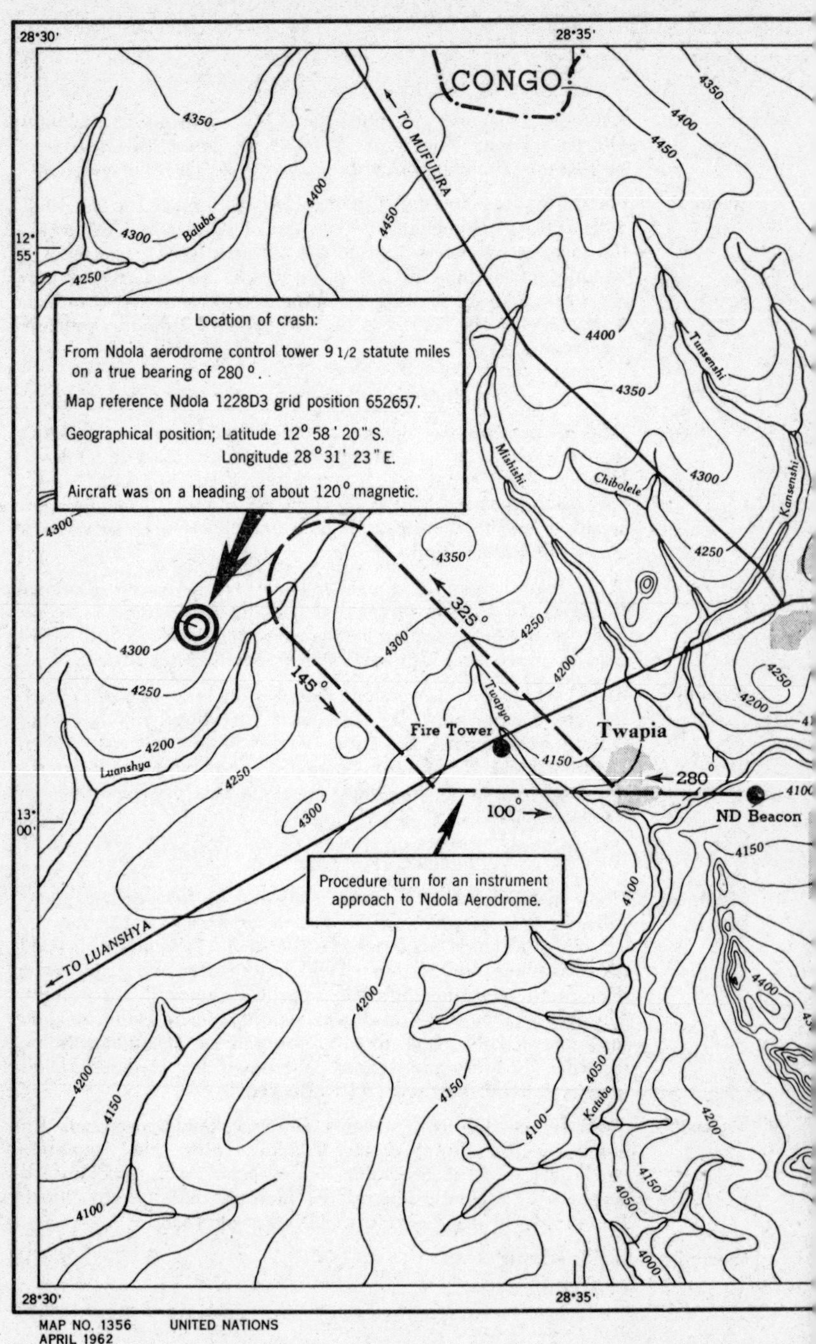

Map from the Report of the Federal Rhodesian Commission which investigated the accident involving Aircraft SE-BDY
Plan from the Report of the United Nations Commission of Investigation

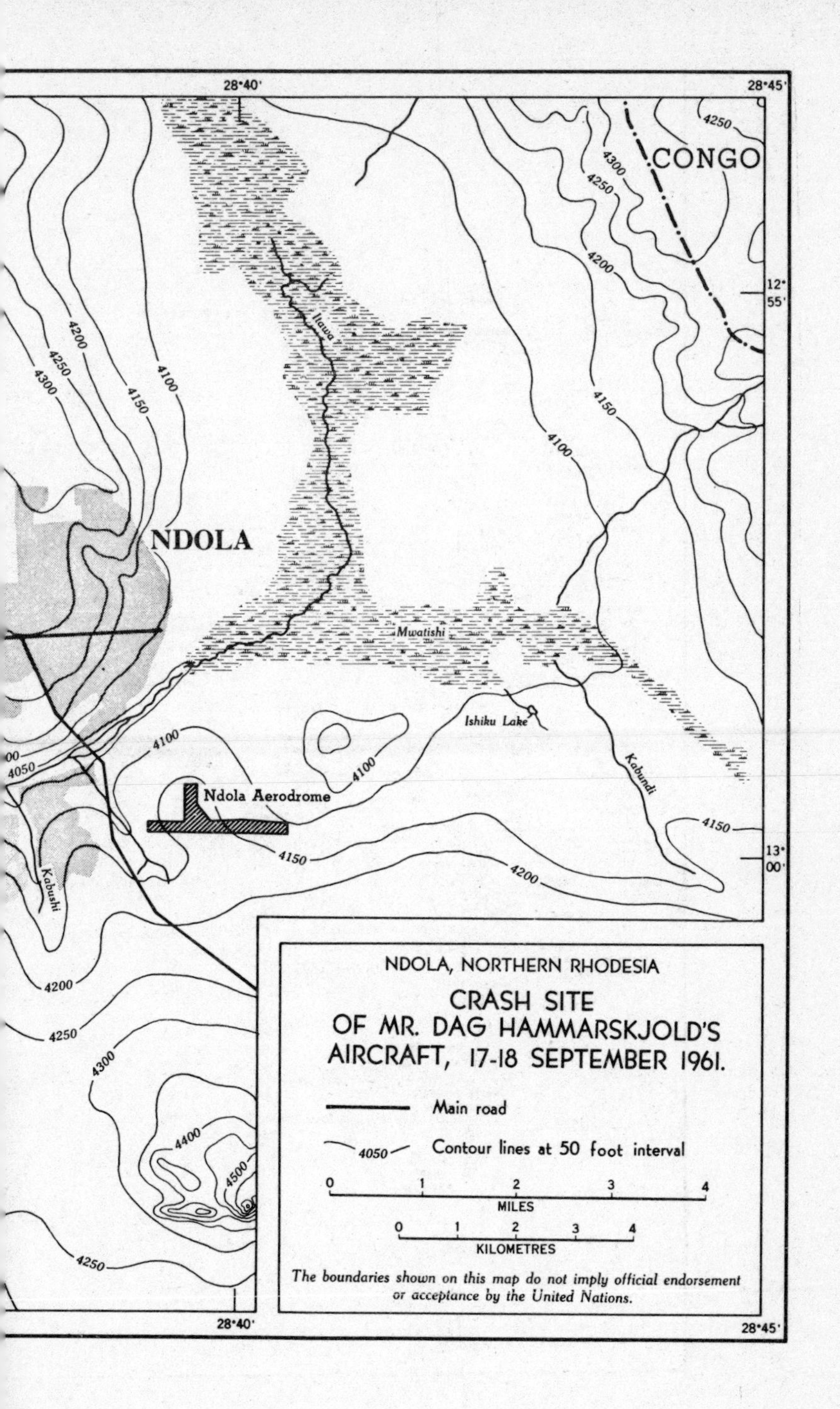
28°40'
28°45'
CONGO
NDOLA
Itawa
Mwatishi
Ishiku Lake
Kabundi
Ndola Aerodrome
Kabushi
12° 55'
13° 00'
4050
4100
4150
4200
4250
4300
4400
4500
NDOLA, NORTHERN RHODESIA
CRASH SITE
OF MR. DAG HAMMARSKJOLD'S
AIRCRAFT, 17-18 SEPTEMBER 1961.
Main road
Contour lines at 50 foot interval
MILES
KILOMETRES
The boundaries shown on this map do not imply official endorsement or acceptance by the United Nations.

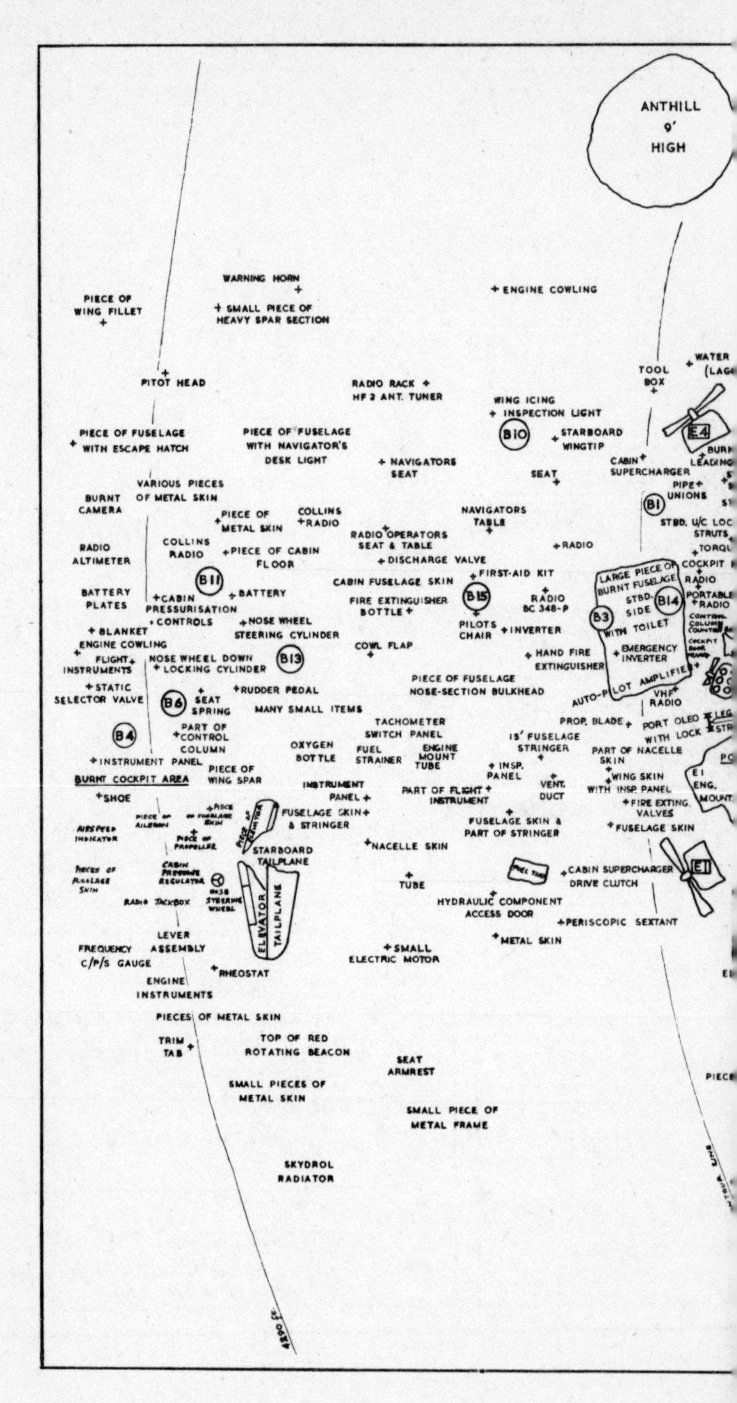

Plan from the Report of the United Nations Commission of Investigatio

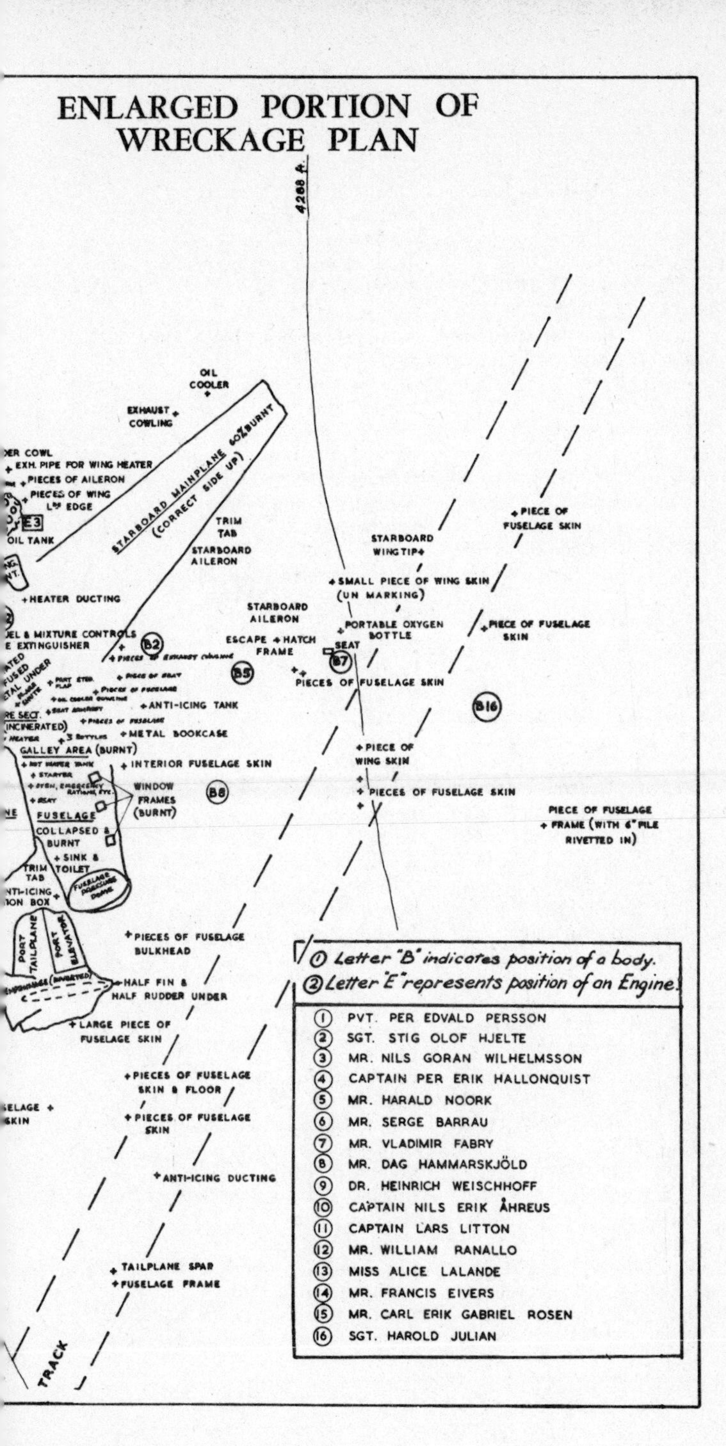
ENLARGED PORTION OF WRECKAGE PLAN
4288 ft.
OIL COOLER
EXHAUST COWLING
STARBOARD MAINPLANE 60% BURNT (CORRECT SIDE UP)
EXH. PIPE FOR WING HEATER
PIECES OF AILERON
PIECES OF WING L'G EDGE
E3
OIL TANK
TRIM TAB
STARBOARD AILERON
HEATER DUCTING
E EXTINGUISHER
B2
STARBOARD AILERON
ESCAPE HATCH FRAME
SEAT
B5
B7
PIECES OF FUSELAGE SKIN
STARBOARD WINGTIP
SMALL PIECE OF WING SKIN (UN MARKING)
PORTABLE OXYGEN BOTTLE
PIECE OF FUSELAGE SKIN
PIECE OF FUSELAGE SKIN
ANTI-ICING TANK
METAL BOOKCASE
GALLEY AREA (BURNT)
INTERIOR FUSELAGE SKIN
WINDOW FRAMES (BURNT)
B8
B16
PIECE OF WING SKIN
PIECES OF FUSELAGE SKIN
PIECE OF FUSELAGE FRAME (WITH 6" FILE RIVETTED IN)
FUSELAGE COLLAPSED & BURNT
SINK & TOILET
TRIM TAB
PORT TAILPLANE
PORT ELEVATOR
PIECES OF FUSELAGE BULKHEAD
HALF FIN & HALF RUDDER UNDER
LARGE PIECE OF FUSELAGE SKIN
PIECES OF FUSELAGE SKIN & FLOOR
PIECES OF FUSELAGE SKIN
ANTI-ICING DUCTING
TAILPLANE SPAR
FUSELAGE FRAME
TRACK
① Letter "B" indicates position of a body.
② Letter "E" represents position of an Engine.
① PVT. PER EDVALD PERSSON
② SGT. STIG OLOF HJELTE
③ MR. NILS GORAN WILHELMSSON
④ CAPTAIN PER ERIK HALLONQUIST
⑤ MR. HARALD NOORK
⑥ MR. SERGE BARRAU
⑦ MR. VLADIMIR FABRY
⑧ MR. DAG HAMMARSKJÖLD
⑨ DR. HEINRICH WEISCHHOFF
⑩ CAPTAIN NILS ERIK ÅHREUS
⑪ CAPTAIN LARS LITTON
⑫ MR. WILLIAM RANALLO
⑬ MISS ALICE LALANDE
⑭ MR. FRANCIS EIVERS
⑮ MR. CARL ERIK GABRIEL ROSEN
⑯ SGT. HAROLD JULIAN

INDEX